HENRY JAMES AND SEXUALITY

In *Henry James and Sexuality*, Hugh Stevens argues for a new interpretation of James's fiction. Stevens shows how James's writing contains daring and radical representation of transgressive desires and marginalized sexual identities. He demonstrates the importance of incestuous desire, masochistic fantasy, and same-sex passions in a body of fiction which ostensibly conforms to, while ironically mocking, the contemporary moral and publishing codes James faced. James critiques the very notion of sexual identity, and depicts the radical play of desires which exceed and disrupt any stable construction of identity. In a number of his major novels and tales, Stevens argues, James anticipates the main features of modern 'gay' or 'queer' fiction through plots and narrative strategies in which heterosexual marriage is at odds with homoerotic friendship. This original and exciting work will transform our understanding of this most enigmatic of writers.

Hugh Stevens lectures in the Department of English at the University of York. He is a contributor to the forthcoming Cambridge Companions to Henry James and D. H. Lawrence, and has published in *The Henry James Review*. He is co-editor of *Borderlines: Gender, Sexuality, and the Margin of Modernism*.

HENRY JAMES
AND SEXUALITY

HUGH STEVENS

University of York

CAMBRIDGE
UNIVERSITY PRESS

PUBLISHED BY THE PRESS SYNDICATE OF THE UNIVERSITY PRESS OF CAMBRIDGE
The Pitt Building, Trumpington Street, Cambridge CB2 1RP United Kingdom

CAMBRIDGE UNIVERSITY PRESS
The Edinburgh Building, Cambridge CB2 2RU, UK
40 West 20th Street, New York, NY 10011–4211, USA
10 Stamford Road, Oakleigh, Melbourne 3166, Australia

First published 1998

Printed in the United Kingdom at the University Press, Cambridge

Typeset in Monotype Baskerville 11/12.5pt [CP]

A catalogue record for this book is available from the British Library

Library of Congress cataloguing in publication data

Stevens, Hugh.
Henry James and sexuality / Hugh Stevens.
p. cm.
Originally presented as author's thesis (doctoral) – Cambridge University
Includes bibliographical references
ISBN 0 521 62259 x (hardback)
1. James, Henry, 1843–1916 – Criticism and interpretation.
2. Homosexuality and literature – United States – History – 19th century.
3. Psychological fiction, American – History and criticism. 4. Sex (Psychology) in literature.
5. Gender identity in literature. 6. Sex role in literature. 7. Desire in literature.
1. Title.
PS2127.s48s74   1998
813'.4–dc21   97–28962   CIP

ISBN 0 521 62259 X hardback

For my parents

Contents

Preface

In the late 1980s, it would not have been obvious that Henry James was to become one of the most discussed figures in literary criticism concerned with sexuality, more specifically with same-sex desire and the development of homosexual identities. Since then, of course, 'queer theory' has gained a foothold in the academy, studies of 'lesbian and gay writing' are more and more frequent in English departments, and literary representations of same-sex desire and dissident sexual identities – in writing from the medieval period onwards – have received considerable attention by literary critics. James himself has become one of the writers most frequently associated with 'queer' literary criticism. As this study developed, so too did the intellectual apparatus with which to consider questions of sexuality in literary texts. Psychoanalytic approaches to sexuality have not been displaced, but critics have increasingly acknowledged that desire and sexuality are constructed differently in different historical periods and cultural locations. Such observations are now commonplace, but are worth repeating in a book on Henry James, for several reasons.

Literary criticism has been reluctant to acknowledge the extent to which James was implicated in the late Victorian culture of sexuality – a culture in which scientific constructions of sexuality gained increasing prestige, and in which a newly punitive legal régime contributed to the stigmatization of the sexual 'deviant'; a culture which witnessed individuals who resisted such stigmatization and criminalization, and who mobilized under the very sign of deviance. This study hopes to demonstrate that while James was not a public participant in the early public manifestations of homosexual culture, his writing shows an informed response to changing notions of homosexuality. In the conclusion I argue that James, in his own select social circle, paradoxically constituted himself as 'queer' – as a desiring male subject involved with other men – without making an identity statement.

A somewhat confused relation between literary criticism and biography has obscured James's relation to his culture. Until recently, critics and biographers have argued that James's supposed abstinence from any form of sexual activity make him an unlikely author of fiction which self-consciously represents same-sex desire between men. Hence erotic moments in his writing are frequently read as unintended. Such a biographical approach is often implicit even in criticism of James which does not specifically refer to James's life. The consciousness of 'Henry James' at the moment of writing is beyond recovery. Nevertheless, I hope to show that James's *writing* is extremely self-conscious about the constraints and injunctions surrounding representations of the erotic and of the deviant. This claim will inevitably affect the way in which we think of James the biographical subject, but this study is more interested in the relation between James's writing and the culture of sexuality it responds to than in the intricacies of James's own psyche. The claims I make for James's writing do not stand or fall on the question of James's own sexual behaviour. Fiction is a mode of writing which teasingly promises to reveal the writing self even as it disavows that self; it is, after all, only 'fiction', and James's own tales about fictional creation remind us that readers will expect to see the writer in the writing even though that expectation can never be properly satisfied. The only biographical claim that follows from a reading which convincingly demonstrates that James's published writing engages with questions of same-sex desire and queer identity is tautological – James was a person who could write and publish such work. Yet this claim is in itself significant.

This study began as an inquiry into the representation of femininity in James's writing. As the study developed, I became increasingly concerned with the representation of same-sex desire in his writing. James's interest in the desiring female subject and his interest in the 'homosexual' subject are not unconnected – they both represent a fascination with the marginal, with alterity – but I would not like to make any essentializing links between them. Perhaps it is worth pointing out what his fiction conspicuously doesn't do – namely, it does not tell the story of the maturing male who makes himself through marriage and the establishment of a family. This plot is noticeably absent from James's oeuvre – it occurs, perhaps, in *The Golden Bowl*, but only to be seen there not as 'normal' but as hyperbolically perverse. At the risk of stating the obvious, the queerness and the perversity of James's writing neither begin nor end with questions of same-sex desire and of homosexuality.

As I write this preface, I am aware that much recent writing has appeared on topics this book addresses with which I have not been able to engage; this book is a contribution to a developing discussion, and I look forward to seeing how critical understandings of sexuality in James's writing continue to develop. I hope that the readings of James's writings offered here do more than contribute to our understanding of James the creative artist. I hope to portray a writer whose work constitutes an intelligent and challenging contribution to cultural understandings of sexuality, a contribution valuable not only to the culture in which he wrote, but to the culture in which we now live.

Acknowledgements

This book began life as a doctoral dissertation, work on which was enabled by generous institutional support. The Cambridge Commonwealth Trust funded my initial three years at Cambridge. The Judith E. Wilson Fund of the English Faculty, Cambridge University, provided expenses for a research trip to the United States. Trinity Hall, Cambridge, awarded me a research fellowship which enabled me to continue work on this project.

Several libraries provided generous access to resources: the University Library and English Faculty Library, Cambridge, the British Library, the London Library, the Widener and the Houghton at Harvard, the Kinsey Institute and the University Library at Bloomington, Indiana, and the University of York Library.

A previous version of chapter 3 appeared in *The Henry James Review* (vol. 14, 1993), and an article containing some of the material in chapters 6 and 7 appeared as 'Homoeroticism, Identity and Agency in James's Late Tales', in Gert Buelens, ed., *Enacting History in Henry James* (Cambridge University Press, 1998).

The personal debts are several. Kathleen Wheeler, my research supervisor, guided me through completion of the dissertation. Maud Ellmann, Adrian Poole and Tony Tanner showed a sustained and valuable interest in my work. I am particularly indebted to Jonathan Freedman, who read through two drafts of this work, and whose advice was invaluable in helping me to revise and reshape the argument.

At Trinity Hall and at York I have had supportive colleagues: in particular I thank John Lennard, Peter Holland, Hugh Haughton, Hermione Lee and Joseph Bristow. Anne Fernihough, Bridget Orr, Louise Watts and Clive Marsland gave valuable feedback at various stages of writing. This book is dedicated to my parents.

Abbreviations

Full details of all works cited are given in the bibliography. The following abbreviations are used throughout the book:

AN   Henry James, *The Art of the Novel: Critical Prefaces*. Ed. Richard P. Blackmur. New York: Scribner's, 1934.

CT   *The Complete Tales of Henry James*. Ed. Leon Edel. 12 vols. London: Rupert Hart-Davis, 1962–64.

HS   Michel Foucault, *The History of Sexuality: An Introduction*. London: Allen Lane, 1979.

CHAPTER ONE

Henry James and the languages of sex

While reading in Henry James's fiction a critique of modern notions of sexuality, this book examines the privileged role sexuality plays in the constitution of the self, or of 'character', in James's writing. It argues that sexuality is an important component in James's conception of identity, even if his fiction might be seen to critique a social formation in which the sexual has a founding, ontological status for the human subject. James's fiction is read in a context in which two questions are being addressed with increasing urgency. Can the 'political' be founded on the notion of an individuated, autonomous subjectivity, and can 'subjectivity' be located according to notions of sexual and gendered identity? It will be argued that 'sexuality' (or the 'erotic') both *constitutes* the Jamesian character in a crucial sense, yet also that for James sexuality marks a space in which the very possibility of selfhood is questioned. For James there is no 'being' or 'essence' of sexuality which precedes the existence of sexuality; nor can sexuality be understood in terms of stable categories. Sexuality is rather a dynamic process, a performance, a story, a narrative, in which the unstable play of desire and identifications can erode the boundaries of the perceived self.

Judith Butler writes in her influential *Gender Trouble* (1990) that 'the gendered body is performative', and 'has no ontological status apart from the various acts which constitute its reality'.[1] This claim, as Judith Butler's work itself shows, is as resonant and productive for conceptualizing 'sexuality' as it has been for thinking about gender. The 'being' of sexuality is always contingent. 'Sexuality' is not simply 'there' to be represented: it is created in its representations.

The insistence that 'sexuality' is 'performative', a 'product of representation', however, does not mean that it is 'free-floating', shapeless, amorphous. Sexuality still has a shape, and its shape may change historically. Yet the 'history of sexuality' is not a straightforward narrative, against which James's fictional texts can be read. Rather, James's writing is part of that history, just as that history unfolds in his writing. Both 'history' and 'James's writing' combine to tell a story of sexuality as a problematic category, a story of sexuality as a conflict of stories.

Any inquiry made today into 'sexuality' needs to place itself in relation to the wide-ranging debate between constructionist and essentialist accounts. This debate, however, is not one that can be 'resolved' in advance of textual analysis. As Diana Fuss has argued, 'constructionism' and 'essentialism' have different contours, different effects, and yield different strategic advantages, depending on their historical and cultural contexts;[2] this applies as well to the very opposition between the two concepts. Indeed, one of the reasons why the constructionist/essentialist debate seems to provide such a useful framework for examining sexuality in James's writing is that in the late nineteenth century this debate had already taken on a decisive importance, in the growth of the social sciences, with their shifting allegiances to ontogeny or to phylogeny, to 'nature' or to 'nurture',[3] and in the development of various clinical discourses on the self – psychiatry, sexology, psychoanalysis. We should not expect, then, to find a James who is either an 'essentialist' or a 'constructionist' (thus discovering in his work either an essential, 'pre-textual' sexuality or a sexuality which is determined solely by its cultural place). Rather, his fiction might be thought of as interrogating these very terms. 'What shall we call our "self"?' Madame Merle asks in one of the most famous exchanges in *The Portrait of a Lady*. 'Where does it begin? where does it end? It overflows into everything that belongs to us and then it flows back again. I know a large part of myself is in the clothes I choose to wear ... One's self – for other people – is one's expression of one's self'. To which Isabel Archer replies both that one has an *inner* core or self – which may or may not be expressed – and that one controls one's own self-representations: 'I don't know whether I succeed in expressing myself, but I know that nothing else expresses me. Nothing that belongs to me is any measure of me; everything's on the contrary a limit, a barrier, and a perfectly arbitrary one. Certainly the clothes which, as you say, I choose to wear, don't express me; and heaven forbid they should!' If Madame Merle has a fault, Isabel thinks, 'it was that she was not natural'; yet Madame Merle does not 'pretend, like some people I've met, to express herself by original signs'. Madame Merle's 'nature spoke not the less in her behaviour because it spoke a conventional tongue. "What's language at all but a convention?" said Isabel.'[4] Here we see James dramatizing the opposition between surface and depth that shapes different conceptualizations of the self. If he is opposing Isabel Archer's naivety to Madame Merle's sophistication, we should remember that his sympathy lies with Isabel.

Perhaps, as Madame Merle says, we find ourselves expressed in languages and conventions that precede us; but might we not also feel, like Isabel, that there are aspects of our 'selves' which exceed or do not meet these terms? James's fiction returns again and again to this difficult meeting of 'culture' and 'the self', a meeting in which the terms of the construction of a sexed, gendered self are always interrogated, never taken for granted.

Reading 'sexuality' in James is framed by the problematic relation of 'then' and 'now': the vocabulary available to James for describing the body is different from our own vocabulary, yet it is not *entirely* different, and reading sexual nuances in his fiction requires an ear both for similarities and differences. We should be aware that his writing spans the era in which our own vocabulary for describing sexuality is being formulated. When he started to write fiction, the vocabulary which we take for granted today – a vocabulary which individuates according to sexual taste (homosexual, heterosexual, masochist, fetishist and so on) – was increasingly used by specialists, 'modern jurists, psychiatrists, writers on forensic medicine' (as J. A. Symonds wrote in 1883),[5] but had yet to achieve general circulation; this vocabulary was to become more widely available in James's lifetime.

This is not to say that James himself adopted modern terminology with enthusiasm. In his fiction, James never even uses the word 'sexuality'; only rarely do we even find the older 'sex'.[6] And, when he does use 'sexuality', in a private context, it is from a standpoint of seeming disavowal. In a letter to Robert Louis Stevenson on 17 February 1893 James writes:

I grant you Hardy with all my heart and even with a certain quantity of my boot-toe. I am meek and ashamed where the public clatter is deafening – so I bowed my head and let 'Tess of the D.'s' pass. But oh yes, dear Louis, she is vile. The pretence of 'sexuality' is only equalled by the absence of it, and the abomination of the language by the author's reputation for style. There are indeed some pretty smells and sights and sounds. But you have better ones in Polynesia.[7]

The letter addresses a topic which James certainly finds sensitive, and wavers between precision and verbal excess. In fact, it is the working of the feminine in this passage which undermines James's masculine control and aggression – signalled by the movement of James's boot-toe, presumably kicking Hardy. (James often places himself in a bodily or even fetishistic relation to writers and to their products, most notoriously in his extensive commentary on George Sand.[8] In an 1876 review of Baudelaire he expresses a painful voyeurism that comes into play when reading *Les Fleurs du Mal:* 'what the reader sees is a gentleman in a painful-looking posture, staring very hard at a mass of things from which, more intelligently, we avert our heads.'[9] The 'sexual passion' of Gabriele D'Annunzio's fiction is compared with 'the boots and shoes that we see, in the corridors of promiscuous hotels, standing, often in double pairs, at the doors of rooms.')[10]

Placing 'sexuality' within quotation marks, James distances himself from and expresses his own cognitive grasp of 'sexuality', which is said, quite strikingly, to be absent from Hardy's work. Yet Tess's presence undermines James's patronizing stance, and tips it over into something resembling hysteria, compromising his aggressive masculinist position. 'But oh yes, dear Louis, she is vile.' Is 'she' '*Tess*' the character or *Tess* the book? – the pronoun 'she' following 'Tess of the D.'s' indicating a slippage between the two. If 'Tess' the woman is vile, is James recoiling before the feminine? Or is 'Tess' the *novel* vile: is he objecting to Hardy's *representation* of the feminine (the creative artist rejecting the artistic practice of a competitor)? It is Hardy's *language* which is an *abomination*, but this response too is more visceral than critical. *Ab-omin-ation:* Hardy's language as ill omen from which James must look away. Do we stare or do we avert our heads? To turn away from or to face the sexual, to open or close one's eyes to it: James's difficulty, even as he disclaims it, has also been a difficulty for readers of James. Do we 'see' the sexual, is it not there for us to open our eyes to, or do we keep our eyes closed so as not to see? And how is the sexual inscribed in his work as a *crisis* of seeing, a trauma of perception?

Yet even as he expresses distaste for 'sexuality' in Hardy, James is making a claim for himself, marking his turf. If Hardy makes a 'pretence' at representing sexuality, can James offer something more authentic? Is the answer to be found in 'vile Tess' herself? For what might James object to in what he calls 'Tess of the D.'s', if not the equation of woman *with* her sex, the equation so many Jamesian heroines (Angela Vivian, Isabel Archer, Milly Theale, Maggie Verver, to name just four) are anxious to deny? Stephen Heath notes that Hardy is dealing with dominant cultural fantasies of 'woman': he writes Tess as 'the primal, tempting, sexually guilty and corrupting woman'. Although the novel is ostensibly a vindication of Tess, as victim, in its 'assumption of "sexuality", . . . she is at fault as woman, the writing moves into the position of her guilt'.[11] The passage Heath quotes from the novel suggests a continuity between Tess's bodily interior and her 'nature': her 'soul' and 'spiritual beauty':

[Tess] had not heard [Angel] enter, and hardly realized his presence there. She was yawning, and he saw the red interior of her mouth as if it had been a snake's. She had stretched one arm so high above her coiled-up cable of hair that he could see its satin delicacy above the sunburn; her face was flushed with sleep, and her eyelids hung heavy over their pupils. The brim-fulness of her nature breathed from her. It was a moment when a woman's soul is more incarnate than at any other time; when the most spiritual beauty bespeaks itself flesh; and sex takes the outside place in the presentation.[12]

In its collapsing of surface and depth, its presentation of the female body as a readable, penetrable collection of signs breathing forth 'the brimfulness' of its 'nature', this passage resonates with the full cultural weight of nineteenth-century medical and psychiatric writing on women.[13] And James's female body, it will be argued, always resists this weight, this point of view as 'factual'. Although novels like *The Wings of the Dove* (1902) and *The Golden Bowl* (1904) might seem to consist of endless attempts to 'read woman', they constitute woman as illegible, as escaping authoritative cultural narratives.

The relation of James to Hardy cannot be expressed, then, as a relationship of genuine product to falsehood, counterfeit. James's fictional concerns are repeatedly close to Hardy's. However, whereas Hardy describes male perceptions which assume a continuum between 'Tess' and her sex, James's fiction is troubled by the very notion of the sexed self. The question asked by *Tess* appears to be: how is femininity, the woman, treated in a given social formation? By contrast, the question returned to in James's fiction is: how is 'femininity', 'the woman', 'female identity' asserted? And, a question which is not really distinguishable from the one just asked: what of 'masculinity'?

The male characters of Hardy's novel (Angel and Alec) assume Tess's 'sexuality' to be legible, and in harmony with her 'sex': a 'prior' to a social surround which suppresses it, refuses to accept it, punishes its expression. In other words, Tess has for them a 'sexuality' and a 'gender': as readers, we are urged implicitly to distance ourselves from Angel, to accept, admire, love Tess's identity rather than be horrified by it. (James, it seems, is horrified: 'she is vile.') In James's writing, by contrast, there is no easy alignment of sex, gender and sexuality. James's presentations of sexuality are quite radical in scope, but do not involve a division between 'conformist' and 'subversive' sexual identities: rather the very construction of sexual identity according to a fixed object-choice is put into question. Which is not to say that the question of sexual identity is avoided in James's writing: this question is always there, but *as* a question, the question of the *possibility* of a sexual identity (or sexual *identities*). The terms of such a construction, the difficulties, the cost, of such a construction, are meticulously examined throughout his work.

Frequently in James's fiction identity is opaque, difficult to discern: it does not readily present itself to an observer, or observers are prone to error in attempting to read other characters. In his *Confidence* (1879), for instance, Bernard Longueville and Gordon Wright find Angela Vivian mysterious: they lack the ability Thomas Hardy attributes to Angel Clare, to '[con] the characters of her face as if they had been hieroglyphics.'[14] Yet this 'illegibility' of the body does not place the body outside history: the 'legibility' of the body is both a historical and novelistic concern. James does not aestheticize the sexual, or enclose the sexual in a sealed aesthetic space. Yet his fiction often comes close to an aestheticization of the sexual, if only to retreat from such an aestheticization at crucial moments.[15] The late fiction critiques the aestheticization of sexuality just as it critiques the medicalization of sexuality, discerning in both the difficulty, the risk, of attempting to represent the body, when the terms available for representation are always already tainted. For James sexuality is always *cultural*, and his fiction responds, in various ways, to the proliferation of discourses, in the late nineteenth and early twentieth centuries, which attempt to 'represent' sexuality, yet are responsible for its very creation.

Writing about 'sexuality' in the late nineteenth century repeatedly comes up against the problem of representation itself. How can one discuss 'sexuality' in James when James himself was so resistant to using this term? Paradoxically, the very *absence* of this term partly demonstrates its importance, highlights its status as that which is difficult to represent. Stephen Heath emphasizes these difficulties in *The Sexual Fix*:

'Sexuality' is the term of our conception and systematization, specific and historical, how we represent the sexual – 'sex' – as an entity, with 'sexology' its study. Sexuality, human experience of the sexual, is as old as language, as old as human being; 'sexuality'[,] particular construction of that experience, goes back little more than a hundred years. One of the difficulties we face is the slide under the same word between these two references: we need the word 'sexuality' in the first sense, but we cannot say or write it today without bringing with it the assumptions, the representation, of the second.[16]

Michel Foucault makes a similar distinction, using different terms – he distinguishes between an *ars erotica* in which 'the truth of sex . . . is drawn from pleasure itself', and the more recent, Western, *scientia sexualis*, in which 'procedures for telling the truth of sex . . . are geared to a form of knowledge-power strictly opposed to the art of initiations and the masterful secret: . . . the confession'.[17]

Given that James is writing in the period in which the *scientia sexualis* is consolidating itself, we would expect to see a certain slippage between terms. Despite this instability, there is still much value in Foucault's conceptualization of 'sexuality' as arising from a formation in which 'erotic' tastes become important both in the role they play in the deployment of discipline and surveillance, and as markers of the self. Whereas the 'erotic' may be assumed to be pleasurable, the 'sexual' may be subject to distaste.

It is useful to think of James both as an erotic writer, and as a writer whose works are marked by the historical development of 'sexuality'. However, if James is an 'erotic writer', his representations of the erotic are never straightforward. Indeed, it is the very elliptical way in which the erotic is so often figured in his writing which marks its importance. Allon White, in one of the best commentaries on James's obscurity, describes James's narrative procedure as involving the

'sublimation' of the positive, elemental and self-contained 'act of a moment' into a form which generates complexity, interrelatedness, negativity and extension until it has lost its 'baseness'; and 'foreclosure' of sexuality by remaining 'outside' the scene of seduction among the hints and clues – by the process of omission and exclusion which we call ellipsis.

Although James frequently tells a 'story of a compromised and compromising seduction', the

'scene of seduction' constitutes a fundamental moment of obscurity and fascination and is characterized by a strange doubleness. It constitutes what Pierre Macherey has termed a 'determining absent centre' to the fiction.'[18]

Here White argues that the obscurity of James's representation of the sexual shows its importance, rather than its irrelevance. White's approach is psychoanalytic in making the 'scene of seduction' the 'determining absent centre'; I argue throughout that the determining absent centre for James is not the scene of seduction as such, but the absence of a language which can adequately describe human affections and erotic attachments.

Erotic silence, or vagueness, needs to be read with great care in James's fiction. Certainly it bears a clear historical relation to the late nineteenth century's injunction to *speak*, to *confess*, which accompanies the very 'taboo' on bringing the erotic into discourse. Thus the dignified silences of *What Maisie Knew* (1897) are part of the same cultural formation as the endless, almost nauseatingly graphic confessions of Walter in *My Secret Life* (ca. 1890). Rather than simply 'escaping' sexuality, *What Maisie Knew*, in constituting *sexual* knowledge *as* knowledge, as the very rationale for narrative, privileges sexuality, in fact *cries out for* sexuality as that which will fill the gaps, occupy the silences, resolve the anxieties of Maisie's hermeneutic enterprise. Yet, silence is never 'filled' by sexuality in a non-problematic fashion: sexuality, like hysteria, is characterized not only by the absence of speech but also by linguistic excess.

James's seeming reluctance to figure the sexual directly cannot be accounted for with reference to a simplistic framework of 'repression'. A novel like *The Wings of the Dove* contains a highly self-conscious commentary on its own methods of figuring the sexual, and exemplifies the sophistication of James's response to the period's discourses on sexuality.[19] There is in James not only a straightforward (and easily documented)[20] desire to conform to public standards of acceptability, to ease the reception of his novels (he abhorred the scandal surrounding Wilde and Hardy, for example). There is also a complex reaction to what might be called an *ontology* of sexuality, an equation of sexual taste, or desire, with being. For James, resisting this equation meant keeping open not only erotic but also aesthetic possibilities.

These claims have to be made with a great deal of care, as they impinge not only on our conceptions of the relation between 'high' and 'low' culture, but also on the iconic status of James the elusive aesthetic fabricator of the incomprehensible, James the canonical Master of early Modernism. James's reputation as a 'Modernist' writer is problematic in that his resistance to identity, and his writing's repeated stressing of the *performative* nature of the self, seems to align him to postmodernism. Although this partly reflects the inevitable difficulty of relating the genealogy of Modernism and postmodernism, there are historical pressures informing this 'postmodernist James' (and also the 'postmodernist Wilde' discovered by recent literary criticism).[21] The very creation of an ontology of gender and sexuality was also an incitement to perform. Resistance is shaped by the 'dominant' discourse in what Jonathan Dollimore, in his recent reading of Wilde, calls the 'perverse dynamic'.[22]

The literary movements of aestheticism and decadence can be seen as participating in this general movement of resistance. Jonathan Freedman has recently argued that 'British aestheticism anticipates the postmodern most fully in its sustained critique of the explanatory syntheses of nineteenth-century European thought.'[23] And the mode of discursive pleasure that Peter Brooks, following Barthes, calls a 'perverse textuality' seems to arise in particular out of fin de siècle decadence.[24] Writers like Beardsley and Wilde developed what Linda Dowling calls a Paterian 'aesthetic of delay',[25] a discursive eroticism in which erotic effects are generated not through the transparency of language and its ability to represent erotic actions, but through language's opacity, through a lingering over the shimmering, wavering instabilities of linguistic effects, through a deferral of cognitive closure.

Such an aesthetic is strongly evident in James's most Paterian novels,

The Wings of the Dove and *The Ambassadors*.[26] In the first chapter of *The Ambassadors*, for instance, Strether 'enjoyed extremely the duration of delay ... There was detachment in his zeal and curiosity in his indifference.'[27] Just as the activity of the pervert, in the view of late nineteenth-century social scientists, threatens social cohesion by privileging individual pleasure over the demands of the group, in the decadent aesthetic the activities of individual words and phrases selfishly destabilize and undermine discursive coherence. These connections were made explicit in Paul Bourget's definition of decadence (which was introduced into British literary life by sexologist Havelock Ellis, writing in 1889). Bourget wrote that a society 'should be like an organism' made up of 'smaller organisms, which may themselves be resolved into a federation of cells', the 'social cell' being 'the individual'. In such a social formation the lesser organisms need 'to subordinate their energy to the total energy'; otherwise, if 'individual life becomes exaggerated beneath the influence of acquired well-being, and of heredity,' an 'anarchy' will arise which 'constitutes the *decadence* of the whole' (the threat of degeneration). Language is governed by a 'similar law', and a 'style of decadence is one in which the unity of the book is decomposed to give place to the independence of the phrase, and the phrase to give place to the independence of the word'.[28]

This view of society as the organic whole constituted by a group of groups, each of which is in itself a group of smaller groups or units, a delicately structured pyramid of hierarchical life forms, helps us see the way in which the Jamesian drawing-room becomes a highly politicized forum, just as the relation of James's characters to marital and sexual life is always resonant with larger social implications. The notion of the organic society was used in a conservative way to underpin existing social arrangements: the departure of individuals from their allotted role in a larger structure appeared to presage the collapse of that whole structure.[29] According to Bourget's definition of the 'style of decadence', the relation of James's novels to what Freedman calls 'the explanatory syntheses of nineteenth-century European thought' corresponds to the relation of the individual life to the larger organism – or, in Freudian terms, to the relation of the pervert to the teleology of sexual life. The Freudian pervert, the exaggerated individual life evoked by Bourget, and the Paterian aesthetic of delay and the performative notion of the self developed by James, all chip away at the authority of a larger narrative structure.

James's fiction then can be characterized as showing an 'incredulity toward metanarratives', a quality which, for Lyotard, is definitive of postmodernism.[30] However, this suspicion is not sufficient to diminish the

importance of the metanarrative: the terms of resistance to such a metanarrative are also dependent on that metanarrative. To read James's
fiction within a framework of resistance to a régime of sexuality is also
to trace the extension of that régime into the personal. If the Jamesian
character wishes to escape the ontology of the sexual, this wish acknowledges the movement of sexuality into the private intimate space of self-
definition, a space which, for all its 'privacy', is deeply marked by the social
circulation of sexual discourse.

Tracing this movement, and resistance to this movement in James's
fiction, does not involve, then, an insistence that what is ostensibly non-
sexual has a 'deep' or 'true' meaning that is in fact sexual. This is important in that it is frequently charged or implied that to read sexual meanings
into James's novels is to vulgarise them. Often it is not clear whether this
critical complaint is directed against sexuality or against homosexuality.
In some discussions of 'political correctness', James takes on strategic
value as the example of the 'great writer' who needs to be preserved
against 'PC' lunacy. The British *Observer*, for example, used James to report
on the lunacy of the American academy, informing its readers of a student
unwilling to take a course on James which would ' "normalise" James. This
meant "teaching him as a great writer, and not as a victim of his homosexuality"'.[31] The desire to separate James's art from his sexuality is also
seen in John Bayley's review of Fred Kaplan's *Henry James: The Imagination
of Genius:* 'Was James ever homosexually active?' Bayley asks. 'Did his
military and mental gaiety go with his being gay in the modern sense?
Fortunately it is a question impossible to answer . . .'[32] This 'Fortunately'
slides over a number of unstated (and offensive) assumptions. Bayley
appears to imply that he would not want a writer like James to be 'gay
in the modern sense', and takes it for granted that his reader will share
this wish.

However, if one does not regard answers to such questions as 'unfortunate', it is certainly possible to think of James's life and work in relation
to modern constructions of sexuality, and, indeed, of homosexuality.
Modern notions of sexual identity inform James's writing profoundly. It
might jar to talk about *What Maisie Knew* and *My Secret Life* in the same
breath (even if we are used to the New Historicist practice of unexpected
conjunctions). Yet these two texts are related inversely to one another, in
that sexual knowledge and its difficult relation to language is a prime
narrative motive in both.[33] Walter continues to recount his sexual exploits
at such length precisely because he obtains pleasure from recounting the
forbidden; Maisie's knowledge is fascinating insofar as it appears to con-

tain, or lack, the sexual. Both the Jamesian narrative, then, and *My Secret Life*, bear a centrifugal relation to the sexual, either as a hallowed absence or as a defiled presence.[34]

One needs then, to insist on the importance of 'the sexual' in James's writing, even as one acknowledges its frequent evanescent, fleeting qualities, the way it shimmers, teasingly appears and disappears in the folds of a vocabulary which is as ambiguous and idiosyncratic as it is erotic. In doing so, it helps to have an attentive ear not only for the period's erotic languages, but for the inflections these languages take in James's own writings. Quite local, specific nuances need to be foregrounded. Consider an example from a slightly later period. Mr. Fortune, the missionary hero of Sylvia Townsend Warner's *Mr. Fortune's Maggot*, a novel published in 1927, thinks to himself that he should not allow Lueli, the Polynesian boy whom he loves and who is his sole convert to Christianity on the fictional Polynesian island 'Fanua', to oil him, as '[o]iling, and all that sort of thing, was effeminate, unbecoming, and probably vicious'.[35] In Evelyn Waugh's *Brideshead Revisited*, first published in 1945, Brideshead, Sebastian Flyte's elder brother, asks Charles Ryder whether he considers 'that there is anything vicious in [Sebastian's] connexion with this German?'[36] Sometime in the first half of the twentieth century, then, 'vicious' appears to have been used as a disdainful term for 'homosexual' – to describe homosexual *vice* – although the *OED* does not record this usage.

Such words have a shadowy existence, but point to the possibility of communications which can convey prescribed meanings not only in secret spaces but in genteel, social forums. They pose a challenge for genealogical inquiry in that they are used, one suspects, precisely for their ambiguity – they lack the harsh clarity of 'homosexual'. In both instances cited here, however, the use of 'vicious' summons up the spectre of the homosexual as a conspicuous absence – one hears 'homosexual' as that word which Brideshead cannot utter, which Mr. Fortune cannot voice, even to himself. Hence to hear 'homosexual' in 'vicious' involves a slight, as to deny being 'vicious' is not only to deny homosexuality, but to avoid the sordidness of speaking its name.

Some of these usages have local, ephemeral lives, avoid the lexicographer's net, and die: 'vicious' is no longer used as a synonym for homosexual. Yet certain words appear to have more persistent homoerotic associations. How are we to read late nineteenth-century utterances of the word 'queer'? In Stevenson's *Strange Case of Dr Jekyll and Mr Hyde* (1886), Enfield calls Dr Jekyll's house 'Black Mail House', and states, 'the more it looks like Queer Street, the less I ask'.[37] What does 'queer' mean in this context? (The current Penguin edition glosses it as 'a term that indicates a case of financial difficulty'.)[38] Does 'queer' already signify 'homosexual' in the 1880s?[39] According to the *OED*, 'queer' only begins to be used as a synonym for 'homosexual' in 1922. Yet if a word like 'queer' takes on the meaning of 'homosexual' in a subcultural (and predominantly oral) context, its date of birth will remain uncertain.

Some readers might like to feel that the name 'Queer Street' is just one uncanny coincidence in a text of uncanny coincidences and doublings; in the nineties, however, it is difficult to deny that 'queer' takes on a more assertive shade of pink. Unsurprisingly, Oscar Wilde is the catalyst for this development. In 1895 the Boston architect Charles Wentworth wrote to his business partner Ralph Adams Cram urging Cram and their third partner, Bertram Goodhue, to be cautious: 'You are two innocents and besides you are both queer and queer things are looked at askance since Oscar's exposé.'[40]

'Queer' then had acquired its modern sense of 'homosexual' as early as 1895; hence it is tempting to think that James was joking on the word in 1893, when he returns J. A. Symonds's 'A Problem in Modern Ethics' to Edmund Gosse and notes that the pamphlet is 'on the whole, I think, a queer place to plant the standard of duty'.[41] Joseph Bristow comments that James here is 'at once concealing and revealing his homophile interest'.[42]

For whom does this usage of 'queer' exist? What does it mean to use 'queer' in this way? What does it signify to others? What can it mean, for instance, when Henry James writes to A. C. Benson in 1906, following the publication of the latter's biography of Pater, talking of how Pater has become a 'figure':

It's a matter almost of tragic or ironic (or even comic) felicity – but it comes here + there to the individual – unawares; ... Well I feel that it has come to dear, queer, deeply individual + homogeneous W.H.P. crowning his strong + painful identity.[43]

Is the comfort with which James calls Pater 'dear' and 'queer' in the same mouthful an indication of James's secret sharing of Pater's queerness? Certainly, in answering these questions, the reader cannot point to the 'authoritative', or 'authorized' meanings of the words involved. James's use of 'queer', in his correspondence, depends not only on a relation between James, his writing, and his subject matter (Pater and Symonds), but on a relation between James and his auditors, men like A. C. Benson and Gosse who are, like James, important in the development of more accentuated homosexual subjectivities and of an élite homosexual circle.

It is important to find ways of discussing the importance of the sexual (and the homosexual) in James's works without reducing their frequent ambiguities, their sometimes infuriating (if immensely pleasurable) vague-nesses, into causal certainties. Such a procedure runs the risk of begging the question of why such involved and involuted rhetorical procedures were in any case necessary. Jamesian ambiguity is important for both aesthetic and historical reasons, and can be accounted for neither by a purely formalist criticism – say, by regarding James's novels as self-referential aesthetic masterpieces – nor by a crude historicism – by referring silence to a framework of 'repression', or by accounting the peculiarities of the text to the peculiarities of James's biography.

An awareness of the manner in which aesthetic strategy may relate to historical context needs to frame our reading of James. James's attempt, in the New York prefaces of 1906 to 1908, to formulate the aesthetic criteria of prose fiction, took place only one decade after the Wilde trials. Although Wilde v. Queensberry (1895) was a case against Queensberry for criminal libel, Queensberry's defence, in seeking to establish that Queensberry's attack on Wilde for 'posing as a somdomite [sic]' was not only based on 'truth' but was also made in the public interest, turned the case around so that it effectively became a trial of Wilde.[44] The case became both a trial of Wilde's aesthetic (in particular, Wilde's insistence that art and morals were radically separate realms) and of Wilde's fiction (Queensberry's plea of justification alleged that *The Picture of Dorian Gray* 'was designed and intended ... to describe the relations, intimacies, and passions of certain persons of sodomitical and unnatural habits, tastes, and practices'.)[45]

Wilde found himself in the awkward position of trying to emphasise a separation of the aesthetic and the ethical, when aesthetic beauty in *Dorian Gray* is frequently said to derive from male physical charm and grace, and thus comes perilously close to the sexual, which *was,* for the Victorians, firmly located within the domain of the ethical. Wilde's defence was unusual in that he found it necessary to advance an aesthetic doctrine – a defence one might expect to be made of a book or work of art (such as in the trial of *Lady Chatterly's Lover* or other obscenity trials) rather than a person. *Dorian Gray* was argued to be non-referential. 'No work of art ever puts forward views', Oscar is quoted as saying in the *Morning Leader* of 4 April 1895.[46] Yet Wilde's insistence that it was invalid to make connections between his sexual behaviour and his artistic production was made difficult in that he had actively participated in a project of constituting *aesthetic style as sexuality.* Neil Bartlett, in *Who Was That Man?* (1988), has shown how Wilde worked at the creation of a sexual language, situated precariously between private and public, with a sophisticated iconography involving the narcissus, the hyacinth, the rose and most notoriously the green carnation.[47] Wilde's fierce cultivation of the (ambiguous) sign of difference combined an excess of *suggestion* with an emptiness of content. The power of his persona derived from its perpetual suggestion of illicit desire accompanied by a refusal to specify, to make concrete. Queensberry's accusation that Wilde was 'posing as a somdomite' repeated the distinction between summoning up the *idea* of the homosexual and actually engaging in illegal sexual practices. By insisting that aspects of Wilde's persona did not merely *suggest* that Wilde was a sodomite but actually constituted the outward signs of the sodomite, the Wilde trials contributed powerfully to the creation of the homosexual as a species. And rather than silencing the creature they set out to condemn, the Wilde trials provided a symbol and a form for the subsequent mobilization of resistance.

The Wilde trials are an important backdrop to James's fiction because they help us recognize the changing contours and implications of same-sex eroticism in his fiction from *Roderick Hudson* (1875) through to late texts such as 'The Jolly Corner' (1908) and 'A Round of Visits' (1910). Reading James's fiction requires a sensitivity to the functioning of silences both in any given text and in that text's contexts. Silence already played an important role in fiction prior to James. In nineteenth-century fiction resonant silences were instrumental in *constituting* the erotic – silence itself was eroticized, and that silence could signal a boundary point where the erotic hovers, at the edge of discourse. John Kucich has alerted us to the importance of libidinal silences in Victorian fiction: what he calls 'eroticized and emotionally expansive refusals of expression' play 'a productive role . . . in the development of Victorian emotional life . . . intensify the circulation of desire and heighten a sense of the self's importance'.[48]

Helpful in reading the significance of silences in James's writing is Eve Kosofsky Sedgwick's recent *Epistemology of the Closet* (1991). Sedgwick argues that 'the modernist impulse toward abstraction in the first place owes an incalculable part of its energy precisely to turn-of-the-century male homo/heterosexual definitional panic.'[49] She demonstrates forcefully how figurations of homosexuality, in the late nineteenth century, oscillated between furious denial and extravagant display.[50] In texts of the period there is often an almost inevitable interpretational movement from silence to sexuality, and from sexuality to homosexuality:

. . . the nineteenth-century culture of the individual proceeded to elaborate a version of knowledge-sexuality increasingly structured by its pointed cognitive *refusal* of sexuality between women, between men. The gradually reifying effect of this refusal meant that by the end of the nineteenth century, when it had become fully current – as obvious to Queen Victoria as to Freud – that knowledge meant sexual knowledge, and secrets sexual secrets, there had in fact developed one particular sexuality that was distinctively constituted as secrecy . . .[51]

This does not mean, however, that a consistent equation between secrecy and homosexuality can be made. For 'secrecy' can have many colourings, and any insistence on secrecy can produce a number of hints as to what the secret in question is.

My reading of *Roderick Hudson* (1876), for example, shows a discrepancy between the novel's denotations and its connotations – between its official text and unofficial subtext of desire. Here the unacknowledged desire of the tale seems to be a homosexual desire, Rowland Mallett's desire for Roderick. However, in *The Golden Bowl* the unstable conjunction of a paucity of denotation and a richness of connotation surrounds a series of sexual fantasies and acts including (quasi-incestuous) adultery and female masochism. The late nineteenth century was not just a period in which the 'homosexual' was created; it saw the birth of the 'pervert', the being whose 'sexual instinct' varied from 'normal heterosexual' desire.[52] Even if it was chiefly homosexuality, as 'the love that dare not speak its name', that was equated with silence, readings proceeding according to this equation can ignore other (potentially more) disturbing meanings. (To see the fin de siècle as an era in which the 'forbidden' in fiction is axiomatically the 'homosexual' is to ignore, for instance, the proliferation of masochistic and incestuous themes in fiction of the period.)[53] In fact, this masking of other sexual meanings may be one of the principle functions of the binary between homosexuality and heterosexuality.

The stigmatization of homosexual desire is in part always also a legitimization of heterosexual desire, but it is also a simplification, a creation of a powerful binary. Discussing such binaries, Sedgwick describes them as 'sites that are *peculiarly* charged with lasting potentials for powerful manipulation', and cautions that resistance to such binaries cannot simply (naively) take the form of an affirmation of the undefined.[54] Sedgwick objects to a deconstructive move which exposes the *constructedness* and instability of such binaries, and then concludes that they are 'inefficacious or innocuous'. She notes that it is 'premature' when Roland Barthes claims that 'once the paradigm is blurred, utopia begins: meaning and sex become the objects of free play, at the heart of which the (polysemant) forms and the (sensual) practices, liberated from the binary prison, will achieve a state of infinite expansion.'[55] This statement by Barthes involves a move from constructionism to essentialism, as it assumes the existence of a pre-social, polymorphous desire which cannot find expression in the language available to describe sexuality. A similar move is found at the close of Stephen Heath's *The Sexual Fix:* 'We need to pose the question [of the importance of sexuality], analyze, understand, refuse – refuse to be heterosexual and homosexual, the opposite sex and a sex at all. . .'[56]

The homosexual/heterosexual binary illustrates how the constructionist/ essentialist debate can function differently around different categories: if categories like 'gender', 'race' and 'sexuality' are constructed, it seems that some categories are more constructed than others. Thus calls to dismantle the very category 'homosexual' seem to be made more freely than calls to dismantle the categories 'female' or 'black'. Yet if a 'deconstruction' of the homosexual/heterosexual opposition is to lead to its dismantling, then deconstruction could very easily become aligned with the insistence of the silencing of the homosexual. The valorization of the 'polymorphous' over the defined (even if contingent, constructed) desire can come close to the demands of 'taste' that insist that the question of homosexuality is one that should not be brought to the study of canonical literature. Antihomophobic criticism is faced then with the tasks of *insisting on* the importance of the category 'homosexual' even while foregrounding its constructed nature, as well as highlighting the role the homosexual/heterosexual binary can play in textual production and reception.[57]

In the speech régime which Eve Kosofsky Sedgwick has memorably analysed as the discourse of the closet, the opposition speech/silence becomes aligned with the opposition between reproductive heterosexuality, which may be named ('love', 'marriage'), and wasteful homosexuality, which 'dare not speak its name'. If this taxonomy – which is the very force of the closet – achieves general cultural currency, then it becomes a powerful means of monitoring behaviour. As the homosexual became identified as a 'type', modes of behaviour which ostensibly need not be classified as 'sexual' could take on a classificatory force. Furthermore, equating the 'unnameable' with the homosexual was a strategy to contain what might be disturbing, unsettling, about desire. What was disturbing *was* homosexual: normality could always be defined, and asserted, as against a demonized homosexual other.

The 'creation' of the homosexual as a particular being can be witnessed in a variety of late nineteenth-century texts, from Krafft-Ebing's *Psychopathia Sexualis* (first English edition, 1892), Havelock Ellis's *Sexual Inversion* (1897), pornographic texts such as *Sins of the Cities of the Plain,* by 'Mary-Ann' (1881), and beseechingly sentimental novels such as Xavier Mayne's *Imre* (1906). Yet the understanding of 'homosexuality' was never as stable as the confident categorizing of sexological texts might suggest. Proscribed forms of behaviour took on the valency of defiant signs of difference, and as such could be actively sought after as well as actively avoided. 'Where there is power, there is resistance', writes Foucault (*HS* 95), and this resistance can take several forms:

Are there no great radical ruptures, massive binary divisions, then? Occasionally, yes. But more often one is dealing with mobile and transitory points of resistance, producing cleavages in a society that shift about, fracturing unities and effecting regroupings, furrowing across individuals themselves, cutting them up and remoulding them . . . (*HS* 96)

The opposition of 'homo' and 'hetero' certainly (as Sedgwick's work shows) moves towards a 'great radical rupture', a 'massive binary division', but it fans out, cuts a swathe across a whole field of disparate modes of existence.

James's late fiction incorporates the changed (and always unstable) nuances of silence in an era in which the homosexual has become an identifiable figure. While this new specification of sexual identity was developing, the passing of the Criminal Law Amendment Act of 1885, which passed penalties not only against 'Buggery committed with Mankind or Beast', but against all 'acts of gross indecency' between adult males,[58] ushered in an intensely punitive legal régime. Anxieties about homoerotic expression were fuelled by specific sexual scandals: not only the Wilde trials but also the earlier Cleveland Street scandal (involving aristocratic customers of a homosexual brothel) in 1889–90.[59] It is ironic how close a description of the reporting of the Wilde trials can come to sounding like a description of one of James's late novels. When Ed Cohen writes that 'in order to mitigate the semantic and commercial consequences that the exclusion of the word "sodomy" threatened to produce, the journalistic texts constructed a complex web of signifiers that endlessly deferred specifying the unnamed and unnameable accusations while explicitly denoting them as an absent site of signification that made their stories useful',[60] he could be describing James's *The Ambassadors* (1903).

The growing visibility of sexual alterity and resistance, signalled more by suggestion than by concrete specification, is noticed by Lambert Strether in this novel. In moving from Woollett, Massachusetts, to London, Strether is overwhelmed by a theatrical display of ambiguous signs of difference. Watching with Maria Gostrey a play in which 'a bad woman in a yellow frock . . . made a pleasant weak good-looking young man in perpetual evening dress do the most dreadful things,' Strether also looks 'beyond the footlights' to take in 'the very flush of English life'. This manifests itself in a variety of 'types':

Those before him and around him were not as the types of Woollett, where, for that matter, it had begun to seem to him that there must only have been the male and the female. These made two exactly, even with the individual varieties. Here, on the other hand, apart from the personal and the sexual range – which might be greater or less – a series of strong stamps had been applied, as it were, from without; stamps that his observation played with as, before a glass case on a table, it might have passed from medal to medal and from copper to gold. (36)

'The personal and the sexual range . . . might be greater or less' because it is unclear whether, in moving from the straightforward division of male and female which characterized Woollett to the 'varieties' of the London theatre, sexual difference is breaking down, being obscured, or whether *new* sexual differences are being created. The personal and sexual express themselves as 'strong stamps' – markers of identifiable individuality put on display as in 'a glass case on a table'. Interestingly, they are 'applied, as it were, from without': their uniqueness depends, in fact, on a mould which precedes them.

The blur around the very word 'sexual' in this passage is potent: is there a greater range of *sexes* – i.e. is the range greater than 'male or female'? – or is a greater range of sexual *tastes* on display in the theatre? Or, given that the dominant trope for homosexuality in the period was of *sexual inversion*, does this ambiguity indicate a mutual dependence between a breakdown in the coherence of gender categories and the surfacing of a sexuality – homosexuality – the existence or creation of which means that the existence of 'natural' sexual taste can no longer be taken for granted? For the 'existence' – or mere spectre – of the 'homosexual' implies firstly that 'heterosexuality' needs to be stated, cannot merely be assumed,[61] and secondly that 'homosexuality' too is only a created category, a stamp on 'the personal and the sexual range'. The spectacle of the London theatre creates for Strether a breakdown in certainty of sexual meanings, and this instability is experienced by him as not only intimidating, but also creative and exhilarating.

The difficulty of naming the sexual is also a source of humour. If the sexual is vulgar, then it must be considered with that other most vulgar article in James, money itself (the passage discussed above, in which 'sexual type' is figured as 'copper' or 'gold', is typical of James in its yoking of sexual and financial metaphor).[62] Humour and pleasure arise in late James from the narrative's inability to name either particular sexual sites or just how fabulously wealthy the protagonists are – or how, indeed, their wealth is generated. This inability to name does not end discourse, it *creates* discourse. Money and sexual desire are the two generative acts of shame in

James's novels. And, in *The Ambassadors*, immediately after Strether witnesses the personal and sexual spectacle of the London theatre, the narrative dwells on the connections between shame, the difficulty of naming, and pleasure. Asked by Maria Gostrey how the Newsomes make their money, Strether refuses to tell her, and thereby creates a pleasure which is peculiarly Jamesian:

His *postponements*, however, made her wonder – wonder if the article referred to were anything *bad*. And she explained that she meant *improper* or *ridiculous* or *wrong*. But Strether, so far as that went, could satisfy her. '*Unmentionable?* Oh no, we constantly talk of it; we are quite familiar and *brazen* about it. Only, as a small, trivial, rather ridiculous object of the commonest domestic use, it's rather wanting in – what shall I say? Well, dignity, or the least approach to distinction . . .'
  'It's a false note?'
  'Sadly. It's vulgar.' (41–2; my emphasis)

Maria Gostrey's insatiable desire for information, her curiosity as to whether the Newsomes manufacture 'clothes-pins', 'saleratus', or 'shoe polish' (42), gives way to other pleasures:

. . . by the law, within her, of the incalculable, her desire for the information dropped and her attitude to the question converted itself into a positive cultivation of ignorance. In ignorance she could humour her fancy, and that proved a useful freedom. (42)

This reading of a small extract from *The Ambassadors* has shown how 'repression' – a refusal to name the sexual – can operate as a productive value in James, creating pleasure, humour, generating narrative itself. A frisson, a readerly buzz or shudder, is created by the un-nameability, by the hint – which won't be confirmed – that the vulgar, domestic article might have to do with bodily functions best left undiscussed. This eroticization of silence – which shows how repression can in fact create desire through prohibition, bring into being that which it ostensibly forbids – is one of the main readerly pleasures in James. In the late fiction, this refusal to name achieves an almost mystical perversity. And if the hovering of the Jamesian narrative around a sanctified silence is in part the very source of the late fiction's beauty, this hovering can also, as it will be shown, bring James's aesthetic project to a point of crisis.

CHAPTER TWO

Gender and Representation in
The Wings of the Dove

Belwood The essential, latent antagonism of the sexes – the armed opposed array of men and women, founded on irreconcilable interests. Hitherto we have judged these interests reconcilable, and even practically identical. But all that is changing because women are changing, and their necessary hostility to men – or that of men to them, I don't care how you put it – is rising by an inexorable logic to the surface. It is deeper – ah, far deeper, than our need of each other, deep as we have always held that to be; and some day it will break out on a scale that will make us all turn pale.
Belinda The Armageddon of the future, *quoi*!

'An Animated Conversation'[1]

I REALISM AND SILENCE

In the dialogue from which I take my epigraph, first published in *Scribner's Magazine* in 1889, Belwood argues that the novel – and, in Belinda's view, '[t]he book today *is* the novel' – 'will contribute in its degree to the great evolution which . . . will certainly become the huge "issue" of the future', namely the 'essential, latent antagonism of the sexes'.[2] What contribution does *The Wings of the Dove* make to such an 'issue'? And how does *The Wings of the Dove* interrogate the very terms with which the 'issue' might be articulated? Perhaps *the* consummate aesthetic structure in the entire Jamesian edifice, *The Wings of the Dove* nevertheless shows a considered response to those 'issues' most prominent in this 'antagonism' at the turn of the century: namely, a crisis in the very manner in which 'femininity', or 'woman', might be represented, and, in turn, the consequences for 'masculinity' of such a crisis.

The Wings of the Dove is remarkable for the level of its engagement with the narrative techniques with which it is constructed: ostensibly a 'realist' text, it repeatedly interrogates its own representational strategies. Terry Eagleton has written that the 'representationalism' of realism effaces the heterogeneity of textual production, insidiously naturalizes the sign, produces discursive closure, homogenizes narrative space and so voids it of contradiction, ranks its codes in a stabilizing hierarchy rather than permitting them to interrogate and contradict one another. And the effect of all this is a fixing of the specular reading or viewing subject in the 'imaginary' plenitude of his or her ideological position.[3]

Yet the 'representationalism' of *The Wings of the Dove* interrogates the 'naturalness' of the sign, fails to reach discursive closure, produces a narrative space replete with contradiction, and sets different narrative codes at war with one another. If 'gender' is interrogated in the novel, then a naturalization of gender is the last thing the novel accomplishes. The novel's embedded critique of its own rhetorical mode is also a critique of the rhetorical procedures through which 'identity' is produced as natural, intrinsic to and essentially attached to the sexed body. And this critique takes place with reference to the highly charged, politicized discussion of sexual difference in turn of the century Europe and America.

Recovering such a context involves negotiating a narrative which appears to create a series of representational voids, or, to use its own terminology, moves in 'abysses'. To read *The Wings of the Dove* several times is to stumble, repeatedly, against prominent gaps in the text, perhaps the most outrageous being that which bridges Book Ninth, ending with Densher farewelling Sir Luke in Venice in early Autumn, and Book Tenth, which begins with Kate Croy asking him, 'in the December dusk of Lancaster Gate':

'Then it has been – what do you say? a whole fortnight? – without your making a sign?' (441)

Absent, then, from the narrative, are Densher's final meeting with Milly, which is referred to only in retrospect in conversation with Kate, and any direct presentation of the final weeks of Milly's life. Before this transition, Densher has reflected that 'Sir Luke's face ... was to be his nearest approach to the utter reference they had so successfully avoided' (439), this being a reference to Milly's illness. The sudden leap to Book Tenth represents then a similar evasion of reference on the part of the narrator. This evasion is comparable to another stunning transition in James's work, the gap, between the end of Chapter 35 and the beginning of Chapter 36 in *The Portrait of a Lady*, which skirts the first three years of Isabel's marriage and the loss of her child. These absences implicate the narrator in the presentation of events in that they resemble lacunae in the characters' own narratives: Madame Merle's suppression of the way her past intertwines with Gilbert Osmond's; the concealment of the emotional bond between Merton and Kate.

Such absences point to a seeming arbitrariness of narrative (it seems the events could have been depicted in another way), yet they are central to the power of narrative. As it is only the narrative that constitutes the events, it is only by reference to the narrative that the presentation of events can be challenged. This leads to a Borges-like paradox by which a valid description of the novel could only consist of a repetition of the novel itself; or to a New Critical position (to which the New Critics in practice did not adhere) that the 'heresy of paraphrase' does 'violence' to the poem.[4] Yet the incompleteness of narrative places the critic in a role analogous to that of each character, attempting to fill gaps in the stories they encounter. From such a position criticism requires a strong intervention with the novel's terms of presentation, even if attempts to fill gaps in the narrative can only ever remain provisional, subject to further re-writings. Moments where the narrative can 'bear without cracking the strongest pressure we throw on it' (AN 304–5) are moments when such criticism is most difficult. Knowledge of this is fully exploited in the characters' attempts to put forward watertight narratives which reveal no 'joint or seam', no 'joint or any piecing'.[5] The gilding over of joints, when done to perfection, represents an art of concealment so finished that one is not even aware that something is being concealed; conversely any showing of a crack reveals the artifice of narrative and leads to a questioning of its terms.

These terms are always a peculiar mixture, made up as they are of the representation by the narrator of the consciousness of the particular character through whose point of view the events are being seen. James's insistence on 'an adopted, a related point of view', the filtering of events through a 'recording consciousness', entails a recognition of the distance between signification and signified, the difficulty of getting to the 'signified' beyond the particular modes of representation used. The interactions of varying points of view portrayed in *The Wings of the Dove* realize fully the act of power in the making of representations. *The Wings of the Dove* 'represents' nothing so much as the process of representation itself. Its language frequently anticipates the terminology of contemporary semiotics, and to follow the sequence of moral dilemmas charted by the novel is to be led through an exploration of the politics of signification.

In the preface James singles out the words 'bristle' and 'portentous' as words he 'rejoiced' or 'delighted' in: both terms suggest the instability of signification, and signal James's pleasure in what, after Barthes, might now be called *jouissance*. The term is particularly appropriate in that Barthes sees *jouissance* arising at a joint, a meeting-point: 'Neither culture nor its destruction is erotic; it is the seam between them, the fault, the flaw which becomes so.' Barthes defines the '*brio* of the text' as its '*will to bliss* [sa volonté de jouissance]: just where it exceeds demand, transcends prattle, and whereby it attempts to overflow, to break through the constraint of adjectives – which are those doors of language through which the ideological and the imaginary come flowing in'.[6]

By such a definition James's desire, expressed in his critical prefaces, that the text should reveal no flaws, no 'joint or seam' (*AN*115), is analogous to a suppression of eroticism, a painting over of the opening to the ideological and the imaginary. Yet James also shows an awareness of the potential for cracks to emerge in any structure, the potential for fragmentation and the subsequent act of reconstitution which the narrative process entails. The eroticism of the Jamesian text may be placed historically with reference to what Foucault calls 'the repressive hypothesis', whereby a repression of sexual discourse, a taboo on 'calling sex by its name', are in fact accompanied by a 'veritable discursive explosion'. The supposed suppression of eroticism in the Jamesian text actually measures an extension of the 'sites where the intensity of pleasures and the persistency of power catch hold', a widening of the domain of the 'sexual', and in this complex relation between repression and a surfacing of what is repressed, '[s]ilence itself – the things one declines to say, or is forbidden to name, the discretion that is required between different speakers, is less the absolute limit of discourse . . . than an element that functions alongside the things said, with them and in relation to them within over-all strategies'. (*HS* 3, 17, 27, 49)

Jouissance then takes on a double significance in James's late work, occurring at a vibration point, the seam, between the repression of and the 'flowing in' of the ideological and the sexual, a silencing the actual effect of which is an intensification of pleasure. Once more such a commentary on the text's rhetorical strategies may be found embedded in the novel as allegorical self-awareness, through Milly Theale's changing response to what she calls 'abysses', a growing realization that joy in the plurisignificance of language is intensified by possible threat.

Nicola Bradbury recognizes the proliferation of linguistic and structuralist terms in the novel, in which, she claims, 'the structuralism of *The Ambassadors* gives way to deconstruction', but her reading of the novel as a celebration of absence, in which Milly is seen as triumphant 'because she has escaped all systems', produces a context-less, apolitical deconstructive reading. Bradbury praises the novel for frustrating 'a structuralist, logo-centric reading'. Such an account works within a structure of binary oppositions which ignores the delicate political nuances associated with varying levels of discursive closure found in the various characters' reading strategies, and the implications in the novel that 'absence' and uncertainty may be just as dangerous as logocentricity, in themselves rhetorical techniques which are not without their ideological accompaniment.[7] James's use of 'absence' and 'silences' anticipates the importance of silence in contemporary drama and music, and in contemporary drama silence is usually threatening, not a cause for celebration. Milly is brought violently into contact with the threat of absence. Early in the novel Mrs Stringham and Milly are attempting to read the 'text' presented by Merton Densher and Kate Croy:

Susie had an intense thought and then an effusion. 'My dear child, we move in a labyrinth.'

'Of course we do. That's just the fun of it!' said Milly with a strange gaiety. Then she added: 'Don't tell me that – in this for instance – there are not abysses. I want abysses.' (133)

Milly's abyss – an erotics of uncertainty – is, later in the novel, a cause of fear:

'Do you mean we should kill you in England?'

'Well, I've seen you and I'm afraid. You're too much for me – too many. England bristles with questions.' (326)

The suppression of knowledge, which in *The Wings of the Dove* is always also sexual knowledge, has become aligned with terror, a terror from which, at the close of the novel, Merton and Kate, and by implication the reader, cannot escape.

II KATE CROY AND THE ART OF POWER

Kate Croy resembles many Jamesian heroines in that her eloquence and elegance seem to bestow her with a raw power quite out of keeping with the social position she occupies. She has two chief means in her bid for power, both strongly emphasized: her ability at self-presentation, and her arts of representation. The novel begins with the classic trope of the woman before the mirror, assessing her own appearance, which is also an act of assessing her power, a power aligned with beauty, charm and grace. James presents Kate's beauty as something which exists in a social relation – 'she was somehow always in the line of the eye' – and as an art which causes admiration in others, 'whose general explanation was to say that she was clever, whether or not it were taken by the world as the cause or as the effect of her charm' (3).

Analysing Kate's discursive arts reveals much about the novel's rhetoric and the commentary it makes on rhetoric. The novel brings different modes of signification into conflict. Each character uses language as if she or he is making impartial claims, yet these claims are always involved, always motivated. The act of utterance becomes inseparable from an act of power. Mark Seltzer's comments on the 'double discourse' of the Jamesian novel apply to the characters of *The Wings of the Dove*, who can be seen as novelists working within the novel, engaged in battles of authority:

> ... the discourse of [James's] fiction is a double discourse that at once represses and acknowledges a discreet continuity between literary and political practices ... [T]he Jamesian aesthetic is elaborated precisely as a way of dissimulating and disavowing the immanence of power in the novel ... James's art of representation always also involves a politics of representation ...[8]

Kate shows her awareness of the politics of representation when she describes how Aunt Maud denies the relation between herself and Merton Densher:

> Aunt Maud's line is to keep all reality out of our relation ... by not having so much as suspected or heard of it. She'll get rid of it, as she believes, by ignoring it and sinking it – if she only does so hard enough. (235)

The immanence of power in Aunt Maud's speech, which Aunt Maud herself would disavow, is insisted on by Kate, whose role as critic in relation to Aunt Maud becomes, then, analogous to that of Seltzer in relation to James:

> The very essence of her ... is that when she adopts a view she – well, to her own sense, really brings the thing about, fairly terrorizes with her view any other, any opposite view, and those, not less, who represent that. (351)

Kate Croy's remarks about Aunt Maud are, of course, ultimately valuable for what they reveal about herself, for in the war of different 'views' she is a practised fighter.

A concern for genealogy and origins is revealed in the way Kate locates (or fails to locate) herself historically:

> Her father's life, her sister's, her own, that of her two lost brothers – the whole history of their house had the effect of some fine florid voluminous phrase, say even a musical, that dropped first into words and notes without sense and then, hanging unfinished, into no words nor any notes at all. (2)

Her bid for power may be seen as a bid to become author of her own narrative rather than subject to another's representations, to take control of her own history: 'She hadn't given up yet, and the broken sentence, if she was the last word, *would* end with a sort of meaning' (3). Yet her narrative is a continuation of a family narrative, re-tracing and continuing the history of a name which has preceded her, that 'precious name she so liked and that, in spite of the harm her wretched father had done it, wasn't yet past praying for' (3). Kate's success will depend on whether she can seize authorship of the family narrative, or whether her life will be written according to its terms.

Kate expresses with vehemence the fear of being the subject of others' representations, of 'being written' rather than 'writing herself'. This fear is shown in her wariness of Susan Stringham: ' "Chop me up fine or serve me whole" – it was a way of being got at that Kate professed she dreaded' (249). Yet Kate is actively involved in manipulating representations of herself and of others, and, as Laurence B. Holland has pointed out, in her own plotting she develops the plot of the novel. Kate and Densher ' "suit the action to the word, the word to the action" of James's novel by agreeing to enact its plot, with Kate forcing Densher to put her plan into words and then joining him in the phrasing of it'.[9] Kate is an artist in a sense defined by Nietzsche: rather than 'know[ing] that something *is* thus and thus' she 'act[s] so that something *becomes* thus and thus . . . *Artists* . . . are productive, to the extent that they actually alter and transform; unlike men of knowledge, who leave everything as it is'. Densher recognizes the artistry in her manipulative skills early in the novel: 'It had really, her sketch of the affair, a high colour and a great style; at all of which he gazed a minute as at a picture by a master' (53). Kate discards the 'will to truth' for a 'will to power': 'If the morality of "thou shalt not lie" is rejected, the "sense for truth" will have to legitimize itself before another tribunal:- as *will to power*.'[10] Truth, though, is preserved as an illusion which is part of the artist's armory. As Seltzer has remarked, the supposed union of form and content – 'James's conviction that the art of fiction is an organic form' – 'allows for a recession of narrative authority and makes for a dispersal of narrative control that is nonetheless immanent in every movement and gesture of character and plot. Moreover, for James, the rule of organic form provides a way of disavowing the violence of authorial manipulation and control even as regulation is secured at every point in the narrative.'[11] James's deconstruction of his own authority is implicit, though, in his depiction of Kate's exploitation of an authority dependent on a logocentricity which is a creation of her own will. A Nietzschean/Foucauldian battle of discourse takes place in which pretences at disinterest, disavowals of power, are in themselves power strategies.

The figures of Kate and Mrs Lowder help place historically a novel which is notoriously free of historical reference. There are no easy chronological placings as can be found in James's earlier novels, such as the chapter in *The Portrait of a Lady* beginning 'One afternoon of the autumn of 1876'.[12] Milly is located more easily through a literary chronology, which identifies her as a post-Dickens, post-Thackeray heroine, than through any reference to political events. Kate and Mrs Lowder's struggles however can be specifically linked with anxieties surrounding gender at the fin de siècle, revolving partly around the figure of the 'New Woman'. The New Woman, in her demands for education and the right to pursue a career rather than marriage, her rejection of the patriarchal family and life of domesticity, and her demand for political power, actively questioned the biological determinism and gender assumptions of the Victorian era.[13] Kate Croy's bid for power is made in terms which are incompatible with the New Woman's agenda – Mrs Stringham is the only woman in the novel who has a profession – yet Kate's (failed) bid for power registers the discontent to which the figure of the New Woman represented only one response. In her disdain for the Mrs Condrips and her own sister's life, and in her desire to resist societal prescriptions as to who she should marry, Kate's battle resembles that of the New Woman, but, like many other Jamesian heroines, her battle is carried out in a private and domestic setting. Olive Chancellor, in her open identification with feminism, is exceptional among James's heroines in that she resists in the public domain.

Smith-Rosenberg writes that 'the New Woman originated as a literary phrase popularized by Henry James', and that his New Woman heroines, such as Isabel Archer and Daisy Miller, 'suffered the consequences of their autonomy'.[14] A central aspect of the autonomy Isabel and Daisy desire is the ability to control their own sexuality; as Linda Dowling remarks, the New Woman 'wanted to reinterpret the sexual relationship ... [T]he heroine of New Woman fiction expressed her quarrel with Victorian culture chiefly through sexual means – by heightening sexual consciousness, candor, and expressiveness'.[15] Such tactics are also those of the melodramatic heroine. This quarrel with socially prescribed terms of sexuality links heroines who identify explicitly with feminism and heroines who appear to accept the terms of patriarchy, defines the common ground of Kate Croy and Olive Chancellor. If Olive is an open feminist, Kate is implicitly so, comparable in many ways to perhaps the most famous

melodramatic heroine fighting for power, Scarlett O'Hara. As Eve
Kosofsky Sedgwick writes,

... in the life of Scarlett O'Hara, it is expressly clear that to be born female is to be
defined entirely in relation to the role of 'lady,' a role that does take its shape and
meaning from a sexuality of which she is not the subject but the object. For
Scarlett, to survive as a woman does mean learning to see sexuality, male power
domination, and her traditional gender role as all meaning the same dangerous
thing.

Noting the dangers of ignoring, in the study of gender, 'historical categories
as class and race', Sedgwick also notes that 'it is *only* a white bourgeois
feminism that [Scarlett O'Hara's view] apotheosizes'.[16] Such a feminism
is implicit in many of James's female characters, who are often consider-
ably empowered by their class and social connections, and, often, their
wealth. A woman like Mrs Lowder can be enormously powerful without
threatening the basic terms of patriarchy: her power is wielded through
the wealth and name bestowed by a dead husband, and is directed towards
making a favourable marriage for a niece and patronizing a male politician. *The Wings of the Dove* expresses the anxieties occasioned by such
feminine power, without explicit reference to the feminist movement in
Britain and America at the turn of the century.

III MERTON DENSHER, THE FATHER, AND THE LAW

Merton provides a critique of Kate's and Maud's aestheticization of
power, yet his critique is wholly ambivalent because of his inability to
establish his own distance from their plotting, to measure to what extent he
is complicit. Aunt Maud dislikes Densher because of his lack of ambition,
his seeming refusal to rank himself in a social and economic hierarchy and
to attempt to rise in that hierarchy. He appears to embody a different conception of the artist from that of Kate, one whose artistry arises from his
detachment and is not an art of power. But the novel brings Densher's
stance of detachment into question, showing how, despite his eagerness to
disavow authority, he comes much closer to Kate and Mrs Lowder and
their arts of power than he would like to see himself.

For Densher also the notion of truth is intimately connected to *action*.
Even a thought can resemble an action: 'He had thought, no doubt, from
the day he was born, much more than he had acted; except indeed that he
remembered thoughts – a few of them – which at the moment of their
coming to him had thrilled him almost like adventures' (428). His sense of
what can constitute action is comparable to a Lockean notion of tacit con-

sent: 'The sharp point was, however, in the difference between acting and not acting: this difference in fact it was that made the case of conscience. He saw it with a certain alarm rise before him that everything was acting that was not speaking the particular word' (428). This suppression – the suppression of his and Kate's secret engagement – stems from a failure to act which is itself an action, and Densher's recognition of the responsibility of silence is a realization that not to challenge actively other narratives is to let them stand, so that, whether he is willing or not, possessing knowledge as he does he will always be involved.

Subject to Kate's manipulations, as the novel proceeds he desires more and more to act himself, and this desire derives from anxieties about how he perceives his own masculinity. The changing dynamics of Kate's and Merton's relationship are central to the novel's portrayal of gender roles. Forced to take a stance towards Kate's plot, and forced to compromise his detachment from action in the realization that such detachment is illusory, Densher begins to question his own passivity, his 'general plasticity' (348), his state of being subjected to another's artistry. Finding himself implicated so deeply in Kate's designs 'wasn't in the least doing – and that had been his notion of his life – anything he himself had conceived'. He is overcome by a 'kind of rage ... an exasperation, a resentment ... in respect to his postponed and relegated, his so extremely manipulated state' (342). The rage is combined with shame when he considers how Mrs Lowder has used him, in terms which portray his relation to her as one of abject servitude: 'His ears, in solitude, were apt to burn with the reflexion that Mrs Lowder had simply tested him, seen him as he was and made out what could be done with him. She had had but to whistle and he had come' (347).

Kate threatens his self-image in a similar way, turning on its head a Victorian ideal of female subservience to male leadership: 'It was beautifully done of her, but what was the real meaning of it unless that he was perpetually bent to her will?' (342) He yearns for a 'decent reaction ... against so much passivity ... His question ... was the interesting question of whether he had really no will left' (343). For Kate's plan to succeed, it is essential that she have from Merton active participation rather than passive compliance. As she cautions him, 'If you want things named you must name them' (378). When it is thus made clear what is asked of him, Merton can use this request as a bargaining point, and in this way effect a crucial change in the distribution of power between them. When Densher asks Kate to come to his rooms we see the distinction between love and power break down, and the blurring of this distinction is, as Mark Seltzer has argued, crucial in James's work.[17]

Both *The Wings of the Dove* and *The Golden Bowl* involve what Seltzer calls the 'vigilance of care', a kindness inseparable from a control exercized through supervision and the manipulation of knowledge. Merton receives such a benevolence from the hands of Mrs Lowder and Kate, that Merton feels himself the recipient of, and smarts under the power involved in this kindness. Recognizing the presence of power in Kate's 'poetic versions' (348) is to question the aesthetic terms in which their love has been figured, and Merton's eventual response, by which he 'emasculates' Kate and empowers himself, does actual violence to these terms by substituting a rhetoric of dominance and slavery for the rhetoric of passion and desire which, until now, has represented their relation:

He had never, he then knew, tasted, in all his relation with her, of anything so sharp – too sharp for mere sweetness – as the vividness with which he saw himself master in the conflict. (383)

Densher's 'mastery' involves, in a typically Jamesian configuration, a physical possession coupled with a regulation of knowledge and represen-tations. Having achieved intimacy with Kate, he begins to build realms of knowledge into which she (and often the reader) is not admitted. His close-ness to Milly, which Kate had so encouraged, excludes Kate as Densher pictures 'the case for Mrs Lowder, but no moment cold enough had yet come to make him so picture it to Kate' (463), and later treasures his corres-pondence with Susan Stringham as 'a secret . . . a small emergent rock in the waste of waters, the bottomless grey expanse of straightness' (498).

Densher's exclusion of Kate is figured as an impossibility of unwriting history: Densher 'saw at moments, as to their final impulse or their final remedy, the need to bury in the dark blindness of each other's arms the knowledge of each other they couldn't undo' (499). Ironically, the truth Kate, Densher and Aunt Maud have wished to 'dissemble' has taken on its own authority. Lord Mark's view, the 'truth' that Kate and Merton are secretly engaged, has been 'terrorized' successfully in the manner Kate has described.

Kate recognizes that Milly – the memory of Milly – has come between them. Densher's separation from Kate is evident in the distance from her he wishes to maintain, even while appearing to share responsibility with her. Although at one point he denies telling lies (359), he later appears to share responsibility with Kate: 'we're together in our recognitions, our responsibilities . . . It isn't a question for us of apportioning shares or dis-tinguishing insidiously among such impressions as it was our idea to give' (448). Very soon after having made this statement, however, he distances himself once more by saying, 'I wouldn't have made my denial, in such conditions, only to take it back afterwards' (450). He is still eager to salvage his conscience. Unwilling to accept the distance between signification and signified, he wants to retain an art of making representations which reduces that distance, is faithful to what is being represented rather than proceeding according to the power effects it can achieve. This is an idealization which will not, however, let him escape the results of his action; as Kate pragmatically observes, '[Milly] never wanted the truth ... She wanted *you*' (451).

Kate's ruthless argument cuts through the finer points of Densher's evasions, and, as she herself notes, Densher cannot save his conscience, cannot redeem the past: 'You've had to take yourself in hand. You've had to do yourself violence' (495). Unable to come to terms with the violence of the past, he begins a kind of lamentation at his own authorship, at the history he has engendered. Flooded by memories, he cherishes 'something rare', which 'while the days melted went with them ... he took ... out of its sacred corner and soft wrappings; he undid them one by one, handling them, handling *it*, as a father, baffled and tender, might handle a maimed child' (502). The loss of Milly's letter is to him 'like the sacrifice of something sentient and throbbing, something that, for the spiritual ear, might have been audible as a faint far wail' (502). This wail forms another parallel to *The Golden Bowl*, the moment when Charlotte's voice 'sounded, for [Maggie], like the shriek of a soul in pain', the sound of 'Charlotte's high coerced quaver before the cabinets in the hushed gallery; the voice by which [Maggie] herself had been pierced the day before as by that of a creature in anguish'.[18] Both Densher and Maggie are faced with the question of whether they can undo the past, and these shrieks and wails suggest that the past may be irrepressible.

This re-emergence of the violence of the past, indicated through Densher's consciousness, is one of the most startling movements from the predominantly social terms of representation of the novel to a private language of metaphors and images describing inner psychological states. This language suggests the uncontrollable relationship of past to present, an inability to suppress the past, to prevent the surfacing of history.[19] The novel links this instability metaphorically to familial relationships. Specifically, the image of the 'maimed child' suggests a radically incomplete mourning and brings forth with frightening vividness the dynamics of the Oedipus complex.

The imaging of Densher as father places Kate Croy in the role of daughter, struggling with desire both for the actual and the figurative father. Her relationship with Densher structurally echoes her relationship with her father, which is partly so resonant because of the barely suppressed eroticism with which it is figured in the first chapter. Here Kate nervously assesses her appearance in anticipation of its being judged by Lionel Croy, and in doing so re-lives the pains of her mother: 'she now again felt, in the inevitability of the freedom he used with her, all the old ache, her poor mother's very own, that he couldn't touch you ever so lightly without setting up' (3). When her father appears she tells him, 'I think we've all arrived by this time at the right word for that: "You're beautiful – *n'en parlons plus,*" ' and 'she virtually knew herself the creature in the world to whom he was least indifferent' (5–6). There is a fearful symmetry in the ending of the novel, which represents another parting between Kate and the object of her affection; this symmetry emphasizes how Densher has taken the place of Lionel Croy – that Kate may still be struggling with paternal authority, even when she believes herself to have escaped it.

Here Kate prohibits mention of her father, and, in another structural echo of the novel's opening, again looks into the mirror with the awareness that her appearance is being assessed. In Lacanian theory, the moment when the child perceives her or his image in the mirror constitutes the mirror stage, which brings on 'the dialectic that will henceforth link the *I* to socially elaborated situations.' This moment initiates the process of socialization mediated 'through the desire of the other', through an identification with the wholeness of the mirror image 'by which the subject anticipates in a mirage the maturation of his power'.[20]

Kate's self-examination in the presence of father-figures suggests the proximity of the mirror stage, the formation of desire, and the Oedipus complex.[21] In Dianne F. Sadoff's analysis of the role of the father in Victorian fiction,

A girl . . . understands without being told that she participates in structures of power only by being possessed by someone who possesses the phallus. The female Oedipus complex ushers in, with the metaphor of castration, the daughter's dependence upon the father and his approbation.[22]

Rather than breaking free from the father, the Victorian heroine often finds paternal authority in a father substitute: often paternal authority returns in spite of determined opposition to it, as in *Daniel Deronda* or *The Portrait of a Lady*. The confusion between 'father' and 'husband' plays a chilling role in James's first novel, *Watch and Ward*, in which Nora Lambert, after the death of her father, is cared for by Roger Lawrence, whose explicit intention is to turn his 'ward' into his 'wife'; recurrent examples of such structural ambiguity can be found in James's fiction.

James, in the preface, calls the absence of the father from much of the narrative a 'lapsed importance', and writes that 'the shame and the irritation and the depression, the general poisonous influence of him, were to have been *shown*' (*AN* 297–8). This criticism is disarming, however, in that this 'deformity' is one of the most alluring features of *The Wings of the Dove*. This gap takes on a peculiar importance. Not only does it echo the gaps in the characters' own narratives; it constitutes an important part of the novel's flirtation with the unspoken, the unspeakable. It seems to take the novel to the edge of what may be articulated.

Kate's father figures as a violence in Kate's past which she wants to redeem; as Holland has pointed out, the name Croy, in a Scots dialect, 'means the legal penalty paid, whether in goods or cash, for murder'.[23] Wanting to heal the 'bleeding wound' (3) in her family name, all of Kate's actions are directed towards escaping an inherited history of violence, yet at the end of the novel it appears that her life has unfolded according to this history's terms. This entrapment in a past dictated by one's family history, by one's blood-line, recalls the bloody demise of Hyacinth Robinson in *The Princess Casamassima*, who reads his assignment to assassinate the duke as the 'horror of the public reappearance, in his person, of the imbrued hands of his mother', an uncanny horror constituted by 'the idea of a *repetition*'.[24] Like Hyacinth, Kate wants to leave untouched 'the old evil, which I keep still, in my way, by sitting by it' (501).

If, as Lacan writes, 'in the *name of the father* ... we must recognize the support of the symbolic function which, from the dawn of history, has identified his person with the figure of the law',[25] then for Kate the law connotes a violence which, despite her efforts to suppress it, insists on surfacing. Despite Kate's active resistance of the roles dictated to her by Victorian society, the name of the father – paternal authority in cahoots with the law – has an uncanny way of returning and intervening in her struggle. This return is figured very much through Densher's person. Densher takes his place in a patrilineal ordering, becomes implicated in a struggle for power despite his intentions. His pleasure at his mastery over Kate, and his awareness of the violence inseparable from his actions, both suggest his involvement in such a struggle. He uses a pose of disinterest as a weapon, regulating the knowledge he will share with Kate, and, towards the end of the novel, testing her moral responses (by seeing what she will do with the letter from Milly's lawyers) without informing her that she is being tested. There is an evident hypocrisy in such behaviour, which, by placing himself in a position of superiority over Kate, emerges as a tactic in a power struggle.

Kate's distinction – '[Milly] never wanted the truth . . . She wanted *you*' (451) – shows the importance of sexuality in the novel in mapping the distribution of power. It is his use of sexuality which enables Densher to effect a power reversal. With Kate's active encouragement, he becomes both the object of Milly's and Kate's desire, both of whom refuse Lord Mark in his favour. This puts Densher in the powerful position of being able to pit his bond with one woman against his bond with another, creating an imitative structure of desire.[26] In encouraging Densher to court Milly, Kate eventually gives reality to a relationship between them, thereby rendering him more desirable, but eventually unattainable.

Writing on erotic triangles, Sedgwick draws from Gayle Rubin a working definition of patriarchal heterosexuality as 'one or another form of the traffic in women: it is the use of women as exchangeable, perhaps symbolic, property for the primary purpose of cementing the bonds of men with men.'[27] The basic assumption of an erotic triangle in such a framework is that two men are rivals for a woman. Yet the erotic triangle in *The Wings of the Dove*, and other Jamesian triangles such as that of *The Portrait of a Lady* and *The Golden Bowl*, figure two women as rivals for a man, a structural echo of the rivalry of daughter and mother for the father. The terms of the Kate/Milly/Merton triangle correspond very much to the Madame Merle/Isabel Archer/Gilbert Osmond triangle, revealing one important aspect in which *The Portrait* can be seen as a rehearsal for the later novel. Both Madame Merle and Kate attempt to use another woman as an object of exchange, passing that woman on to a man with whom they have a sexual bond. By refusing Mrs Lowder's terms, which involve both the opportunity to make a prestigious marriage and an accompanying financial reward, Kate endeavours to become subject of her own sexuality, making her own object choice and endeavouring through her own means to acquire a fortune. The stakes are high: she wants to reject the position offered her by her family and the limitations placed on her by her gender, yet gain power in the same society which so restricts her. Likewise Madame Merle, marginalized by her adultery and alienated from her illegitimate child, aims to retain power by an active regulation of knowledge which enables her to marry Isabel to Osmond and thereby bring her daughter into the line of Isabel's wealth. Yet the necessity to suppress the knowledge that she is Pansy's mother enables Gilbert eventually to banish her, meaning that she loses all status as mother, having no recognition in the official ordering of Pansy's parentage. Gilbert's status and power as father remain unchallenged, and Isabel ends up occupying the dubious position which was once Madame Merle's. Similarly Milly, used as an object of exchange by Kate, ends up by displacing Kate in Merton's affections.

The power reversal takes place when a sensitive nerve in Densher makes him dissatisfied with his own passiveness, so that he begins his own regulation of knowledge, and uses his position at the apex of the erotic triangle to play off his attraction to Milly against his attraction to Kate, thereby making Kate the object of his own sexual choice rather than the subject of her own sexuality. His gender anxieties, induced by a fear of subjection to women and by his contempt of his rival, Lord Mark, motivate his attempt to gain male entitlement. His apparent lack of ambition suggests that he is not motivated merely by the desire for money and prestige: rather what is at stake is (male) identity itself, and what James shows Densher going through before his bid for mastery is analogous to the homosexual panic Sedgwick finds in 'The Beast in the Jungle'. By the time Densher figures himself as a 'father, baffled and tender, ... handl[ing] a maimed child', he has gone through a considerable change in his relation to power. Like Marcher he has exchanged his status of son for that of father, and asserted his identity with the Law.

IV MILLY THEALE AND THE DOCTOR: THE REPRESENTATION OF ILLNESS

To what extent does James's own fictional practice embody the Law? In examining the representation of illness in *The Wings of the Dove*, I shall be asking to what extent James's art is complicit with what Teresa de Lauretis calls the 'discourse of the sciences of man,' which

constructs the object as female and the female as object. This, I suggest, is its rhetoric of *violence*, even when the discourse presents itself as humanistic, benevolent, or well-intentioned.[28]

De Lauretis examines the gender dynamics in what Michel Foucault has called 'discourses on sex', emerging, in the nineteenth century, in the domains of pedagogy, medicine, psychiatry, psychology and law. The inquirer after truth is male, the object of that inquiry is 'woman': this paradigm could apply to *The Wings of the Dove*. Yet, I shall be arguing, deconstructive moments in the text undermine the logocentricity, the closure and naturalization of the sign integral to such a discourse. 'Woman' is figured in the novel, yet the novel differentiates itself from writing of the period which asks after her 'true nature' by putting the process by which that nature is figured under scrutiny.

The novel achieves this by refusing to endorse any point of view, repeatedly narrativizing moments in which the female subject becomes object, and analysing the intricate movements of the gaze which constitute this process. One such moment is Milly Theale's first visit to Sir Luke, when 'perhaps what made her most stammer and pant was its thus queerly coming over her that she might find she had interested him even beyond her intention, find she was in fact launched in some current that would lose itself in the sea of science' (164). Her anxiety as to what constitutes the ideal relationship between 'lady' and 'physician' indicates the absence of clear boundaries demarcating 'scientific' activity. There is an ambiguity in the means of generating the 'truth' of Milly, deriving from what Foucault has called the 'interference between two modes of production of truth: procedures of confession, and scientific discursivity' (*HS* 64–5).

Both modes are involved in the diagnosis, the 'production of the truth', of Milly's malady, and neither manages entirely to gain the upper hand. 'After much interrogation, auscultation, exploration, much noting of his own sequences and neglecting of hers' (174), Milly asks for the 'great man's' (163) judgment:

'So you don't think I'm out of my mind?'
'Perhaps that *is*,' he smiled, 'all that's the matter.' (176)

Milly is left in confusion: is her illness an illness of 'mind' or 'body'? Unspoken by Sir Luke, but implicit in his treatment of a 'physical' illness by focusing on Milly's romantic life, is the nineteenth-century assumption that woman's value was defined by her reproductive function, the instabilities of which subjected her to a variety of nervous disorders. Debate on woman's nature formed part of the 'woman question', described by Nietzsche, with characteristic verve and irreverence, in 1885:

Supposing truth to be a woman – what? is the suspicion not well founded that all philosophers, when they have been dogmatists, have had little understanding of women? that the gruesome earnestness, the clumsy importunity with which they have hitherto been in the habit of approaching truth have been inept and improper means for winning a wench? Certainly she has not let herself be won – and today every kind of dogmatism stands sad and discouraged.[29]

For a generation which had 'begun by hoping more from science than perhaps any generation ever hoped before',[30] the 'riddle of femininity'[31] located a flaw in the scientific endeavour, that point where scientific discourse let its own assumptions collapse, felt the need to move beyond its own rules and boundaries so that supposedly impartial representations were in fact active interventions containing *a priori* judgments which preceded inquiry. For woman 'was an enigma to the medical profession, an enigma that grew first from an imperfect apprehension of her disorder, and was confused even further by the dialectical skills of the physician-philosophers of the age and their efforts to deal with the implications of feminism in a male-oriented society'. Such uncertainty did not prevent medicine harnessing 'scientific method' to depict women 'as creatures inferior to men yet somehow kin to the angels'.[32]

Much recent work has shown how cultural ideals informed scientific representations of the 'nature' of woman, and how scientists used the idea of natural gender (and class) differences to justify social inequalities.[33] Such a constellation has been repeatedly observed in the way nineteenth-century medicine depicted gender, 'nature' and disease. As Catherine Gallagher and Thomas Laqueur write, Victorian woman 'was conceptually disembodied, but only to the extent that she was biologized; she was denied sexual feeling, but only to the extent that she was often imagined as wholly sexually determined'.[34] In considering the representation of illness in *The Wings of the Dove*, it is important to ask how such ideals of femininity shaped the understanding of 'physical' illness, particularly those illnesses which had no stable etiology and no developed cure, for which cultural attitudes could supplement concrete 'scientific' description.[35]

As Susan Sontag has demonstrated in *Illness as Metaphor*, tuberculosis, in its many representations in novels, plays and films, acquired an extensive metaphorical gloss, part of which involves a sentimentalization of the tuberculosis victim. Tuberculosis was seen to affect a certain personality type. It was a disease of 'passion, afflicting the reckless and sensual'; the tubercular was 'melancholy, . . . sensitive, creative, a being apart'. Yet the attributes of the tuberculosis victim are often contradictory: tuberculosis could also affect 'someone (like a child) thought to be too "good" to be sexual: the assertion of an angelic psychology'.[36]

Sontag argues convincingly that such metaphorical linkages stigmatize the sufferer and, by suggesting that susceptibility to the disease stems from fundamental aspects of one's nature, hinder the healing process. Such an argument, however, isolates representations of disease from their historical, social and literary context, attention to which would link 'illness as metaphor' to the nineteenth century's medicalization of sexuality. The metaphorical overload Sontag attacks derives from and contributes to quite specific ideological formations.

The linkage of disease and sexuality is implicit in the sentence Sontag quotes from Thomas Mann's *The Magic Mountain*: 'Symptoms of disease are nothing but a disguised manifestation of the powers of love; and all disease is only love transformed.'[37] If disease is love is disease, a new conception of the role of the doctor is required. Such an attitude derives from and facilitates the growth of the paternalistic powers of the doctor accompanying the development of psychology and the 'helping professions'. The important role played by the doctor in the life of the Victorian woman is noted by Alice James's biographer, Jean Strouse, who writes that in the James family 'the concern elicited by illness passed for love – and doctors were the scientifically sanctioned personification of solicitude and care'.[38]

Disease a metaphor of sexuality: such a (crude) formula illuminates the contradictions between the ubiquity of sexuality in James's work and the discretion with which this sexuality is figured. Foucault has described the paradox of an official 'suppression' of discourses on sexuality coupled with an actual proliferation of such discourse, in which metaphor and euphemism take the place of a forbidden terminology; in such a context Freud develops a discourse of transformation, a means to re-write narratives, both oral and written, so that their 'truth', which is their 'sexuality', may be known, so that the implicit may become explicit. The figurations of 'sexuality' in literary discourse delicately tread the balance between the sexualization of woman and social insistence on her innocence, between representing individual drives and satisfying censorial literary standards.

The influence of these contradictions is evident in the mutation the well-defined scenario James first outlines in his notebook, in November 1894, undergoes when transposed into the public discourse of the novel. James wonders whether his 'own' aesthetic values, and furthermore the English reading public, can accomodate the ugliness of his plot. The public, in their prudery, restrict artistic freedom and would reject the scenario for reasons quite distinct from James's own:

If I were writing for the French public the whole thing would be simple – the elder, the 'other', woman would simply be the mistress of the young man, and it would be a question of his taking on the dying girl for a time – having a temporary liaison with her. But one can do so little with English adultery – it is so much less inevitable, and so much more ugly in all its hiding and lying side.[39]

The sexuality of the scenario emerges then in metaphorical guise, meaning that James's 'realism' takes on the 'hiding and lying side' he deplores in the English public. In wanting to satisfy that public, James cannot help being tainted by the hypocrisy he deplores. Thus we see in his writing the violence of a conflict between an apparent curbing and control of sexuality and the strong expression of an (often unconventional) sexuality.

Milly's illness carries much of the sexual charge James wants in his novel, but he fears that the coupling of illness with sexuality could justify a charge of sensationalism deriving from a reductive reading of his work:

... this idea of the physical possession, the brief physical, passional rapture which at first appeared essential to it; bothered me on account of the ugliness, the incongruity, the nastiness, *en somme*, of the man's 'having' a sick girl: also on account of something rather pitifully obvious and vulgar in the presentation of such a remedy for her despair – and such a remedy only. 'Oh, she's dying without having had it? Give it to her and let her die' – that strikes me as sufficiently second-rate.[40]

James is worried that the result of representing such vulgarity will be ugly, yet in failing to do so would he not be guilty of the ugly 'hiding and lying' manner in which the English refer to adultery? Wondering whether the representation of something ugly can be beautiful exposes the tensions between the demands of 'representationalism' and those of 'poetry' which make up James's realism.

His response is to aestheticize the situation, and in the preface he describes how it could be made beautiful. Although James seems to find illness a dubious foundation for art, if the poet 'deal[s] with the sickest of the sick, it is still by the act of living that they appeal to him, and appeal the more as the conditions plot against them and prescribe the battle' (*AN* 289–90). The gender of the subject would help render her fit for artistic treatment, 'since men, among the mortally inflicted, suffer on the whole more overtly and grossly than women, and resist with a ruder, an inferior strategy' (*AN* 290). Here the 'humanistic, benevolent, well-intentioned' nature of James's 'aesthetic' seems to correspond exactly to the 'rhetoric of violence' de Lauretis describes.

Yet traces of the 'vulgar' element he wishes to avoid remain in the novel. Certainly the novel is read this way by Susan Sontag: 'In *The Wings of the Dove*, Milly Theale's doctor advises a love affair as a cure for her TB; and it is when she discovers that her duplicitous suitor, Merton Densher, is secretly engaged to her friend Kate Croy that she dies.'[41] Here are present all the elements of a modern valorization of the power of sex, as descibed by Foucault:

The Faustian pact, whose temptation has been instilled in us by the deployment of sexuality, is now as follows: to exchange life in its entirety for sex itself, for the truth and the sovereignty of sex. Sex is worth dying for. It is in this (strictly historical) sense that sex is indeed imbued with the death instinct. When a long while ago the West discovered love, it bestowed on it a value high enough to make death acceptable; nowadays it is sex that claims this equivalence, the highest of all. (*HS* 156)

James's eschewal of an explicit sexual vocabulary in figuring Milly does not mean that her being is not sexualized, for the sexual pervades the rhetoric of heightened emotion, of sentiment, which dominates the novel.

This sexualization is present in Milly's encounters with Sir Luke. Sir Luke is one of the most evasive figures in the novel, and he is subject to a number of contradictory figurations. Seen primarily through Milly's eyes, he creates in her an anxiety as to how she will be diagnosed or represented. As such he operates as a metaphor for James himself, the omnipresent but invisible author.

Milly's meetings with Sir Luke are charged with the resonance of an ambiguous Jamesian sexuality, in which love and care are conflated with power and masculine force. In 'pitifully obvious and vulgar' terms, Milly falls in love with the doctor. Like Alice James, Milly brings 'extraordinarily high expectations to these encounters'.[42] After her first consultation, Milly announces, 'He knows all about me, and I like it'. Sir Luke looked 'to her fancy, half like a general and half like a bishop' (306), and Milly finds herself in the 'temple of truth' of this 'smooth strong director' (306) 'secretly romancing . . . all over the place' (169). Milly finds the ambiguous nature of the encounters titillating, observing to Sir Luke 'that I visit you in secret' (170), and indulging in joking banter with Kate:

Kate's eyes never quitted her. 'He must have liked *you*.'
   'Oh – doctors!' Milly said.

A lexical slippage operates so that 'knowledge', 'truth', 'happiness' and 'living' all become (un-named) 'sex': the equivalences of the Faustian pact Foucault describes. Sir Luke's instructions to Milly are not medical (or physical) so much as verbal initiations, permission to partake of 'life': 'You must accept any form in which happiness may come' (173); 'isn't to "live" exactly what I'm trying to persuade you to take the trouble to do?' (176).

Yet Milly perceives it not as a pleasure, but as a danger that Sir Luke is 'exceptionally moved', that she has caught him 'in the act of irrelevantly liking her' (180). It is her 'doubt', 'fear', and 'danger' that he 'perhaps wouldn't even take advantage of her being a little romantic to treat her as romantic altogether' (169). She experiences his 'compassion' as 'directly divesting, denuding, exposing'; it 'reduced her to her ultimate state'. Here his gaze appears to be experienced as a metaphorical rape. As Sir Luke is seen through Milly's eyes, it is impossible to gauge the part he plays in such an eroticism. He remains blank and enigmatic. Is he merely the primitive, uninteresting male, the bland, unthinking face of patriarchy?

James's perspective shows how power can best be measured through its effects. Milly's response to Sir Luke highlights his paternalism, his willingness to give commands without giving a clear diagnosis, his support which Milly comes to call 'bolstering – the bolstering that was simply for the weak; and she thought and thought as she put together the proof that it was as one of the weak he was treating her' (179). Vagueness of diagnosis accompanied by clear instructions for 'treatment': such was the patronizing treatment the Victorian woman could hope for from her physician. Thus Alice James could welcome the clear verdict of breast cancer as freeing her from subjection to the sympathy of the doctor:

Ever since I have been ill, I have longed and longed for some palpable disease, no matter how conventionally dreadful a label it might have, but I was always driven back to stagger alone under the monstrous mass of subjective sensations, which that sympathetic being 'the medical man' has had no higher aspiration than to assure me I was personally responsible for.[43]

Milly's illness lacks a conventional label (the word 'consumption' is used only once in the novel, by Kate in converation with Densher), and this lack delivers her into the hands not only of the 'smooth strong director', the 'medical man', but also of literary critics. In the verdict of Virginia Fowler, Milly's illness is a 'symbol' of 'her own character and personality', and Milly 'is doomed as much by her own psychology as she is by her illness'.[44] And according to Alfred Habegger, Milly is a distorted version of James's cousin Minny Temple, lacking Minny's rebelliousness, her freedom and strength.[45]

My objection to such moves is not only that they involve the reduction of ambiguity to certainty, but that in talking of Milly's 'character and personality' as clear, unproblematic entities, they ignore the extent to which Milly is *all representation*. Milly's 'character' or 'being' is subject to the constructions of others, and the representations she has to choose from – a 'princess', the sufferer of a physical disease which denotes a highly sexualised self, the sufferer of mental conditions caused by her femininity, the embodiment of a 'beauty' sinisterly close to delicacy and weakness – bring her to a state of crisis, evoked most vividly in her confrontation with the Bronzino portrait at Matcham.

Kate's assessment of self before the mirror, her fear of Susan Stringham's narrative arts, and Milly's crisis before the Bronzino: these are the novel's three chief instances of the desire to avoid the violence of representation. When Milly faces the Bronzino, a painting which threatens to displace her ('Lady Aldershaw meanwhile looked at Milly quite as if Milly had been the Bronzino and the Bronzino only Milly' (159)), she sees her self as already written: 'Then I'm not original', she remarks, 'which one always hopes one has been' (158). Her fluidity, her Emersonian self-reliance, are threatened by the passivity and stasis of the portrait, her construction as object, the relegation of her self to the field of the *represented*. Milly is both 'at one' with and apart from the image; like Lacan's child before the mirror, her equation of self with representation brings her into a structure of alienation, difference and division. And if, in Lacan's mirror stage, the subject anticipates 'the maturation of his power' through identifying with the wholeness of the mirror image, this maturation is only possible with a degree of self-authorship.

In answering such an attack as Habegger's, or claims that James has, in Milly, created a 'beautiful victim', account must be made of how James, his own first critic, is also his own *self-accuser*. Insight into James's criticism of the art of representation may be gained by comparing Milly with a recurrent type of 'beautiful victim', the tubercular heroine of nineteenth-century sentimental fiction. Such a heroine wore the signs of her disease visibly, and they rendered her more beautiful, sexualized her very being. In Dumas *fils' La Dame aux Camélias* Armand says of Marguerite that 'even her thinness became her', and 'either because it was her nature or else an effect of her state of health, her eyes flickered intermittently with flashes of desire which, if spoken, would have been a heaven-sent revelation to any man she loved.'[46]

Marguerite's being is constituted through the appraisals of the male gaze. The novel's mode of representation is fully complicit with the economy of exchange in which it figures its heroine. In its avoidance of a female point of view it repeats the power distributions of patriarchy rather than criticizes them. Marguerite, and other French tubercular heroines of the period, such as Mimi or Germaine, show no rage at their objectification, pose no threat to the sexual order.[47] The greater sexual explicitness of such fiction, then, does not indicate an absence of 'repression' but a mirroring of the sexual ideology which forms the text.

Whereas the narrative voice of Dumas *fils* does not vary in tone, James, by fragmenting point of view, shows the *effects* of such an economy, and asks what is involved in the attempt to find 'the truth that was the truest about Milly' (431). The novel persistently asks: what is it to know, or to represent a woman; what is it to diagnose her illness? In Kate's analysis, Milly's being eludes one's evaluating gaze:

One *sees* her with intensity – sees her more than one sees almost any one; but then one discovers that that isn't knowing her and that one may know better a person whom one doesn't 'see', as I say, half so much. (246)

Through 'seeing' Milly one attempts to constitute her being, yet, as if realizing that 'seeing' in this way is merely 'representing', Kate acknowledges that her 'being' may escape such a representation. The novel escapes such an equation of 'being' with 'representation' above all in its avoidance of a deathbed scene. The death of the consumptive heroine might be expected to reveal her 'sublimated essence': such an expectation was found across nineteenth-century culture, in medicine, the visual arts, opera and medicine.[48] (A classic example is the death of Violetta in Verdi's *La Traviata*.)

For Densher, a relation between 'seeing' and 'being' underpins the ideology of the aesthetic. Realizing that Milly's being may not correspond to the image that has been made of it brings him to a crisis which diagnoses the very terms of James's art. His meditation at this point deserves quotation in full:

> He hadn't only never been near the facts of her condition – which counted so as a blessing for him; he hadn't only, with all the world, hovered outside an impenetrable ring fence, within which there reigned a kind of expensive vagueness made up of smiles and silences and beautiful fictions and priceless arrangements, all strained to breaking; but he had also, with every one else, as he now felt, actively fostered suppressions which were in the direct interest of every one's good manner, every one's pity, every one's really quite generous ideal. It was a conspiracy of silence, as the *cliché* went, to which no one had made an exception, the great smudge of mortality across the picture, the shadow of pain and horror, finding in no quarter a surface of spirit that consented to reflect it. 'The mere aesthetic instinct of mankind -!' our young man had more than once, in the connexion, said to himself; letting the rest of the proposition drop, but touching again thus sufficiently on the outrage even to taste involved in one's having to *see*. (431–2)

Densher's remarkably perspicacious critique discerns a disjunction – expressed in the formulation 'beautiful fictions' – between ethics and aesthetics, between truth and beauty; in doing so it touches James's greatest anxiety in his attempts to lay an aesthetic foundation for his art. It questions his desire to avoid 'the ugliness, the incongruity, the nastiness, *en somme*, of the man's "having" a sick girl'; his claim that the poet can only deal with 'the act of living'. Densher is 'actively' involved in making fictions or remaining silent; he recognizes the power involved in the disavowal of power, the ideological factors forming the construction of an 'aesthetic' which, rather than forming the 'precondition of truth and virtue',[49] seems to render truth and virtue impossible. As a persuasive recent study by Jonathan Freedman suggests, we can see in passages such as these James's immersion in and his departures from British aestheticism. We see here what Freedman calls a 'Ruskinian fusion of aesthetic and social criticism',[50] a fusion which calls the aestheticist project into question. Densher's Paterian valorization of intense sensation collapses at the very point where he realizes the horror of, the 'outrage to taste' involved in what he has 'to *see*'. The aesthete's dream of a redemptive space cannot be realized.

Which leads to another possible interpretation of Milly's illness: as protest, as refusal of idealization. This is implicit in Bradbury's claim that Milly is triumphant 'because she has escaped all systems'. Milly would then be comparable to another famous 'heroine', also struggling with an uneasy relationship with a doctor: Dora. Her withdrawal can be compared with Dora's strategies of absence and refusal.[51] Before one is tempted, however, to let such an interpretation endorse a 'celebration of absence', one should remember at what cost such an escape is made. The novel ends, after all, with Milly's death; and a 'celebration' of absence always involves replacing absence with presence.

CHAPTER THREE

Sexuality and the aesthetic in The Golden Bowl

'Is there a mode of civilized discourse which might at least partially
dissipate our savage sexuality?'

Leo Bersani, *The Freudian Body*

In the prefaces James seems to waver between two notions of what would
constitute the 'ideal' novel: the self-contained organic whole and the refer-
ential narrative. This hesitation between two different ideals leads him to a
dilemma, as he discerns a disjunction between the novel's aspirations to
'beauty' and its obligation to 'truth'. In *The Golden Bowl* and *The Wings of
the Dove* dramatic tension arises from this disjunction. *The Golden Bowl* is a
narrative which seems to portray – in a parthenogenetic *mise en abîme* –
itself being created. It begins by postulating the idea of the artwork as
civilized form, and in a seemingly natural juxtaposition locates civilized
form in the institution of marriage. The civilized discourse which is
marriage is constituted in the repudiation of 'our savage sexuality'.[1] Yet
sexuality in the novel is *that which cannot be figured*, that which is always
alluded to but rarely directly portrayed. The novel returns again and again
to the question of the marriage, which survives through the renunciation
of incest and the denial of adultery. Ubiquitous desire is replaced by an
insistence that sexual desire can be channelled solely through the marital
bond.

Marriage then, like the poem in New Criticism, or the organic whole
of the Romantics, is a form resolving all conflicts of its disparate parts.
If deconstruction has taught us to mistrust such resolutions in literary
criticism, we may be similarly suspicious of this aestheticization of the
marriage bond. This teleological progression – a renunciation of polymorphous perversity for a socially sanctioned genital (hetero)sexuality – is
of course the story told by two of the most eminent theorists of sexuality
and civilization: Sigmund Freud and Claude Lévi-Strauss.

Freud turned on its head the dominant nineteenth-century narrative of

45

sexual development – in which the innocence of childhood yielded to the corrupting experience of sexual maturity, in which perversion, or sin, was the result of straying from the well-lit road which led to a monogamous, child-bearing union. In *Three Essays on the Theory of Sexuality* (1905) normal development is the path along which the polymorphously perverse child, passing through the vicissitudes of the Oedipus complex, acquires 'normal' genital sexuality. Similarly Lévi-Strauss's work reverses the Christian narrative of an originary innocence (Eden) followed by a fall from grace: civilization becomes instead a state which follows the prohibition of savage incest.

Both these narratives – Freud's tale of sexual development in the individual subject, Lévi-Strauss's account of the formation of civilization – suffer from an instability occasioned by the repression of an originary desire. (In 'psychoanalytic jargon', as Roland Barthes writes, 'all repudiation is avowal'.)[2] The continuance of incestuous desire is in fact measured by the strength of this desire's prohibition; the institution of psychoanalysis survives by satisfying a need which exists because so many individual subjects do not go through the 'normal' sexual development psychoanalytic literature describes. In *Three Essays* Freud struggles with the term 'perversion', wondering if it can be appropriate to describe conditions which appear so prevalent. The distinction between 'normal' and 'perverse' is one he has difficulty maintaining. The perversity of the child seems to persist into adult sexuality, and can be traced in the slips, the gaps in adult speech which point to unresolved childhood complexes.[3] In *The Golden Bowl* violent fantasy can be implicit in the most delicately mannered settings, and 'sexuality' consists not so much in bodily contact as in the endless working out of scenarios, and of variations of scenarios. James has created sexuality as discourse: a formidable eroticism of the text.

The Golden Bowl is James's most passionate novel. In it *the* question is the sexual question – in its most mundane form, 'are the Prince and Charlotte having an affair?' Fanny and Bob ('the Colonel') Assingham, James's two *ficelles*, pose that question repetitively, and augment the erotic tension of the novel by subjecting it to the fervid curiosity of the voyeur – a voyeurism which is theirs and that of the reader.[4] The Colonel watches Fanny perform her mental acrobatic stunts 'very much as he had sometimes watched at the Aquarium the celebrated lady who, in a slight, though tight, bathing-suit, turned somersaults and did tricks in the tank of water which looked so cold and uncomfortable to the non-amphibious' (85). Images of the body in pain, on display, as spectacle, are to recur throughout the novel, though not always in such a grotesque and amusing form.

In a passage from *The Pleasure of the Text* (1973) Barthes opposes 'perversion (which is the realm of textual pleasure)' to 'corporeal striptease' and 'narrative suspense'. The two latter are comparable because in both

there is no tear, no edges: a gradual unveiling: the entire excitation takes refuge in the *hope* of seeing the sexual organ (schoolboy's dream) or in knowing the end of the story (novelistic satisfaction).

In textual pleasure or perversion, however,

there are no 'erogenous zones' (a foolish expression, besides); it is intermittence, as psychoanalysis has so rightly stated, which is erotic: the intermittence of skin flashing between two articles of clothing (trousers and sweater), between two edges (the open-necked shirt, the glove and the sleeve); it is this flash itself which seduces, or rather: the staging of an appearance-as-disappearance.

To this pleasure corresponds 'not the anecdote ... but the layering of significance; as in the children's game of topping hands, the excitement comes not from a processive haste but from a kind of vertical din (the verticality of language and of its destruction)'.[5]

According to Barthes' taxonomy (a medicalizing of texts), narrative pleasure in *The Golden Bowl* is perverse. It might be objected that Barthes is staging the act of reading as an encounter between male spectator and female body-as-object, although in fact the body on display, as described by Barthes, is, with its 'open-necked shirt', either ungendered or masculine. Many attempts to theorize the gaze have dwelt on the (symbolic) gender of the viewer and of the displayed body. Laura Mulvey, in 'Visual Pleasure and Narrative Cinema' (1975), her influential attempt to theorize cinematic pleasure, found it necessary to postulate a *male* viewer. Mulvey writes that 'an active/passive heterosexual division of labour has ... controlled narrative structure': consequently pleasure is only available to the female viewer through an identification (in fantasy) with the male viewing position.[6]

Both Barthes and Mulvey (whose essay draws on a psychoanalytic framework similar to that used by Barthes) are attempting to describe the scopophilic economy of patriarchy. In the work of both writers can be felt the influence of Freud's essay 'Medusa's Head', in which the spectacle of Medusa is said to represent the mutilated male genitals, and functions apotropaically to ward off castration fears. Mulvey writes that 'woman in representation can signify castration, and activate voyeuristic or fetishistic mechanisms to circumvent this threat'.[7] This is the voyeuristic scenario Bob Assingham undergoes at the aquarium, and returns to when confronted with his wife's great eloquence, an eloquence which, in Freud's analysis, may be compared to woman's love for plaiting and weaving, an achievement echoing nature's 'causing the growth at maturity of the pubic hair that conceals the genitals', the castration scar.[8] Bob replaces the articulate woman with the cold and uncomfortable woman in her 'slight, though tight, bathing-suit', consoles himself in the face of the phallic powers of 'Fanny' with a vision of the woman in pain, the woman whose meaning is, ultimately, sexual difference, and thereby assures himself of his own possession of the phallus.

If Bob Assingham wants to comfort himself with a fantasy of woman as sexual difference, this is in part because, in *The Golden Bowl,* sexual difference is on the verge of a breakdown. Roland Barthes has noted that in Balzac's *Sarrasine* the 'symbolic field' of gender 'is not that of the biological sexes, it is that of castration: of *castrating/castrated, active/passive*'.[9] Barthes is very close here to Lacan, who sees castration as a central term in the constitution of the subject and the scopic drive: who has the phallus, who lacks it. The male gaze, focusing on the figure of the castrated woman, assures the gazer of his mastery.[10]

Castration is important, in Lacanian theory, in the symbolic dimension, and does not indicate a simplistic division according to biological sex. The phallus is seen as mark of division. As Jacqueline Rose remarks: 'the phallus relegates sexuality to a strictly other dimension – the order of the symbolic outside of which, for Lacan, sexuality cannot be understood'.[11] This implies that the workings of sexual difference in the psyche can vary historically, and *The Golden Bowl* is marked with an understanding that the psychic process of gendering is historically inflected. Charlotte notes that the 'position of a single woman to-day is very favourable' (80): although women in the novel are not expected to find fulfilment in marriage as is the Victorian 'angel in the house', Charlotte's statement is disingenuous in that (as her own progress in the novel indicates) the economic pressure on women to marry was often considerable. (Despite the presence of the New Woman, upper-class women were often discriminated against in inheritance, as Vita Sackville-West, barred from inheriting Knoles, her family's estate, was to experience.[12] The anger of a powerful, creative woman unable to live in her dead husband's home is, of course, the story of James's *The Spoils of Poynton* (1897).)

This relationship between a psychoanalytic division of power (according to who possesses the phallus), and a historical account of power struggles (the woman's movement in Victorian and Edwardian England), measures a discrepancy between a patriarchal *fantasy*, in which women hold no power, and a patriarchally ordered society in which women are engaged in political action, fighting for power. James's novels focus on how this discrepancy is played out in the individual: interest is directed to how these women wrestle with that fantasy and the hold it takes on their psyche. If a symbolic patriarchal ordering does not prevent women from holding power, or wielding influence (on any part of the political spectrum), it may also produce femininity as a difficulty, a problem emerging from the cost in that order.[13] In *The Golden Bowl* James pays attention to an inner life of fantasy, in particular on the part of Maggie, but does not draw simplistic parallels between the movements of fantasy and her behaviour. Instead the novel focuses on the question of how Maggie wrestles with the hold fantasy has on her.

Through the figure of Maggie the novel asks the banal question of psychoanalysis – what does a woman want? (in Freud's words the 'riddle of femininity') – and comes up with some disturbing answers. Maggie indulges in masochistic fantasies, figuring herself as the abused woman in a mimetic triangle of desire:

One of the most comfortable things between the husband and the wife meanwhile ... was that she never admired him so much, or so found him heart-breakingly handsome, clever, irresistible, in the very degree in which he had originally and fatally dawned upon her, as when she saw other women reduced to the same passive pulp that had then begun, once for all, to constitute *her* substance ... [E]ven should he some day get drunk and beat her, the spectacle of him with hated rivals would, after no matter what extremity, always, for the sovereign charm of it, charm of it in itself and as the exhibition of him that most deeply moved her, suffice to bring her round. (156–7)

The passage implies a savage sexuality lurking beneath civilized ('comfortable') form. This opposition structures much writing on sexuality in the period's new disciplines – sexology, psychiatry and sociology – in which the spectre of an ancient, passive femininity, deriving pleasure from a violent system of sexual exchange epitomized by wife-capture, is summoned to 'naturalize' existing social arrangements and simultaneously to pathologize female resistance. Thus Richard von Krafft-Ebing, in *Psychopathia Sexualis*, writes that 'under the veneer of polite society the instinct of feminine servitude is everywhere discernible'.[14] Maggie occupies with peculiar force the very clichés of femininity (a 'passive pulp' desirous of violence and abuse), which she opposes to, in fact sees engendered by, a hackneyed image of masculinity – violent, 'heart-breakingly handsome, clever, irresistible'.

Part of the novel's power lies in its re-working of clichés both of masculinity and of femininity. In the Prince James examines the code of *machismo*, according to which women are important only as sexual objects, and are categorized accordingly. The Prince divides women into those to whom he has or hasn't 'made love':

He liked in those days to mark them off, the women to whom he hadn't made love: it represented – and that was what pleased him in it – a different stage of existence from the time at which he liked to mark off the women to whom he had. (42)

For him an encounter with a woman involves an approach and a surrender, a stage of waiting for 'the thing always as certain as sunrise or the coming round of saints' days, the doing by the woman of the thing that gave her away' (74). Being thrown together with Charlotte involves for the Prince a fundamental challenge to his masculine identity, 'as if a galantuomo, as *he* at least constitutionally conceived galantuomi, could do anything *but* blush to "go about" at such a rate with such a person as Mrs Verver in a state of childlike innocence, the state of our primitive parents before the Fall' (275).

In the terms of the fantasy outlined above, Charlotte, as the Prince's other woman, would merely be a part of Maggie's sexual scene; Maggie, desiring 'the spectacle of [the Prince] with hated rivals' (as Severin, in *Venus in Furs*, is wildly excited at Wanda's coupling with the Greek), can thus be seen as culpable for her own status as victim. The problem with such a reading is its lack of attention to the problems posed by fantasy. The fantasy seems at odds with the ending of the novel, in which Maggie terminates the very scene she is shown, at the beginning of the novel, to desire so strongly, as if, once in possession of it, she finds it dispensable. Maggie's fantasy life poses difficult problems to the reader in that it seems to locate a split in subjectivity: what she fantasizes about, and what she wants, cannot be equated. (Her masochistic desires have some affinities with the Princess Casamassima's radical chic – a flirtation with tokens of alterity which might not be so attractive if they were imposed rather than freely chosen.) In James's fiction it is not only women who feel this desire for self-obliteration: Spencer Brydon, the protagonist of 'The Jolly Corner' who has recently discovered a talent as building entrepreneur, is also absorbed in a fantasy of self-obliteration, an encounter with 'the hot breath and the roused passion of a life larger than his own, a rage of personality before which his own collapsed'.[15] James's writing is sensitive to the different ways in which male and female characters respond to similar fantasies. Although both Spencer Brydon and Maggie eroticize a violent masculine figure, they place themselves very differently in relation to him.[16]

Maggie's eroticization of violence (constructing an order with the classic definition of patriarchy as an economy in which women are objects of exchange[17]) signals not so much a surrender to as an ambivalence towards this violence, the sexual pleasure that can 'bring her round'. The problem of how pain could be actively sought out ('The Economic Problem of Masochism') was one which bothered Freud, as he could not reconcile it with the workings of the pleasure principle. In 'A Child is Being Beaten' (1919) he attempts to explain this problem with reference to a fantasy, similar to that of Maggie's, which he claims is frequently encountered in clinical situations. This fantasy is drawn from an Oedipal situation of sibling rivalry, and is said to differ for the boy and the girl. For the girl the fantasy passes through the following three stages:

1 My father is beating the child whom I hate.
2 I am being beaten by my father.
3 A child is being beaten.

The transition from the first stage to the second stage represents a movement along the activity-passivity polarity, which Freud, in 'Instincts and Their Vicissitudes' (*'Triebe und Triebschicksale'*, 1915) classifies as the 'biological polarity', one of 'the three great polarities that dominate mental life', the other two being 'that of ego-external world as the *real*, and finally that of pleasure-unpleasure as the *economic* polarity'.[18]

'Masochism' was named and defined by Richard von Krafft-Ebing in the first edition of his *Psychopathia Sexualis* (1886). Curiously, although nearly all of the case-studies of masochism in *Psychopathia Sexualis* were men, Krafft-Ebing makes some remarks which typify the association of masochism with femininity to be found in many subsequent writers:

... it is easy to regard masochism in general as a pathological growth of specific feminine mental elements – as an abnormal intensification of certain features of the psycho-sexual character of woman – and to seek its primary origin in the sex ... It may, however, ... be ... that, in woman, an inclination to subordination to man (which may be regarded as an acquired, purposeful arrangement, a phenomenon of adaptation to social requirements) is to a certain extent a normal manifestation.[19]

Krafft-Ebing, playing the scientific fence-sitter, commits himself neither to the viewpoint that masochism is a female perversion nor to the viewpoint that in a woman an 'inclination to subordination to man' is normal. For many commentators masochism seems to be more disturbing in a man than in a woman, in that it subverts the common equation of masculinity with activity.[20] Although *Psychopathia Sexualis* represents a frenzied creation of taxonomies of the 'abnormal', it also enshrines nineteenth-century notions of gender difference in a clinical context. Krafft-Ebing insists on female passivity, and thereby makes a pathology of female desire. He writes:

[Man's] love is sensual, and his choice is strongly prejudiced in favour of physical attractions. A mighty impulse of nature makes him aggressive and impetuous in his courtship . . . Woman, however, if physically and mentally normal, and properly educated, has but little sensual desire. If it were otherwise, marriage and family life would be empty words. As yet the man who avoids women, and the woman who seeks men are sheer anomalies.

Woman is wooed for her favour. She remains passive. Her sexual organization demands it, and the dictates of good breeding come to her aid.[21]

Krafft-Ebing is unable to choose between a biological or social explanation for female passivity, or what he regards as only a more extreme manifestation of this passivity, female masochism.

Later accounts firmly linked the phenomenon of masochism to the workings of a primordial feminine passivity, evidence for which can be found everywhere in nature. G. Stanley Hall writes in 1904 that in sexual selection 'woman may acquire a Massochistic [sic] love of violence and pain for the ideal of pleasure, [and] abhor the bashful man'.[22] The most extreme linkage of femininity and masochism occurs in Havelock Ellis's 'Love and Pain' (1903), which claims that insight into 'the relationship of love and pain' can be gained 'by returning to the consideration of the essential phenomena of courtship in the animal world generally'. Noting that among mammals 'the male wins the female very largely by the display of force', and that 'marriage by capture' is the norm among a number of primitive tribes, Ellis claims that '[t]he masculine tendency to delight in domination, the feminine tendency to delight in submission, still maintain the ancient traditions when the male animal pursued the female'. Violence arises in a patriarchal ordering 'when there are rivals for the possession of one female'.[23] If the account of sexual difference found in sexologist tracts resembles closely the version of sexual difference informing Maggie's fantasy life, it is important to note how Maggie does not play a static role in this fantasy. James's account of Maggie's fantasy life resembles Freud's accounts of female masochism, which is played out in the framework of what may now be seen as a particular, historicized, late nineteenth-century bourgeois family.

By comparing Freud to Krafft-Ebing, Havelock Ellis and G. Stanley Hall, we can see to what extent Freud was escaping the nineteenth-century biologism of the sexologists, who referred to states of primitive humanity and to animal life in order to justify (or protest) contemporary social orderings. In trying to account for masochism, Freud is torn between a biologizing explanation and an explanation which draws on his work on infantile sexuality and the structure of the Oedipus complex. In 'The Economic

Problem of Masochism' (1924) he attempts to locate the workings of masochism in the individual organism, and to do so makes use of his theorization of the death drive. He writes that

In (multicellular) organisms the libido meets the instinct of death, or destruction, which is dominant in them and which seeks to disintegrate the cellular organism and to conduct each separate unicellular organism into a state of inorganic stability . . . The libido has the task of making the destroying instinct innocuous, and it fulfils the task by diverting that instinct to a great extent outwards . . . A portion of the instinct is placed directly in the service of the sexual function, where it has an important part to play. This is sadism proper. Another part does not share in this transposition outwards; it remains inside the organism and, with the help of the accompanying sexual excitation described above, becomes libidinally bound there. It is in this portion that we have to recognize the original, erotogenic masochism.[24]

In making a connection between this *biological* masochism existing at the level of the organism and a masochism to be found in individual subjects, Freud finds it necessary to refer to the figure of the father. He writes, 'We now know that the wish, which so frequently occurs in phantasies, to be beaten by the father stands very close to the other wish, to have a passive (feminine) sexual relation to him and is only a regressive distortion of it.'[25] If the gaze, in early feminist theory, was seen as giving reassurance that one possesses the phallus, then masochism, as Freud conceives it, arises from a position of lack, a desire to possess the phallus of the father. Thus Freud writes, with reference to 'characteristic situations' of female-ness that resemble those described by Havelock Ellis in 'Love and Pain', that

The fear of being eaten up by the totem animal (the father) originates from the primitive oral organization; the wish to be beaten by the father comes from the sadistic-anal phase which follows it; castration, although it is later disavowed, enters into the content of masochistic phantasies as a precipitate of the phallic stage of organization; and from the final genital organization there arise, of course, the situations of being copulated with and of giving birth, which are characteristic of femaleness.[26]

Jean Laplanche notes that 'in the transition to phase 2 [of the beating fantasy] *the fantasy, the unconscious*, and *sexuality* in the form of *masochistic excitation* together emerge in a single movement'.[27] The fantasy is important, then, in locking the figure of the father into the psyche, and in *The Golden Bowl* the bond between Maggie and her father is returned to repetitively. Freud, in his essay 'Analysis Terminable and Interminable' (1937), writes that some women are unable to renounce the Oedipus complex,[28] and the novel can only end – analysis can terminate – with Maggie's renunciation of her father.

The question of Maggie's agency is central to an understanding of the novel. The novel frequently aligns her with the figure of the virginal, passive victim. Before the marriage the Prince remarks that 'the Blessed Virgin and all the Saints . . . have her in their keeping' (76), and even after the marriage Maggie the 'nun' (172), who 'wasn't born to know evil' (94), continues to be figured as virgin. As a vessel unable to be violated she comes to resemble the golden bowl itself, only the bowl 'as it *was* to have been . . . with all our happiness in it . . . without the crack' (475).[29] Thus Fanny Assingham can remark that Maggie is 'the creature in the world to whom a wrong thing could least be communicated. It was as if her imagination had been closed to it, her sense altogether sealed' (310). Yet Maggie's 'substance', her identity, is not, despite the above quotation, a mere passive pulp. The novel shows her in negotiation with the fantasy of passivity: the question of her 'identity' remains unanswered, her 'femininity' divided, incomplete.

If Freudian psychoanalysis normalizes masculinity and pathologizes femininity, describing a tortuous, circuitous route which the biological being must follow to 'become a woman', Maggie attributes the difficulties of this path to difficulties created by social relations instead of to an ahistorical castration complex. Maggie reflects that Amerigo '*had* a place, . . . something made for him beforehand by innumerable facts, facts largely of the sort known as historical, made by ancestors, examples, traditions, habits' (548–9), whereas she has only an

improvised 'post' – a post of the kind spoken as advanced – with which she was to have found herself connected in the fashion of a settler or a trader in a new country; in the likeness even of some Indian squaw with a papoose on her back and barbarous bead-work to sell. Maggie's own, in short, would have been sought in vain in the most rudimentary map of the social relations as such. The only geography marking it would be doubtless that of the fundamental passions. (549)

This complex passage invokes two contradictory notions of feminine identity. If Maggie is the settler, femininity is an identity that has to be colonized, acquired. Unlike the Prince, she cannot take up a gendered identity which is culturally endowed. The Edwardian period witnessed a fierce debate over what constituted 'femininity'; so Maggie must discover femininity in a 'new country'. Yet, as the Indian squaw, she would have recourse to a primitive, 'barbaric' femininity, one not socially constructed, not 'in the map of social relations', but dependent on the 'fundamental passions' (these are the two poles along which gender is constructed in the writings of the sexologists). The passage is juxtaposing a set of oppositions: feminine/masculine, natural/cultured, primitive/developed, colonizer/ colonized. The Indian squaw suggests a primal female principle, but, as Italian princess and American heiress, Maggie seems to see the squaw as 'other'.

Maggie's eventual assumption of agency involves an assertion of the sexual bond between her and her husband and a banishing of Charlotte, not only to American City but, in a series of revealing fantasies, to the position of a savage, primal femaleness, the place of the 'other woman'. Following Maggie's lead, criticism has tended to forget Charlotte, just as criticism often tends to forget the other woman, whether as third term of a triangular structure of desire, or as the servant or black woman erased from the canvas (in, for example, Vermeer's *Mistress and Maid* or Manet's *Olympia*).[30]

Charlotte as other woman is a problematic figure because she seems necessary to Maggie's marriage (she institutes the structure of mimetic desire which brings Maggie closer to her husband) yet needs to be banished so that the marriage may take on the aesthetic form of the bowl 'without the crack' (475). This act of banishment takes on a dimension of psychic cruelty. In Maggie's imagination her father becomes a Sadeian master, holding Charlotte in a 'long silken halter' (523) which is to become a 'silken noose, his wife's immaterial tether' (553) used in a horrific picture of Charlotte's execution:

Mrs Verver's straight neck had certainly not slipped it; nor had the other end of the long cord – oh quite conveniently long! – disengaged its smaller loop from the hooked thumb that, with his fingers closed upon it, her husband kept out of sight. (554)

With the prince, too, Charlotte enters a sexual economy which objectifies and suffocates her:

[The Prince] knew above all the extraordinary fineness of her flexible waist, the stem of an expanded flower, which gave her a likeness also to some long loose silk purse, well filled with gold pieces, but having been passed empty through a finger-ring that held it together. (73)

In both scenes – that created by Maggie and that by the Prince – Charlotte is held in, imprisoned, by the long cord (of bondage), a finger-ring (of marriage?), by a purse (the body as commodity), by the notion of identity itself, identity seen as restriction rather than growth, an entry into a tight constricting space enclosed by an imaginary master, a femininity defined by lack, castration. Critics trying to evaluate James's sexual politics would do well to attend to the complexity of such passages.[31] While the images evoked are specifically horrific, James is complicating the issue of participation. Both Maggie and the Prince are involved in similar fantasies, but their involvement takes different forms. Maggie escapes from her 'bath of benevolence' or 'gilded cage', yet the door which opens to permit her 'desired flight' (355) is firmly bolted on Charlotte:

The cage was the deluded condition, and Maggie, as having known delusion – rather! – understood the nature of cages. She walked round Charlotte's – cautiously and in a very wide circle; and when inevitably they had to communicate she felt herself comparatively outside and on the breast of nature: she saw her companion's face as that of a prisoner looking through bars. (484)

Maggie, the civilized woman, projects onto Charlotte the image of the primitive beast, and with this beast enters into a pained relationship of identity and difference suggestive of Lacan's mirror stage: '[Maggie] had had, as we know, her vision of the gilt bars bent, of the door of the cage forced open from within and the creature imprisoned roaming at large' (521).

This creature, like the beast in the jungle, resists easy interpretation. That Charlotte is the creature indicates that Maggie is moving positions in the beating fantasy, from 'I am being beaten by my father' to 'My father is beating the child whom I hate'.[32] Adam as Charlotte's master is a vision which can console Maggie for the loss of her father, yet more importantly, project onto Charlotte the negative effects of the male logos, femininity in the economy of the phallus (thus leaving, presumably, Maggie free).[33] Maggie's urge to keep the creature in the prison (which was formerly her own place) also suggests an urgent need to repudiate, keep away from herself, aspects of femininity she sees as primeval, savage. Here the James of *The Golden Bowl* can be read as a cultural anthropologist, defining the differences between civilization and barbarity. James's repeated use of kinship terminology in the novel – 'stepmother-in-law' (207), 'the parent and the child' (357), to name just two instances – gives the characters status as icons, so that the novel can be read as an exploration of what is acceptable in our culture. Maggie's development in the novel can be simultaneously read as passage through the Oedipus complex, and, with reference to Lévi-Strauss, as defining the boundary between the primitive and the cultured.

The novel invokes several notions of Maggie – Maggie the virgin, Maggie the daughter, and Maggie the wife and Maggie the mother – and sets these 'Maggies' into conflict with one another. Fanny Assingham invokes the figure of the Virgin Mary – wife and mother of God the Father – as the protective vessel which can embrace all these differences, talking to Maggie of the 'little silver cross you once showed me, blest by the Holy Father, that you always wear, out of sight, next your skin' (402), and, when visiting Maggie on the occasion when the bowl is to be broken, feeling 'as the truly pious priest might feel when confronted, behind the altar, before the festa, with his miraculous Madonna' (430).

It is an astute move of Fanny, the novel's best literary critic, to absorb Maggie's conflicts into the image of the Madonna. Earlier Fanny has noted how Maggie's incestuous attachment to her father is responsible for driving the Prince and Charlotte together:

[Maggie] began with wanting to show [Adam] that his marriage could never, under whatever temptation of her own bliss with the Prince, become for her a pretext for deserting or neglecting him. Then that ... entailed her wanting to show the Prince that she recognized how the other desire – this wish to remain, intensely, the same passionate little daughter she had always been – involved ... neglecting and deserting *him*. (317)

The frustration of this attachment, and the need to renounce it, is suggested with unusual directness towards the end of the novel:

It was positively as if in short the inward felicity of their being once more, perhaps only for half an hour, simply daughter and father had glimmered out for them and they had picked up the pretext that would make it easiest. They were husband and wife – oh, so immensely! as regards other persons ... (501)

Here a syntactical ambiguity directs the reader's attention towards a possibility the passage seems to be rejecting – that instead of being 'husband and wife' to Charlotte and the Prince, Adam and Maggie are 'husband and wife' to each other. Maggie's 'sacrifice' of Adam is represented as the passage from girlhood into adult sexuality, an abandonment of the dolls of the nursery:

The only way to sacrifice him would be to do so without his dreaming what it might be for. She kissed him, she arranged his cravat, she dropped remarks, she guided him out, she held his arm, not to be led, but to lead him, and taking it to her by much the same intimate pressure she had always used, when a little girl, to mark the inseparability of her doll ... (382)

In assuming agency Maggie will abandon her father for her husband, allying herself with the cultural forms of sexuality. For, in the words of Claude Lévi-Strauss, 'the incest prohibition is at once on the threshold of culture, in culture, and ... culture itself'.[34]

This action, however, involves upturning the dynamics of her relationship with the Prince, reversing the interplay of machismo and sadomasochism which earlier in the novel seemed to characterize their relationship. Maggie's assumption of power would be unlikely in a mid-Victorian novel, or in a novel from James's middle period (it is a much stronger gesture than that of Isabel Archer at the close of *The Portrait of a Lady*), and reflects the changes of the position of women in marriage from the Victorian to the Edwardian period. A comparison of Maggie's progress through the stages of the Oedipus complex with that of Kate Croy or Charlotte would suggest that money, and economic autonomy, are factors of great import- ance to which Freud pays insufficient attention. Also, in the context of the novel, Maggie's power represents a displacement of a feudal code of masculinity by commodity capitalism. Maggie's economic power displaces the strength of the Prince's masculinity. For the Prince has already been turned into a commodity at the beginning of the novel, where Maggie tells him, 'You're at any rate a part of his [Adam's] collection ... a rarity, an object of beauty, an object of price' (49). As such his feudal machismo, although posing a threat to Maggie, comes to seem an anachronism.

Maggie's repudiation of a femininity figured in terms of the 'Indian squaw', or 'things of evil when one's nerves ... had left one in a darkness of prowling dangers that was like the predicament of the night-watcher in a beast-haunted land' (532), suggests more, however, than a line which, across history, across cultures, defines the meeting-point between barbarity and civilization. It recalls imperialist novels of the late nineteenth century such as Rider Haggard's *She* (1887) and George MacDonald's *Lilith* (1895) which depict colonialism as an encounter between Christianity and barbarism, civilization with a primeval femininity.[35] A logic of purity informs such an encounter, a fear of contamination present in the very desire to have the bowl 'without the crack'.

This logic is strengthened by a quiet anti-Semitism in the novel, an anti- Semitism of snide references, joking remarks. The Prince's younger brother has taken a wife 'of Hebrew race, with a portion that had gilded the pill' (53); Charlotte, we are told, is 'neither a pampered Jewess nor a lazy Creole' (64). The most heinous description is that of Mr Gutermann- Seuss's relatives, 'the graduated offspring, ... the fat, ear-ringed aunts and the glossy cockneyfied, familiar uncles, inimitable of accent and assumption' (190). This description recalls the tourist described in 'Covering End' (1898) as 'a matron of rich Jewish type, with small nippers on a huge nose and a face out of proportion to her little Freischütz hat', whose presence indicates a fear of contamination in a tale about a struggle for possession of an old English country home.[36]

In *Powers of Horror* Julia Kristeva writes that the abject figure of the Jew is invoked whenever identity is at stake, that when 'a scription on the level of identity' (which is a fine description of *The Golden Bowl*) 'comes face to face with abjection, it enters into competition with biblical abominations and even more so with prophetic discourse'.[37] We see, accompanying Adam's ambition to see his own life as connected with the production of the beautiful, and to forge his own identity as the cultured Anglo-Saxon (Aryan) millionaire, a projection of the sordid aspects of money-making activities onto the figure of the Jew.

Jonathan Freedman has recently analysed the significance of the Jewishness of the vendor of the golden bowl: the 'queer little foreign man' (406) who owns the little shop in Bloomsbury. (The novel is infuriatingly vague about his ethnicity – he denies being English or Italian.) Freedman draws attention to the Prince's pronounced loathing of the vendor, and his obsession with the price of the bowl.[38] The Prince cautions Charlotte that the price asked for the bowl is too high, and, even as Maggie is telling the Prince that she knows of his liaison with Charlotte, he is anxious to know what Maggie paid for the bowl, and whether the vendor offered to refund her purchase when he came to tell her the bowl was flawed. The legalism with which the vendor points out the bowl's flaws – but does not expect this to negate the contract made between vendor and purchaser – is consonant with a long history of associations of Judaism and legal cunningness.

This reading has fascinating implications for the discussion of abjecting mechanisms presented here. Whereas the Prince loathes the vendor – he thinks of him as a 'horrid little beast' – Maggie is glad to have found 'such a friend' (Charlotte also shows an obvious fondness for him) (460). This movement of the Jewish vendor into the most intimate spaces of Maggie's and the Prince's marriage constitutes one of the most cruelly ironizing gestures of the novel: the Prince resorts with obsessive blindness to the question of the Jew's financial integrity at the same time as Maggie, her blindness in retreat thanks to the revelation offered by the Jew, confronts him with 'having for so long so successfully deceived me' (462).[39]

That Maggie acquires her empowering knowledge from a Jew impacts on and complicates the intricate movements of abjection which take place across the novel. If many critics read the novel as a celebration of Maggie's acquisition of agency and 'adult sexuality', this is because the narrative structure is one of a teleological drive towards Maggie's final actions, which are enshrined, mystified. As Charlotte observes of Adam's buying the Damascene tiles from Mr Gutermann-Seuss, Maggie's actions have, 'for a finish, the touch of some mystic rite of old Jewry' (192). Yet reading

The Golden Bowl as a victory of the aesthetic and of marriage involves a repetition of Maggie's removal of Charlotte to American City. Such a reading defines its own place as culturally central even as it is marred by its failure to move from that place. For it requires an endorsement of Maggie's point of view at the expense of Charlotte's, a repetition of the novel's highly skewed mode of perception, a silencing of the 'other woman'.

As the act that straddles 'nature' and 'culture', Maggie's renunciation of incest for desire within marriage is an activity suggesting the golden bowl itself – a structure designed to hide its fundamental flaw. This is the very structure of the aesthetic in *The Golden Bowl*. Repeatedly the novel portrays the construction of the 'beautiful' as something rooted in the cultural process of exclusion (of the Jew), of repudiation (of 'the creature', of a 'savage sexuality'). The novel's crisis of representation arises from the always incomplete nature of this exclusion: what is repudiated always hovers on the margins, so that at the end of the novel Maggie is filled with 'pity *and dread*' of the Prince's 'strangely lighted' eyes (550; my emphasis).

Maggie's actions bring onto her the weight of shaping the novel, are an assumption of authorship, in which case the novel represents authorship – the aesthetic – as *the strict adherence to a decorous lie*.[40] Criticism's portrayal of Maggie as redeemer quells the other voices of the novel which are so forcefully and painfully repressed. The apparent victory of the aesthetic and marriage which ends the novel depends on a forgetting of the sound of 'Charlotte's high coerced quaver before the cabinets in the hushed gallery; the voice by which [Maggie] had been pierced the day before as by that of a creature in anguish' (528).

CHAPTER FOUR

The eroticism of prohibition: masochism and the law in Roderick Hudson

'Constructivism needs to take account of the domain of constraints without which a certain living and desiring being cannot make its way. And every such being is constrained by not only what is difficult to imagine, but what remains radically unthinkable: in the domain of sexuality these constraints include the radical unthinkability of desiring otherwise, the radical unendurability of desiring otherwise, the absence of certain desires, the repetitive compulsion of others, the abiding repudiation of some sexual possibilities, panic, obsessional pull, and the nexus of sexuality and pain.'

Judith Butler[1]

I JAMES AND HIS CRITICS

Over the next four chapters I will be discussing fictional texts by James published between 1875 (the date of the American publication of *Roderick Hudson*) and 1910 (when James's last short story, 'A Round of Visits', was published), and showing that James's writing persistently concerns itself with same-sex eroticism, and the relation between same-sex passion and 'identity'. Homoeroticism and the question of homosexual identity are, according to the reading offered here, important in James's writing both before and after the formation of recognizably modern homosexual identities in 1890s Britain and America.

This reading represents a departure from a critical view of James as only exploring homoeroticism and homosexual identity timidly, or views which argue that such themes have a subtextual presence in James's work, but were not necessarily intended by James. Recent readings by critics such as Eve Kosofsky Sedgwick, Wendy Graham, Eric Savoy, Terry Castle and Michael Moon reflect a crucial shift in James studies, which have begun to take seriously his work's engagement with homosexuality.[2] This reading of homoeroticism in James's fiction is necessary, not only because homoeroticism plays such an important role throughout James's fiction, but because it will reveal the importance of James's 'queer writing' to subsequent lesbian and gay writing, and acknowledge one of the most important cultural commentaries made by James.

Eve Kosofsky Sedgwick and Jonathan Freedman have considered the absence of such readings. Sedgwick suggests a number of reasons for such an 'active incuriosity', ranging from 'a desire to protect James from homophobic misreadings in a perennially repressive sexual climate', a fear of marginalizing James 'as, simply, *homosexual*', a desire to avoid anachronism, a belief that James's work leaves no mark of a homosexuality which has been successfully transmuted into heterosexuality, or a belief that an interrogation of homoerotic themes in his work could only proceed from an ' "attack" on James's candor or artistic unity'. (I am sure Segdwick is accurate here, but she is also very charitable. What she does not suggest is that James's critics might, quite simply, not want to discuss homoeroticism in the fiction due to their own homophobia.[3]) The 'net effect' of such reasons, the motives of which are 'understandable', is nevertheless, Sedgwick argues, 'the usual repressive one of elision and subsumption of supposedly embarrassing material'.[4]

In his study *Professions of Taste: Henry James, British Aestheticism, and Commodity Culture*, Jonathan Freedman argues that this absence in Jamesian criticism arose at the very moment James was being made such an important figure in institutional literary criticism, in the 1940s and the 1950s. Critics of the period avoided relating James's work to British aestheticism, Freedman argues, because such an inquiry would 'focus explicitly on those elements of James's character and art that the anti-Jacobites had attacked, ... not only on his expatriation or his dedication to an idealized form of art, or even on the voyeuristic dimensions of his techniques of "point of view", but also on James's homoeroticism, an unspoken subject that clearly underlies the language of effeteness and effeminacy that anti-Jacobites persistently used to describe James's putative aestheticism, and for which the term "aesthete" long served as a virtual synonym'.[5]

Of course, this absence is only part of a much larger structuring absence: it is only recently that any sophisticated hermeneutic apparatus has become available for addressing the relationship of homoeroticism to any writer's work. Before Foucault's questioning of the *constructedness* of sexual identities, the role the literary text plays in such constructions had not been the focus of criticism. Rather an unsophisticated mode of Freudian enquiry treated the literary text as symptomatic of already existing identities, the 'normal' or pathological nature of which could be read in terms of a 'sexuality' seen to be reflected in the text itself. Before Foucault, this mode of Freudian enquiry was the most prestigious model of interrogating sexuality within literary criticism. Edel's biography views James through such a Freudian lens, but reassuringly ushers the Master into the safe realms constituted by a fear of sexuality: if sexuality is unsavoury, at least the Master had the decency to retreat from it.[6]

Such an absence, then, is best thought of in terms of the institutional siting and history of Jamesian criticism. What Sedgwick calls an 'active incuriosity' is not necessarily an inability to *hear* homoerotic nuances in James's fiction. Rather, it has been assumed possible to read James's fiction while ignoring homoerotic elements in his work. Such an assumption has left many important issues in James's texts unaddressed.

Interestingly, the homoeroticism of James's writing has occasionally been identified by critics hostile to James. For Maxwell Geismar, a 'perversity' in James's writing constitutes a ground for dismissing James's importance. Writing about 'The Jolly Corner' in *Henry James and his Cult*, Geismar claimed that the 'complexity' of style in the tale masks 'a virtual absence of content'; yet this absence – the tale's supposed aesthetic distinction – is a mark of James's failure to develop sexually. Geismar writes that James's 'whole view of sex and love was on the oral, infantile, pre-oedipal and pre-sexual level'.[7] Whereas many critics see 'The Jolly Corner' as a high Modernist narrative resistant to any form of interpretation,[8] Geismar attacks James's story both for its 'absence of content' and for the 'view of sex and love' it manages to express, despite such an absence!

Whereas much criticism of *The Bostonians* advanced recognizably homophobic attacks on the character of Olive Chancellor, Geismar's attack is directed at James himself; the deformities of James's prose are related to the supposed deformities of James's person. Geismar's crudely dismissive gesture might be seen as a transitory moment in Jamesian criticism, but in 1982 Alfred Habegger could write that James 'failed to earn masculinity in the ways that American boys and men had to earn it. He grew up a gender-less man with a dark suspicion that all sexual roles and functions are sinister. His own social function was to write a body of fiction about sensitive, genderless minds, usually devoid of desire, who discover the secret shameful facts of life about a species essentially alien.' According to Habegger, New York critics in the 1930s and 1940s canonized James because they were 'in precisely the same limbo that has always engendered or promoted genteel culture under whatever name it goes by. The Partisan Reviewers loved James because his fiction supplied the ideal material prop – highbrow fantasy masquerading as realism – for mandarins on the margin of American political life.'[9] Here effeminacy is equated with a social, political and critical uselessness.

The vituperative rhetoric adopted by Geismar and Habegger nevertheless plays across an important tension in James's writing and in Jamesian criticism. This tension concerns the construction of James as the master of a certain Modernist sensibility – perpetually keeping aesthetic sensation in play and warding off cognitive closure through strategies of deferral and verbal ambiguity – played out against the realization that perhaps, nevertheless, there is something sexual at stake in James's 'play'. In addressing such a tension in Modernism, Sedgwick suggests that 'there is a case to be made that the modernist impulse toward abstraction in the first place owes an incalculable part of its energy precisely to turn-of-the-century male homo/heterosexual definitional panic'.[10] It is also true that such abstraction, in so far as it derives from Pater, can be seen as a 'non-panicked' response to Darwinism. The teleological Darwinist plot of fertility and reproduction, preoccupied with growth and transformations, was re-worked in British Aestheticism to a valorization of the *non-evolutionary* and the *non-reproductive*, of sensations which could not be assimilated into an evolutionary narrative. This strain of Pater is taken up most enthusiastically by Wilde, who writes derisively of 'Mr Herbert Spencer, scientific historians, and the compilers of statistics' in 'The Decay of Lying', in which he advocates that art is a performative space which 'life – poor, probable, uninteresting human life' can only imitate.[11] In Max Nordau's *Degeneration* (translated into English in 1895) Wilde is considered as an ego-maniacal example of a literary degenerate, in a chapter which attacks literary decadence for its failure to embody an ideal of healthy masculinity.[12] Such a response indicates that at the moment of its inception Pater's advocacy of using our 'interval' 'in getting as many pulsations as possible into the given time', while only being 'sure it is passion', was read as a threat to a normative reproductive sexuality.[13] Freedman has shown the extent to which James, in his fiction, appropriates a cultural agenda drawn from Pater and literary decadence and makes it his own. (Think for instance of Milly Theale, imaged by James as 'passionately desiring to "put in" before extinction as many of the finer vibrations as possible' (*AN* 288).) Such a cultural context shows that Jamesian aesthetic 'vibrations' and 'absences' are never neutral, that what he calls 'the shy and illusive, the inscrutable, the indefinable' (*AN* 344) operates in negation of an ethos of fullness, an ideal of the expressive and reproductive body. (In the prefaces, James frequently speaks of his works as deformed, disfigured, maimed and mutilated – a vocabulary which parodically re-enacts the scorning of the degenerate body.[14])

If James, in his late fiction, moves towards an anti-essentialist critique of gender, he nevertheless advances, throughout his fiction, a critique which has strong affinities with late twentieth-century 'identity politics'. In particular, his work is sensitive to the ways in which the social context of gendered identity can frustrate the development of an identity which will admit same-sex attachment. His work persistently interrogates homosexual prohibition, and is sensitive to the different ways in which such prohibition might operate: whether as a prohibition of homoerotic *acts*, of same-sex *affection*, or of homosexual or lesbian identities. This sensitivity makes it necessary to differentiate between two prohibitive régimes which broadly characterize his fiction. James's fiction written before 1890 shows considerable freedom in its exploration of same-sex affection, which is not in and of itself associated with 'homosexual identity'. After 1890, the very expression of same-sex desire becomes anxious, as the person who shows such desires faces the risk of identification as 'homosexual', an increasingly recognized character type. The existence of two such discursive régimes, however, should not be taken to imply that James himself had no conception of a 'homosexual identity' before 1890. Discussions of *Roderick Hudson*, *The Princess Casamassima* and *The Bostonians* in this and the following chapter will show that James was always interested in the character whose same-sex affections exceeded the terms of 'normal' friendship. In these three novels, James explores the melancholia associated with the inability to find a bond which would recognize such extraordinary affection. These novels also anticipate many major motifs and plot strands of twentieth-century fiction about male and female homosexuality. Before they are discussed as 'lesbian' or 'gay' novels, however, it is still necessary to ask: what homosexuals do these novels talk about? Are they in fact talking about 'homosexuals'? Did homosexuals exist when they were written?

II WHAT HOMOSEXUAL SUBJECT?

At the close of James's *Roderick Hudson*, Rowland Mallet mounts a long vigil over his friend Roderick's dead and 'admirably handsome' body. Rowland's loss is described in terms which recall Othello's ranting at his belief that Desdemona has been unfaithful: 'Th'immortal Jove's dread clamours counterfeit, / Farewell! Othello's occupation's gone.'[15] The narrator tells us that this 'most rational of men was for an hour the most passionate . . . Now that all was over Rowland understood how *exclusively*, for two years, Roderick had filled his life. His occupation was gone.'[16]

Can an 'exclusive' interest, an 'occupation' that 'fills' one's life, be called an 'identity'? If Roderick has filled Rowland's life 'exclusively', then that other interest, on which the novel insists at various points, namely his interest in Mary Garland (Roderick's cousin and fiancée), seems not to have been worth terribly much. In fact, this other interest *is* worth a lot to Rowland, and the form it takes is addressed in the next two paragraphs, the last paragraphs of the novel, when the body beautiful is borne to its bereaved mother and fiancée:

> In the doorway, clinging together, appeared the two bereaved women. Mrs Hudson tottered forward with outstretched hands and the expression of a blind person; but before she reached her son Mary Garland had rushed past her and, in the face of the staring, pitying, awe-stricken crowd, had flung herself with the magnificent movement of *one whose rights were supreme*, and with a loud tremendous cry, upon the senseless vestige of her love.
>
> That cry still lives in Rowland's ears. (388; my emphasis)

Rowland's private vigil contrasts markedly with the publicity of Mary's magnificent gesture, and this emphasis on Mary's 'rights' recalls many other moments in this novel, which is studded with references to the law. Mary's double claim is of course not a terribly effective hold on the steamy Roderick, but with Roderick safely dead it will at last remain unchallenged. And it is a claim which Rowland strongly envies (perhaps naively). He takes every opportunity to 'instruct' his protégé on filial and familial duty, even before he has met the principle claimant of such obeisance: ' "I have not had the pleasure of seeing your mother, but I will lay you a wager that this is where the shoe pinches. She is passionately fond of you, and her hopes, like all intense hopes, keep trembling into fears." Rowland, as he spoke, had an instinctive vision of how the beautiful youth must be loved by his female relatives' (75). Later in Rome, he takes 'extraordinary pleasure' in a letter from Mary Garland which quite drips with affection for Roderick, and dwells on how the familial space remains intact, despite the strains his own actions have placed on it: 'The monotonous days of the two women seemed to Rowland's fancy to follow each other like the tick-tick of a great timepiece, marking off the hours which separated them from the supreme felicity of clasping the far-away son and lover to lips sealed with intensity of joy' (134–5).[17] This is an envy and *Schadenfreude* laced with respect (Rowland's hostility to Roderick's mother becomes more marked towards the end of the novel).

That Rowland finds Roderick sexually attractive has been noticed by James's critics (it is hard to escape). In 1978 Robert K. Martin persuasively read *Roderick Hudson* as a gay novel, with detailed analysis of the text.[18] More needs to be asked, however. Did James intend to make the relationship between Roderick and Rowland so strongly erotic? If he did, what commentary was he making on such a relationship? How does such a commentary speak to the social conditions in which it is written? I want to show that the novel makes homoerotic affection much more than a casual aspect of Rowland Mallet's character. In its foregrounding of questions of legal status, and its exploration of Rowland's melancholic resignation, the novel specifically explores the cost of relinquishing same-sex attachment.

Yet such a reading of homoeroticism in *Roderick Hudson* risks begging an important historical question: to what extent was the representation of homoeroticism, or of a 'homosexual identity', possible at the time of the novel's writing? This question can, however, result in a tautological double-bind: a reading of a novel like *Roderick Hudson* could be said to show the (minimum) extent of such a possibility. And if the novel does thematize homoerotic desire, the question of the extent to which such a thematization might also involve a conception of a 'homosexual identity' naturally arises. James began writing *Roderick Hudson* in 1874. What kind of 'homosexual identity' might be found in a novel written before the invention of the homosexual? *What homosexual subject?*

The word 'homosexual' only passed into medical currency in the States in the early 1890s. However, notions of 'sexual perversion', a 'perverted sexual instinct', 'normal love' and 'normal sexuality' were current in the 1880s; the 1880s also saw an increasing pathologization of same-sex intimate friendship. The designation of same-sex friendship as unhealthily eroticized arose not only in medical literature but in newspapers.[19] The writing of *Roderick Hudson*, however, precedes such a pathologization. Before the 1880s, much freer expression of same-sex affection was possible. Steven Seidman writes that in Victorian America '[r]omantic friendships or love between women and, to a lesser extent, love between men was [sic] fairly typical and carried no trace of wrongdoing or shame'.[20]

Current historiography cannot establish that the formation of homosexual identities, or various precursors to such identities, such as the 'invert' or the 'pervert', took place in the States before 1880. It might seem common-sensical to suggest that the first medical and psychiatric case-studies of urban 'perverts' would have to post-date the formation of perverse identities, but of course it was the medicalization of sexuality that shaped the construction of such identities. Foucault argues convincingly that prior to the construction of the 'invert' and the 'homosexual' same-sex erotic activity was seen as 'a temporary aberration', and although he provocatively gives the 'date of birth' of the 'homosexual' as 1870 (Ulrichs had already developed notions of the development of congenital theories of homosexuality in the 1860s), this birthdate cannot be assumed in an American context (*HS* 43).[21]

Such an attempt at historical reconstruction then cannot frame a reading of homoeroticism in *Roderick Hudson* with any certainty. That homoerotic expression was legible and enjoyed a great deal of freedom in the period seems to be a consequence of two factors: this 'legibility' was not a legibility of a certain *identity*, and such 'expression' – an expression of homoerotic desire – did not accompany any visible genital contact.[22] Further, the publication and reception of *Roderick Hudson* has not left us with a record of contemporary readers who associated the novel with perversity.[23] This in itself is not of great significance. Any contemporary responses to *Roderick Hudson* are obviously informed by the same historical context which can account for the novel's peculiar mix of great boldness and intangibility.

Eve Kosofsky Sedgwick has shown in *Epistemology of the Closet* that homosexuality made its way into late nineteenth-century literature as a textual dissimulation, calling for a reading highly sensitive to nuances which are registered in textual silences, interstices and ambiguities. But these literary strategies – reading and writing in the 'closet' – presume a notion of homosexual identity that is distinct enough so that a subject can feel it needs to be concealed. If the closet is defined by a threshold, and *defines* a threshold – a barrier intended to keep secrecy from becoming disclosure, ignorance from becoming knowledge – then *Roderick Hudson* is poised on the threshold of a threshold.

Whether or not a homosexual 'identity' was legible in American literature before James, representations of *homoeroticism* were commonplace in both the American and European literature he was familiar with before writing *Roderick Hudson*. The third edition of Walt Whitman's *Leaves of Grass*, which included the *Calamus* poems, appeared in 1860; in 1871 Whitman published his essay 'Democratic Vistas', in which he advocated his doctrine of 'adhesive love'.[24] James will also have been familiar with the pronounced homoeroticism of Melville's *Moby-Dick* (1851). One year after the publication of *Roderick Hudson* he was able to write of Baudelaire that '[t]here is little in "Les Fleurs du Mal" to make the reader of either French or English prose and verse of the present day even open his eyes', and claims that when Baudelaire 'makes an invocation to "la Débauche aux bras immondes" one may be sure he means more by it than is evident to the vulgar – he means, that is, an intenser perversity'.[25] His response to Whitman is equally instructive. In 1865, reviewing Whitman's *Drum-Taps* at the age of 22, James wrote, '[i]t has been a melancholy task to read this book; and it is a still more melancholy one to write about it'. He talks of a 'certain precise instinct of conservatism, which is very shrewd in detecting wanton eccentricities', and to which 'Mr. Whitman's attitude seems monstrous. It . . . outrages the taste.' James ends the review with a long diatribe in which he offers Whitman advice: Whitman must not 'amass crudity upon crudity', art 'requires a suppression of one's self, a subordination of one's self to an idea'; 'You must respect the public which you address; for it has taste, if you have not', and '[i]t is not enough to be rude, lugubrious, and grim'.[26] If James here advances a 'conservative' reading of Whitman which finds the poetry distasteful, he does so from a position of knowledge, proclaiming his ability to detect 'wanton eccentricities'. (It is only fair to add that in 1893, writing to Manton Marble, James refuses to divulge the location of this review, which he refers to as a 'deep and damning' disgrace, one of the 'abominations of [his] early innocence'.)[27] James's 1875 review of Swinburne's *Essays and Studies* is also interesting, and seems to contain a number of (intended?) jokes: Swinburne was 'at pains . . . to quicken the apprehension of American readers', his tone 'is in need of a correction', Swinburne's writing can 'lapse into flagrant levity and perversity of taste', one cannot find 'a single case in which the moral note has been struck'. The problem with Swinburne is not that he 'does not understand morality – a charge to which he would be probably quite indifferent; but that he does not at all understand immorality'.[28] Anticipating his later derogatory remarks on Hardy (see chapter one), James, in these reviews of Baudelaire and Swinburne, makes it clear that *he* understands the 'immoral' and the 'intenser perversity'; through this stance of superiority he is staking out his own claims as a writer who understands the (perverse) erotic.

It is, moreover, possible to resolve the apparent invisibility, in historical documents, of the availability of a homosexual subjectivity in 1870s America with the pronounced thematizing of homoerotic desires in *Roderick Hudson*. In fact, the novel can be seen as a response to such an absence. The initial Whitmanic 'adhesiveness' of the two men is abandoned in the novel for a Europeanized eroticization of hierarchy, subordination and domination.[29] Partly at stake is a difference between Whitman's lyric exuberance and Utopianism and James's narrative precision and fuller social contextualization. The Whitmanic possibilities established in the opening chapter of the novel are only established to be subject to systematic 'disintegration'.

At issue here is not only the task of establishing that the young James, capable of reading homoeroticism in the writing of others and responding either with censoriousness or with blasé acceptance, possessed such an insightful writerly and intellectual apparatus that instances of homoeroticism in his own early work need not be regarded as sublimatory or accidental. This is however important in terms of our perceptions of James. (Sedgwick writes that in reading James she is 'very eager that James's sexual language be heard, but that it not be heard with this insulting presumption of the hearer's epistemological privilege'.)[30] Understanding the workings of homo-eroticism in *Roderick Hudson* is necessary if we are to recover the novel's powerful cultural response. This understanding enables us to perceive a more dynamic relationship between text and historical context, one in which fiction actively questions its own cultural framework. If *Roderick Hudson* mourns the absence of cultural legitimation of certain desires, then the possiblity of such a legitimation has at least a ghostly presence in the text. It is interesting then to establish that such a response is not unique to *Roderick Hudson*. Bayard Taylor's *Joseph and His Friend: A Story of Pennsylvania*, a novel published in 1870, expresses such a mourning clearly. And whether or not James had read this novel (James wrote an unenthusiastic review of Taylor's 1865 novel, *John Godfrey's Fortunes*, in which he complained of the novel's 'general tone of vulgarity'), *Joseph* shows the extent of what was possible in 1870s America.[31]

Roger Austen, in a literary study which came out of 1970s 'gay libera-tion', called *Joseph and His Friend* America's 'first gay novel'.[32] The novel, which ran into several editions, articulates an explicit conflict between 'a woman's love' and 'a man's perfect friendship'[33] (the novel takes as its epigraph two lines from Shakespeare's 144th sonnet: 'The better angel is a man right fair; / The worser spirit a woman colour'd ill.'). It moves towards an uncomfortable resolution in a marriage plot: at the end of the novel, Joseph, now a (merry) widower, seems set to marry Madeline, the woman whom Philip apparently loves. Philip looks on, and, in a distorted echo of the sonnets' arguments that the young man should reproduce, thinks, 'I must be vicariously happy, warmed in my lonely sphere by the far radiation of their nuptial bliss, seeing a faint reflection of some parts of myself in their children' (361). However, the novel shows considerable hostility towards marriage – which seems most important for its ability to separate the two male protagonists, Joseph Acton and his 'friend', Philip Held. When Joseph's wife dies, having taken an overdose of the arsenic she uses to preserve her complexion (surely a 'woman colour'd ill'!), 'Philip's heart gave a single leap of joy' (270).

Joseph and Philip are repeatedly propelled together in moments of crisis. They first meet on a train, after Joseph has arranged his marriage to the duplicitous Julia Blessing, and Joseph's eye is 'attracted by a new face . . . It was not long before the unknown felt his gaze, and turning slowly in his seat, answered it' (90–1). ('The usual reply to such a gaze is an unconscious defiance: the unknown nature is on its guard: but the look which seems to answer, "We are men, let us know each other!" is, alas! too rare in this world' (91).) A convenient train accident facilitates the bodily contact the two men seem to crave: the injured Joseph finds himself nursed by Philip's '[s]trong and gentle hands', and 'looked wistfully in the stranger's face' (92). The two men find places together on the recovered train, Joseph leaning 'his head back on [Philip's] supporting arm', and feeling that 'a new power, a new support, had come into his life' (93). The scene is set for one of the novel's many romantic outbursts:

'... there is no high or low, knowledge or ignorance, except what applies to the needs which most men have, and go all their lives hungering for, because they expect them to be supplied in a particular form. There is something,' Philip concluded, 'deeper than that in human nature.'

Joseph longed to open his heart to this man, every one of whose words struck home to something in himself. (95)

The absence of a 'particular form' in which men's 'needs' and 'hunger' might be supplied is this novel's repeated lament, most forcibly expressed in a chapter entitled 'A Crisis', in which the two men struggle with their desire to escape the 'distorted laws of men'. Philip attempts to persuade Joseph to leave his yet-living wife, for a life in the West where they could be 'outlaws ... in our freedom! – here we are fettered outlaws'. Joseph feels 'a mighty temptation in [Philip's] words: they could lead me to snap my chains, break violently away from my past and present life, and surrender myself to will and appetite.' However, Joseph argues that even if the 'laws of men' are distorted, they still need to shape their lives 'according to the law which is above'. Hearing Joseph's argument, it becomes 'Philip's turn to be agitated ... Both natures shared the desire, and were enticed by the daring of his dream; but out of Joseph's deeper conscience came a whisper, against which the cry of passion was powerless.' Joseph's 'deeper conscience' does nevertheless allow an unusual amount of bodily contact, which grows out of a tender resignation: 'Each gave way to the impulse of his manly love, rarer, alas! but as tender and true as the love of woman, and they drew nearer and kissed each other'. The bodies brought together in such passages are clearly zoned: a certain yearning is legible, but there is an avoidance of the genitals at all costs. Head to shoulder, torso to torso, mouth to mouth: such contact is permitted, even while submitting to the 'law which is above'. But more is obviously being asked for; a certain 'cry of passion' is still not being placated (215–17).

What is interesting in *Joseph and His Friend* is not only its subject matter but its rhetoric of 'nature', 'instinct' and 'selfhood'. '[W]hat a luxury it is, just to be one's true self', the arsenic-user Miss Blessing exclaims (18), and this sentiment, which allows a distinction between a 'true' and a 'false' self, an 'inner' and an 'outer' self, recurs throughout the novel. The true self is not the self one necessarily knows: one must endeavour to find it. Thus Joseph, we are told, '[i]f he had not been quite so unconscious of his inner nature as he was over-conscious of his external self, ... would have perceived that his thoughts dwelt much more on Philip Held than on Julia Blessing. His mind seemed to run through a swift, involuntary chain of reasoning, to account to himself for his feeling towards her, and her inevitable share in his future; but towards Philip his heart sprang with an instinct beyond his control' (96). The body – in particular those organs concealed or located below the neck – has an instinct, a nature, a 'will and appetite' of its own which the 'over-conscious ... external self' denies. Further, these inner, concealed selves can be divided into categories. Joseph and Philip feel that they 'stand above the level of common natures, feeling higher needs and claiming other rights' (214). Philip argues that a man's (and a woman's!) 'nature' dictates with whom – with what nature of a person – he or she should spend his life:

Two natures, as far apart as Truth and Falsehood, monstrously held together in the most intimate, the holiest of bonds, – two natures destined for each other monstrously kept apart by the same bonds! Is life to be so sacrificed to habit and prejudice? I said that Faith, like Law, was fashioned for the average man: then there must be a loftier faith, a juster law, for the men – and the women – who cannot shape themselves according to the common-place of society, – who were born with instincts, needs, knowledge, and rights – ay, *rights!* – of their own! (214)

This appeal to 'nature' and 'instinct' predates the 'invention of the homosexual'; nor can it be seen under the rubric of 'sexual inversion' – the friendship of the two men is assertively masculine. (This rhetoric shows that sodomy – or male-male sexual activity – was certainly seen as more than a 'temporary aberration' before what Foucault calls 'a new *specification of individuals*' arising in clinical literature (*HS* 42–3). Necessary to the history of late Victorian clinical writings on sexual perversion is that history's *pre-history*, namely, the way in which transgression of the *law* was already seen as demarcative of a certain identity before the terms of such an identity were rigidly categorized.)[34] 'Man's perfect friendship' in this novel is not only an eroticized friendship, but a friendship which is outlawed, which marks those who seek it as having particular 'natures'. *Roderick Hudson*, unlike *Joseph and His Friend*, does not create such a transparent ontology out of desire. However, it shares many qualities with *Joseph and*

His Friend. The influence of the earlier novel can be felt in *Roderick Hudson*'s eroticization of prohibition and its foregrounding of a forced submission or sacrifice to the law, a law which nevertheless imposes its power.

The identifiability of the 'homosexual' in fiction of the 1890s (and, in Britain, in the 1880s) meant that homoerotic desires between men led to a certain traumatizing. For the masculine subject, homoerotic desire – or even *the possibility of its suggestion* – came to mean a forced negotiation with what Sedgwick has identified as 'homosexual panic'. The turn-of-the-century gentleman who remained in 'the treacherous middle stretch of the modern homosocial continuum', who failed actively to assert a hetero-sexual interest, made himself vulnerable to homosexual panic. Under such a structure, the 'bachelor' ceased to become an innocent construct.[35] This panic emerges in literary texts as representations of violence which also constitute a *representational violence*, a textual instability arising from the legibility of that which should not be written. The representational violence of *Roderick Hudson* takes a different form. The bachelor Mallet's desires are presented with a certain freedom which results from the fact that they are not seen to mark him as 'a homosexual'.

This freedom is evident in the way the other characters in the novel read Mallet. In the first chapter Cecilia argues that Rowland needs an interest in his life, and interprets a long speech of his in which he claims that '[t]rue happiness . . . consists in getting out of one's self', as 'an immense number of words . . . to say you want to fall in love!' She offers to introduce him to some of the 'excellent' and 'very pretty' girls of Northampton, Massachusetts, but then rather abruptly changes her mind: 'I don't think there are any worth asking. There are none so very pretty, none so very pleasing.' On his next visit she makes a different offer, an offer which moves Rowland much more powerfully than the offer of prospective fiancées to which Rowland has responded with a 'little profession of ideal chivalry'. 'If I refused last night to show you a pretty girl', Cecilia says, 'I can at least show you a pretty boy.' Noting Rowland's 'exclamation of surprise', she 'gave him a rapid glance, perceived that her statuette was of altogether exceptional merit, and then smiled knowingly, as if this were a familiar idea'. That the statue, which she has campily opposed to the offer of 'pretty girls', should afford Rowland such scopic pleasure is not a surprise to her. Later in the novel Christina Light comments on the spectacle of what her mother calls 'Mr Mallet and Mr Hudson sleeping under a tree' with the words: 'Don't you know that Mr Mallet is Mr Hudson's sheep-dog? . . . He was mounting guard to keep away the wolves.' Rowland immediately responds that Christina's appearance means that his efforts have been made '[t]o indifferent purpose'. (Christina's comment follows on her instruction to her poodle Stenterello to wake Roderick up, which he does by extending 'a long pink tongue' and licking Roderick's cheek.) Christina continues the exchange, adopting the role of the indignant schoolmistress who has discovered an indiscretion on the part of her charges: '"Is that the way you spend your time?" Christina demanded of Roderick. "I never yet happened to learn what men were doing when they supposed women were not watching them but it was something vastly below their reputation."' (53–9, 199)

The freedom with which Christina comments on Rowland's desire for Roderick finds a parallel in the novel's portrayal of the relationship between the two men, in which gestures which could be read as flirtational elicit no violent reaction from either man, nor any particular narrative comment. (Such a freedom does not obtain in the male bonds in James's late short fiction.)[36] Rather the narrative focuses on the initially pleasurable but increasingly painful nature of Rowland's emotional involvement. When Rowland first meets Roderick he is able to lay 'a kindly hand on his shoulder', and the discussion of Roderick's statuette of 'a naked youth drinking from a gourd', a figure who 'might have been some beautiful youth of ancient fable – Hylas or Narcissus, Paris or Endymion',[37] enables their conversation to be safely charged with an eroticism in which Rowland's admiration of the statue stands in for the 'great fancy' he takes to Roderick (66, 59, 68). (The figure, with his 'loosened fillet of wild flowers about his head' (59), recalls the flagrant display of male beauty so often found in Keats, as the comparison with Endymion hints; think for instance of the 'sleeping youth / Of fondest beauty' in Keats's poem, whose 'face repos'd / On one white arm, and tenderly unclos'd / By tenderest pressure, a faint damask mouth / To slumbery pout,' and above whose head, 'Four lily stalks did their white honours wed / To make a coronal.')[38]

Roderick, meanwhile, animated by Rowland's flattery and seemingly already aware of the value of Rowland's patronage, seems more than happy to engage in a verbal flirtation which is aided by his coquettish gestures:

'Did you mean anything by your young Water-drinker? [asks Rowland] Does he represent an idea? Is he a symbol?'

Hudson raised his eyebrow and gently stroked his hair. 'Why, he's youth, you know; he's innocence, he's health, he's strength, he's curiosity. Yes, he's a good many things.'

'And is the cup also a symbol?'

'The cup is knowledge, pleasure, experience. Anything of that kind!'

'Well, he's guzzling in earnest,' said Rowland.

Hudson gave a vigorous nod. 'Aye, poor fellow, he's thirsty!' And on this he cried good night, and bounded down the garden path. (66)

When Roderick appears a couple of evenings later, they walk together 'over hill and dale, through woods and fields', to 'the generous Connecticut', by which they 'flung themselves on the grass'. This very American land-scape is an idyllic setting for what Whitman called 'a new friendship', which 'shall be called after my name, / It shall circulate through the States, indifferent of place, / It shall twist and intertwist them through and round each other – '.[39] Roderick's familial name happily contributes to this Whitmanic grandeur, to which Rowland draws attention with an exuberant speech: 'This is an American day, an American landscape, and American atmosphere' (69). The two young men are brought into sensual contact with an environment which is alive with erotic movement and touch: 'Rowland watched the shadows on Mount Holyoake, listened to the gurgle of the river, and sniffed the balsam of the pines. A gentle breeze had begun to tickle their summits, and brought the smell of the mown grass across from the elm-dotted river-meadows. He sat up beside his companion and looked away at the far-spreading view' (69).[40] However, even as it exults in the communion of the two men, the novel prepares the reader for the many ways in which such peace will be ruptured: 'It seemed to [Rowland] beautiful, and suddenly a strange feeling of prospective regret took posses-sion of him. Something seemed to tell him that later, in a foreign land, he should remember it with longing and regret' (69).[41]

James has set up with ease the pattern which is to structure the novel: erotic anticipation will only meet with disappointment. The landscape passes further commentary on this melting together of two young men: Roderick 'passe[s] his hand through Rowland's arm' and they walk to the Hudson house, which is 'flanked with [Keatsian] melancholy hemlocks' (71). A number of interests have been established for the reader. That Rowland accepts his bachelor status, as the first paragraph tells us, is ques-tioned by Cecilia's claim that he wants to fall in love; this is a clear comic signal for the reader to expect an intrigue of some sort. Cecilia then fails to introduce him to any young women but instead shows him the beautiful statue, then introduces him to the statue's beautiful creator. Rowland is ecstatic at having met Roderick, yet the novel gives off signals that his happiness is not destined to last.

That Rowland should be plunged into melancholy is inevitable given that his object makes himself so readily available for multiple appreci-ations. This brief erotic idyll in Arcadia is only the prelude to the long

narrative of pain which puts more and more distance between Rowland
and the 'remarkably handsome youth' with whom, as he informs Roderick's
mother, he has 'become so suddenly intimate', despite having known him
'[o]nly three days', as he confesses to Mr Striker, the lawyer for whom
Roderick works (84). Having used the power of patronage to remove
Roderick from employer, mother and his cousin Mary Garland, Rowland
leaves the shadows of Mount Holyoake and its gentle breeze, but only to
walk into an 'elaborately-devised trick' played by fortune which 'had lured
him out into mid-ocean and smoothed the sea and stilled the winds and given
him a singularly sympathetic comrade, and then . . . turned and delivered
him a thumping blow in mid-chest' (102). If the pleasure principle seeks out
stillness, Freud wondered why the subject could seek out thumping blows
which disrupt such stillness. Rowland's first blow – Roderick's announce-
ment that he is engaged to Mary Garland – is received even before he
reaches Rome. Persuading himself that he is disappointed because of his own
affection for Mary, this affection becomes a further pretext for Rowland to
stay with Roderick – he can watch over Roderick on Mary's behalf.

Rowland's 'love' for Mary also helps him account for the emotions he
feels observing Roderick's various amatory entanglements. Roderick is
that sort of dangerous flirt who shoots out more enticing arrows than he
wants to take responsibility for, but Rowland is unconcerned – or gratified
– at the sight of Roderick's disappointed lovers: 'when those who loved
him were in tears, there was something in all this unspotted comeliness
that seemed to lend a mockery to the causes of their sorrow' (114).

Desire for the object, identification with and envy of those who have a
claim on that object: these need not add up to a 'homosexual identity',
although the very historical project of reading historical 'identities' out of
complex inscriptions is of course one which needs to proceed with care.
Sedgwick, when reading Shakespeare's sonnets, asks: 'what on earth does
it take to be homosexual? One thing that it takes is a cultural context that
defines the homosexual as against the heterosexual.'[42] James, it will be seen
(section IV), later in life, not troubled with the many problematizations
arising out of the New Historicism, appealed to such a law of binary oppositions to read, tentatively yet assertively, a notion of 'identity', predicated
on Rowland Mallet's directional desire. He used the word 'nature'.

III VIOLENCE, PROHIBITION AND THE LAW

Roderick Hudson presents a stunning eroticization of power. In the New
York preface James refers to the novel as 'my first attempt at a novel, a long

fiction with a "complicated" subject' (*AN* 4). This statement orphans, or renders illegitimate, his first novel, *Watch and Ward*, the engaging and quasi-incestuous romance which describes the relationship between Roger Lawrence and the orphaned Nora, who becomes firstly his charge and then, after much intrigue, his wife (*Watch and Ward* was written in 1870 and serialized in *The Atlantic*; James published it in book form in 1878).[43] If *Watch and Ward* examines the workings of power and desire within a relationship of paternal 'benevolence', then the networks of power and desire in *Roderick Hudson* are even more complicated.

The physicality of the language and the proliferation of violence in *Roderick Hudson* are astonishing. The novel is full of beatings, of physical and mental cruelty. This cruelty is frequently located within marriage. The first example of such marital excess is a portrait-painter known to Roderick's mother, 'who used to drink raw brandy and beat his wife' (76). Madame Grandoni's marriage is similarly unfortunate: her husband, 'a Neapolitan music-master, ten years younger than herself and with no fortune but his fiddle-bow ... was suspected of using the fiddle-bow as an instrument of conjugal correction. He had finally run off with a *prima donna assoluta*, who it was to be hoped had given him a taste of the quality implied in her title' (121). (Whereas in *Watch and Ward* James's sexual innuendos are heavy-handed, in *Roderick Hudson* they are effortlessly absorbed into the narrative flow. This violent non-reciprocity and asymmetry in personal bonds becomes almost a working assumption in the novel.) It is, moreover, not only husbands who administer beatings in the novel. Madame Grandoni tells Roderick about Herr Schaafgans, another painter, who attempts to be a 'Beato Angelico' but is not successful. (Beato Angelico was a Florentine painter of religious frescoes, who led a holy life of self-denial as a Dominican monk.)[44] Instead he marries a Roman model, who takes up a career as a washerwoman, begins to 'beat him ... and ... make him go and fetch the dirty linen' (126).

In particular, Christina Light, the heroine, who would make, Gloriani claims, 'a magnificent Herodias' (170), has a (matri)lineage of quite shameless husband beaters.[45] Her maternal grandfather, also a painter, is named 'Savage', which 'used to make everyone laugh, he was such a mild, melancholy, pitiful old gentleman'. He has the misfortune of marrying 'a horrible wife, an Englishwoman who had been on the stage', who (as Madame Grandoni tells Rowland Mallet) 'used to beat poor Savage with his mahlstick, and, when the domestic finances were low, to lock him up in his studio and tell him he couldn't come out until he had painted half a dozen of his daubs ... She would go forth with the key in her pocket ...' (152).

Christina's mother, it is gently hinted, may even be a husband-slayer (in her case the name 'Miss Savage' is not so inapposite). Her husband, 'a mild, fair-whiskered young man, with some property', 'had not been married three years when he was drowned in the Adriatic, no one ever knew how' (152–3). Mrs Light also has a liaison with the Cavaliere Giuseppe Giacosa (Christina's father), the '*l'ami de la maison*' who 'used to hold her bouquets, clean her gloves and satin shoes, run her errands, get her opera-boxes, fight her battles with the shopkeepers' (153). Her 'shabby treatment' (318) of the Cavaliere is expressed succinctly in this account of his fetishistic relation to her gloves and shoes. Madame Grandoni says that although Mrs Light 'pretends to be a great lady, ... I consider old Filomena, my washerwoman, is in essentials a greater one' (153). Thus the Cavaliere's degradation and humiliation is comparable to that of the linen-carrying Herr Schaafgans.

This physical cruelty is related to (and not necessarily worse than) forms of psychic cruelty which proliferate in the novel. If Roderick's mother is 'a little timid tremulous woman who is always on pins and needles about her son' (James's metaphors are 'painfully' vivid) then it may only be speculated what sort of a relation she had to her husband, 'a Virginia gentleman – an owner of lands and slaves' who 'drank himself to death' and squanders the familial wealth, combining, it seems, destruction and self-destructiveness (67). The relationship of Rowland's parents is characterized more fully – his mother, whom Rowland thinks of as a 'saint' and a 'singularly unhappy woman', 'found nothing to oppose to her husband's rigid and consistent will but the appearance of absolute compliance' (57).

James quite explicitly relates the volatile entanglement of his three main characters to the sordid dynamics of the relationships of their parents – although these connections are far from systematic. For Rowland and Roderick the possibility of identification with the father is far from an attractive or obvious choice. Roderick adores and idealizes his plaintive mother, subject of one of his most successful sculptures, but has more than a passing resemblance to his bibulous spendthrift father. Rowland certainly sides with his mother against his father, 'a chip of the primal Puritan block, a man with an icy smile and a stony frown' (54). However, the relation is ambivalent. He 'had no desire to make money', and 'disentangled himself from business' (58), whereas his father was a shrewd businessman. However, he has 'an uncomfortably sensitive conscience' and makes 'a rule to render scrupulous justice to fine strokes of behaviour in others' – marks of a punishing superego (49, 58). His youthful consciousness has been 'chilled by the menace of long punishment for brief transgression' (54). Rowland may be making 'a parade of idleness' and want to be 'a graceful *flâneur*' or 'a vigorous young man of genius without a penny' (58), but importantly, there is also in him a strong desire to identify with the law.

Christina's gnarled family tree – an important part of it (the father) not legible by the law – prepares her for the role of the cruel woman, a role she is certainly not happy with. Although she treats her father, the Cavaliere, shabbily, as does her mother, she is also genuinely fond of him and it is as a result of his intervention that she eventually marries the Prince Casamassima. In these transactions Christina is seen as being shamefully degraded by the submission into which she is forced by the Cavaliere and (more importantly) her mother. These transactions are complicated in that Christina does not know the Cavaliere is her father. It is when she finds this out that she agrees to marry the Prince.

These ambivalences feed into the triangle of Rowland, Roderick and Christina. Within this triangle, the circulation of erotic energies, of what Freud, in *The Ego and the Id*, calls 'the great reservoir of the libido',[46] does not allow for a resolution which might enable a stable positioning of each participant in the scene.

Crucial to this volatility is the availability of the male body as erotic object (and to a male gaze) – an availability which is quite striking in the novel. D. A. Miller has written that 'a prerequisite for the success of the ambitious young man from the provinces is the course in body *Bildung* that instructs him on how to withdraw from the pleasures and dangers of visibility, from an *object* position where he might be desired, circulated, wounded. In the canonical story of making it, Balzac's *Père Goriot*, Rastignac requires a body whose power and prestige depends on its vanishing into a gaze that cannot effectively be returned.'[47] Roderick's body, by contrast, is constantly on display and available for erotic circulation (if not consumption) and for wounding. From his first appearance, when he is wearing a 'white linen suit', 'a bright red cravat, passed through a ring altogether too splendid to be valuable', twisting 'a pair of yellow kid gloves' and flourishing a 'light silver-tipped walking-stick', this 'tall slender young fellow, with a singularly mobile and intelligent face', which is, moreover, 'remarkably handsome', draws attention to himself in a variety of voguish striking poses (64).[48] Roderick is subject to a continued lingual caress, a narrative gaze which lingers over his body, the body of 'a beautiful, supple, restless, bright-eyed animal, whose motions should have no deeper warrant than the tremulous delicacy of its structure and seem graceful even when they were most inconvenient' (69).

Narrative interest in the novel derives, however, from the spectacle of

this 'bright-eyed animal' in pain, from increments of tension which strain
and strain further the supple body beautiful, and any claim Rowland
might make on that body. It is Rowland Mallet who brings about the first of
many structural disturbances to Roderick's frame, just as Roderick is
responsible for a 'distinct commotion' (*AN* 17) in Rowland's more stoic,
'pliable, frank' structure, which could 'never [be] accused of anything
more awkward than a manly roundness' (56). That he takes an active interest in such a straining is evident early in the novel, when he tells Cecilia:

'Of course when a body begins to expand, there comes in the possibility of burst-
ing, but I nevertheless approve of a certain tension of one's being. It's what a man
is meant for.' (81)

Christina Light contributes marvellously to the realization of Rowland's
doctrine of male expansion and explosion. She pumps Roderick up and
lets him down as one might an inflatable plastic duck.

Christina Light, cruel woman (and soon to be princess), arrives like the
Prince in Sacher-Masoch's *Venus in Furs* to add a few turns to the screw of
Rowland's discomfort. All women *are* cruel to the extent that they can draw
Roderick from Rowland; as the narrator tells us: 'Women are said by some
authorities to be cruel; I know not how true this is, but . . . Mrs Hudson
was intensely feminine' (336). (James makes it clear that Rowland's and
Roderick's perceptions of Christina's cruelty are projections, drawing
from a rich realm of fantasy.)[49] The novel's erotic triangle consists of a
dominant tableau, in which Rowland, as spectator, looks on at the flirtatious interactions of Christina and Roderick. This tableau eroticizes the
spectacle of Roderick's suffering, but this suffering is subsumed within
what might be called, variously, an economy of cruelty, of beating, of
pain, of need. This economy might productively be called a 'masochistic'
economy – but such a label is misleading to the extent that masochism has
predominantly been theorized as a perversion in the individual subject.
And there is something quite radical in the play of identifications, the
movement of roles, within the erotic triangle of *Roderick Hudson*, which
cannot be contained by an analysis of an individual subject taking up a
position within a fantasized scene.

The radical masochistic economy of *Roderick Hudson* derives from
complex and multiple movements of ungratified desire and unstable identifications. For Rowland's desire for Roderick, and Roderick's desire
for Christina, comes full circle (or full triangle) in Christina's desire
for Rowland. Mapping these movements is at the least very tricky in a
novel which takes advantage of so many rhetorical strategies – camp,

negation and denial, disavowal, identification – to indicate and reiterate desire.

The most elusive link in the chain – and one suggested rather than fully portrayed – is Christina's desire for Rowland. Roderick points this out at the end of the novel, but Rowland could surely have been aware of it had he been a sharper reader. (Christina continually controls the stakes of legibility in their transactions: for instance, when Rowland asks her to leave Roderick behind on Mary Garland's behalf, she is perfectly aware of Rowland's own investment in their separation.) With Christina writing him notes asking him to 'Begin and respect me!' (235), and the Cavaliere telling him he is 'the only man whose words she remembers' (307), Roderick's claim that Rowland is 'obtuse' is fairly well-grounded.[50]

Roderick makes this claim with great viciousness. 'There are certain things you know nothing about,' he tells Rowland, at which Rowland turns pale:

'These things – what are they?' Rowland asked.

'They are women, principally, and what relates to women. Women for you, by what I can make out, mean nothing. You have no imagination – no sensibility, nothing to be touched!'

'That's a serious charge,' said Rowland gravely. (373)

A charge, however, which Roderick presses home, referring to Rowland's 'grossly obtuse' treatment of Christina, who 'took a fancy to you':

'There is something monstrous in a man's pretending to lay down the law to a sort of emotion with which he is quite unacquainted – in his asking a fellow to give up a lovely woman for conscience' sake when *he* has never had the impulse to strike a blow for one for passion's!'

'Oh, oh!' cried Rowland. (374)

These violent outbursts, laced with slurs, 'bristling' with suggestions, put pressure on a structure, a 'canvas', containing a 'boundless number of . . . distinct perforations for the needle' and covered with 'the weaving of silver threads and tapping on golden nails' (*AN* 5, 69).[51]

The novel opposes a current of desire to a current of cruelty, flowing in different directions around the erotic triangle. Each love object is cruel to the lover by turning their attention to another object.[52] The dominant configuration of the triangle is certainly that in which Rowland is spectator, but the vitriolic counter-attack launched by Roderick at the novel's close suggests that Roderick has been participating much more intensely – at least, with an unselfconscious abandon – in his own eroticized tableau in which the cruel Christina is trying in vain to attract his 'obtuse' patron.

Each of the three is both spectator and participant: it has already been shown that Christina employs the tongue of her poodle Stenterello to separate 'sheep-dog' Rowland from Roderick, and shatter the tranquil shared slumber of the two men, and Roderick's failure to tell Rowland of Christina's 'fancy' for him is anything but an innocent omission. Similarly, Rowland both enjoys watching Roderick's and Christina's flirtatious involvement, and stepping in to ruin it (see especially chapter thirteen of the novel). The circuits of cruelty, like those of desire and of rivalry, however, do not follow fixed routes.

This spinning, collapsing and expanding triangle sets up multiple matrices of identification and desire, which cannot be disentangled to constitute a heterosexual or 'nuclear-familial' frame. Further, the dynamics of desire and fantasy within the triangle are fully informed by the respective economic and gendered statuses of the participants. (Rowland's financial status, Roderick's economic dependence on Rowland, and the degraded submission to which Christina is eventually forced by her family are the most obvious factors impacting on and corrupting the symmetry of the triangle. If Roderick and Rowland fantasize about Christina as representing a dynamic female activity and evil – even when they first see her they compare her with Mephistopheles and designate her 'dangerous', and 'the incarnation of evil' (110) – she is of course unfortunate in her parents, with a mother who can abuse her 'as if [she] were the vilest of the vile' and an apparently submissive father holding the 'sword of Damocles' (315) over her head.)

Two visual icons play a privileged role in the triangle: the framing of Christina as cruel woman and *femme fétiche*, and the spectacle of Roderick Hudson's suffering body. For both the swift and chaotic narrative action is interrupted; a freezing, a delay, a suspension of temporality takes place. When, for instance, Christina interrupts Madame Grandoni's party, she stands in Orientalized splendour at the focal point of every spectator's gaze:

> They were of course observing her. Standing in the little circle of lamplight, with the hood of an Eastern burnous shot with silver threads falling back from her beautiful head, one hand gathering together its voluminous shimmering folds and the other playing with the silken top-knot on the uplifted head of her poodle, she was a figure of radiant picturesqueness. She seemed to be a sort of extemporised *tableau vivant*. (290)[53]

When the narrative, a few pages later, pauses on Roderick, he is supine, passively withdrawn, his senses pained with 'drowsy numbness' (Keats) and his body abandoned in an erotic, deathlike (and similarly extemporised) stillness:

Roderick lay motionless . . . He was smelling a large white rose, which he continued to present to his nose. In the darkness of the room he looked exceedingly
pale, but his handsome eyes had an extraordinary brilliancy. He let them rest for
some time on Rowland, lying there like a Buddhist in an intellectual swoon,
whose perception should be slowly ebbing back to temporal matters. (302)

This pre-Raphaelite spectacle tropes on late Romantic figurations of
death, recalling in particular Keats, for whom, as Adrienne Donald writes,
'the paradigm of all experience – sexual or otherwise – is . . . passive transgression'.[54] (Roderick is fulfilling the prophecy made by Gloriani early
in the novel: 'You will become weak. You will have to take to violence, to
contortions, to romanticism in self-defence' (125).)

Gilles Deleuze writes in *Coldness and Cruelty* (in which he takes Sacher-
Masoch's novels as paridigmatic of masochism) that the aestheticism of
masochism depends on waiting and delay, postponement and suspense:
the masochist 'waits for pleasure as something that is bound to be late, and
expects pain as the condition that will finally ensure (both physically and
morally) the advent of pleasure'.[55] In the preface to the novel James complains that '[e]verything occurs . . . too punctually and moves too fast',
claiming that the 'exhibitional interest' of 'Roderick's disintegration',
which derives from its being 'gradual and occasional', is compromised by
its speed (*AN* 12). A more ideal or 'exquisite' interest would arise from a
slowing of the narrative tempo. And certainly, as James's career develops
the element of 'suspense' in his work increases; the late novels seem to
move into a number of formal tableaux, spatial visualisations in which the
characters are placed according to the rules of perspective, only to be
broken up by the temporality of narrative. The consecutive sequence of a
freezing-up followed by a shattering comes to be the dominant rhythm of
James's writing.

Deleuze's *Coldness and Cruelty* describes masochism as a particular erotic
subjectivity available to the masculine subject. *Roderick Hudson*, however,
portrays what I have called a 'masochistic economy', an economy in which
desire is never gratified and always punished, but in which a certain
pleasure derives from that very punishment. James himself expresses
anxiety that Roderick's speedy decay might render 'the whole view a
disservice of appearing to present him as a morbidly special case' (*AN* 12).

The very fact of prohibition and its extension across the novelistic canvas
is what stops the novel and its characters from being merely 'morbidly
special'. At one point of the novel, watching Roderick's absorption in
Christina, Rowland wonders whether 'there was not a larger moral law
than for narrow mediocrities like himself' (170). If Roderick accuses

Rowland of 'lay[ing] down the law' (374), then Rowland's interest in whether or not Roderick will submit to it is considerable.

Roderick's passivity is thematized as an imperfect submission to the law. Roderick is unassuming and disarmingly frank in his self-assessments. 'I am very weak!' is a characteristic cry (282). He tells Rowland early in the novel: 'I have been a mollycoddle. I have been sprawling all my days by the maternal fireside, and my dear mother has grown used to bullying me . . . She would fain see me all my life tethered to the law, like a browsing goat to a stake' (75–6). In taking a hammer to destroy the bust of his employer, Mr Barnaby Striker ('he dealt a merciless blow upon Mr Striker's skull' (73)), he makes an attempt to break out of servitude, the first of many attempts which inevitably fail.

Mary Garland appears to see Roderick kicking the 'shapeless fragments' of this skull; she lets out her first 'cry of horror', anticipating the cry which closes the novel. Mary asks her cousin what he has done, and he replies: 'I have driven the money-changers out of the temple!' Mary is dismayed at the thoughtless behaviour of the boy Jesus, and understands that the 'young man's allegory . . . must be an evil one from being expressed in such a lawless fashion' (73).

James is invoking a law of sacrifice, a law inscribed across the novel in serious and comic registers. (Stenterello the poodle is called a 'ram for sacrifice' on his first appearance (109).) Christina, cast as Herodias by Gloriani (but resembling Salomé more closely), helps frame the sacrificial body attractively. *Roderick Hudson* doesn't advocate joining those you can't beat, but beating those you can't have. Rowland, in his paternal role of patron, lays down the law which manages eventually to pacify the criminal Roderick. (By Roderick's dead body 'he accused himself of cruelty and injustice' (387).) If it is tempting to conflate Roderick's name to Rock, then the novel brings a Mallet to Rock Hudson. Whereas *Joseph and His Friend* ends with the disappointed Philip Held trying to gain vicarious pleasure from Joseph's marriage, Rowland is left with the even more dubious pleasure of identification with a widow. Prohibition has been eroticized, but at what a cost.

IV THE 'DANGER TO VERISIMILITUDE': JAMES READING JAMES

In writing the preface to the novel and also, importantly, in revising the text, the older James provides us with an interesting reading of the artistic output of his younger self, an output he calls, in the preface to *The Golden Bowl*, his 'uncanny brood', 'the first-born of my progeny', the 'reappearence' of which is figured 'as a descent of awkward infants from the nursery to the drawing-room' (*AN* 337). James appeals to a process 'of drawing-room discipline, . . . the purification, in other words, of innocent childhood', which is necessary to make his 'brood more presentable under the nobler illumination', but notes the absence of any judge who can 'kindly measure out . . . the appropriate amount of ablutional fluid' (*AN* 338). The 'act of revision, the act of seeing . . . again, caused whatever I looked at on any page to flower before me as into the only terms that honourably expressed it; and the "revised" element in the present Edition is accordingly these terms, these rigid conditions of re-perusal, registered' (*AN* 339).

Sedgwick's 'Shame and Performativity: Henry James's New York Edition Prefaces' interrogates the movements of 'exhibitionistic flirtation' in James's prefaces, which are 'gorgeous with the playful spectacle of a productive and almost promiscuously entrusted or "thrown" authorial narcissism', a spectacle attended by a powerful shame (and shaming), which, through revision, is nevertheless rendered 'narratively, emotionally, and performatively productive.'[56] The power of her reading may be measured in the last paragraph of James's last preface, in which James notes that shaming and embarrassing 'connexions' need not be disavowed:

Our noted behaviour at large may show for ragged, because it perpetually escapes our control; we have again and again to consent to its appearing in undress – that is in no state to brook criticism. But on all the ground to which the pretension of performance by a series of exquisite laws may apply there reigns one sovereign truth – which decrees that, as art is nothing if not exemplary, care nothing if not active, finish nothing if not consistent, the proved error is the base apologetic deed, the helpless regret is the barren commentary, and 'connexions' are employable for finer purposes than mere gaping contrition. (*AN* 348).

In reading the first of his 'uncanny brood' he owns up to, James considers the 'connexions' or 'relations' in the novel without using large quantities of 'ablutional fluid'. He shows himself highly attentive to the eroticism of the novel (an awareness shown in every preface). I have quoted often from James's prefaces in presenting this reading because of the very intelligence they display, not only in their interrogation of novelistic and aesthetic questions, but in the eloquent erotic vocabulary they provide.

The preface to *Roderick Hudson* raises many of the questions I have been addressing, not least the question of Rowland's identity, or what James calls his 'consciousness, and the drama is the very drama of that consciousness' (*AN* 16). James takes a highly circuitous and comic route to account for the 'danger to verisimilitude' arising from the fact that the reader has not been 'put into position to take more closely home the impression made [on Rowland] by Mary Garland' (*AN* 17). It is difficult to extricate James's argument from the gymnastics of his prose, which, despite its procrastination, manages elegantly to make a certain assertion through negation:

> ... though there was no reason on earth (unless I except one, presently to be mentioned) why Rowland should *not*, at Northampton, have conceived a passion, or as near an approach to one as he was capable of, for a remarkable woman there suddenly dawning on his sight, a particular fundamental care was required for the vivification of that possibility. The care, unfortunately, had not been skilfully enough taken, in spite of the later patching-up of the girl's figure. We fail to accept it, on the actual showing, as that of a young person irresistible at any moment, and above all irresistible at a moment of the liveliest *other* preoccupation, as that of the weaver of (even the highly conditioned) spell that the narrative imputes to her. The spell of attraction is cast upon young men by young women in all sorts of ways, and the novel has no more constant office than to remind us of that. But Mary Garland's doesn't, indubitably, convince us; any more than we are truly convinced, I think, that Rowland's destiny, or say his nature, would have made him accessible at the same hour to two quite distinct commotions, even a very deep one, of his whole personal economy. (*AN* 17)

James produces a remarkable definition of the novel's most 'constant office': to remind the reader of 'the spell of attraction cast upon young men ... by young women'. According to this law, then, *Roderick Hudson* has failed dismally to discharge its office, and the reason for this, the second reason, which is 'presently' given, after an inevitably lengthy diversion, is, beyond that of the *girl's* figure not presenting itself as irresistible 'at a moment of the liveliest *other* preoccupation', precisely this *other* preoccupation. We cannot believe that Rowland's *nature* 'would have made him accessible at the same hour to *two* quite distinct commotions'. James's indiscreet discretion may be measured in the fact that he never mentions what the 'first' commotion or the 'other' preoccupation are, although he draws his reader in to this realm of unspecified knowledge: 'each of these upheavals of his sensibility must have been exclusive of other upheavals, yet the reader is asked to accept them as working together. They are different vibrations, but the whole sense of the situation depicted is that they should each have been of the strongest, too strong to walk hand in hand' (*AN* 17–18). Obviously, the strong 'vibration' created by *Roderick* is the disabling force which prevents Mary Garland from producing more than a slight tremor in Rowland.

James then sees the 'damage to verisimilitude' arising out of a difficulty of controlling the terms of sameness and difference – the *other* preoccupation, the 'spell of attraction cast upon young *men* by young *women*', the way one 'upheaval' excludes the *other*, the incompatibility of the *different* vibrations 'to walk hand in hand'. In the next paragraph he observes that '[o]ne is ridden by the law that antitheses, to be efficient, shall be both direct and complete ... [T]he ideal antithesis rarely does "come off," and ... has to content itself for the most part with a strong term and a weak term, *and even then to feel itself lucky*' (*AN* 18; my emphasis). If the workings of 'same' and 'different' within the preface bear a relation to what Sedgwick calls 'the inaugural discourses of modern homo/heterosexuality', and the 'historical specificity of homosocial/homosexual definition',[57] James's awareness of the rarity or impossibility of the 'ideal antithesis' complicates such oppositions, recalling the unstable asymmetry of bonds linking 'strong' and 'weak' terms within his novel, suggesting that such bonds are neither categorizable in terms of equality or of subordination. Such a volatility would frustrate an easy mapping of 'strong' and 'weak' terms onto the very binary oppositions which are encouraged in terms of the 'law' James is aware of being 'ridden' by.[58] Although the bonds foregrounded in the novel seem divisible into 'strong' and 'weak' term (patron/artist, lover/cruel woman), the dynamics in any bond are shown to proceed according to complex negotiations of empowering and disabling mechanisms. Similarly, the strong term 'hetero', the term identified with the law which states that novels should portray the 'attraction' of 'young women' (in the preface Christina is the 'strong term' displacing Mary's weakness), finds no 'ideal antithesis' with a weak term, the term disregarding the law, and the term which has considerable strength in the novel, the term of the spell of attraction cast upon young men by young *men*.

Thus the novel's failure to reproduce and advocate the law of the attractiveness of young women to young men opens up a discursive space in which the failure of young men to comply with this law might be articulated. Just as Cecilia, failing to show Rowland a pretty girl, shows him a pretty boy instead, *Roderick Hudson* foregrounds the spectacle of an attractive young man casting spells in a way which seems 'monstrous' to a 'precise instinct of conservatism'. How might this failure of the novel correspond to the failures within the novel? How are submission – and failure to submit – played out in preface and novel?

If Rowland is the novel's most active homoerotic fantasizer, his own psychic punishment takes the form of the destruction of the body of Roderick, Rowland's romantic and beautiful Sebastian. The ending of the novel, expressed in a re-working of the Freudian geometry of beating ('A Child Is Being Beaten'), might read, 'My father (who is myself) is beating the child (whom I love and hate and who hasn't loved me).' This accompanies a string of other fantasies: 'My love object is being cruel to me', 'The woman is being cruel to my love object (and consequently also to me.)' As Wilde was later to write in 'The Ballad of Reading Gaol', 'all men kill the thing they love'.[59]

When revising the novel James re-works and expands its use of the story of Salomé, even re-working the language of the novel with, as Adeline R. Tintner has pointed out, allusions to Moreau, Huysmans and Wilde.[60] James's novel both anticipates and echoes Wilde's play in making a sacrificial spectacle of the unavailable erotic male body.[61] Roderick's death is fully consonant with Rowland's survival. Rowland, although he enjoys and contributes to the spectacle of Roderick's martyrdom, survives intact. If not entirely happy with the 'prospect of bachelorhood', the painful and ecstatic trajectory through which he is drawn by his love for Roderick is perhaps sufficient to convince him to stick with it. And by the end of the novel, sticking with it is surely a point of honour. For he has become a widow. Rowland's Puritan childhood has amply prepared him, as the novel tells us, for 'the menace of long punishment for brief transgression' (54).

Roland Barthes writes that 'the only biography is of an unproductive life', and his 'biography', which 'must all be considered as if spoken by a character in a novel', begins with the gesture with which *Roderick Hudson* ends: the 'demand for love'.[62] Consider that the novel is initiated by this demand, and that the movements this demand will make, the identifications it will inspire, are difficult to circumscribe. 'There's nothing I can't imagine! That is my difficulty!' as Christina Light exclaims (231).

The mature Henry James recalls that trying to 'draw, by a geometry of his own, the circle' within which relations might 'happily *appear*' to stop, the 'young embroiderer of the canvas of life began to work in terror, fairly, of the vast expanse of that surface, . . . The very meaning of expertness is acquired courage to brave one's self for the cruel crisis from the moment one sees it grimly loom' (*AN* 6). Rowland's 'cruel crisis' arises from possessing no 'rights' – as does Mary Garland – to make this demand. Yet his identification with her does not 'feminize' him: he wants to displace her rather than be her. Or to displace anyone who can make a claim on Roderick.

The performative geometry of the novel consists in a brutal reiteration of the law, through a sacrifice which re-affirms Rowland's bachelor status, a status perhaps more palliative for its crossing over into the status of widowhood. Rowland wavers and trembles between the demands of the law and his own demands, which are only defined to the extent that they are refused recognition by the law. This refusal means his demands are only articulated through remaining inarticulate. For Rowland's desire for Roderick, made hugely apparent to the reader, is principally legible to

Rowland to the extent that he can read that desire in others – only at the novel's close does he voice to himself 'how exclusively . . . Roderick had filled his life' (387).

The scenario offered in *Roderick Hudson* might appear to be a scenario of doom, a 'cruel crisis' which one might only brave with 'acquired courage'. Rowland's love is not the love of the closet, the 'love that dare not speak its name', but the love that cannot find its name. The knowing and articulate circle that James draws around such inarticulate relations – which stop nowhere and do not even *appear* to do so – remains a paradoxical miracle that no amount of theorizing can properly account for. The novel of an unproductive life need not be an unproductive novel; it can instead be a productive failure.

To talk of the 'demand for love' is to beg another question. I have been talking of *Roderick Hudson* as an intricate structure of desire, of thwarted desire. But of course, it is also a novel about love, particularly in its concern with the law. The relation of desire to the law cannot be considered apart from the relation of love to the law. This question will be considered more extensively in chapters six and seven; to quote James once more (from the preface to *The Wings of the Dove*), it 'leaves me with a burden of residuary comment of which I yet boldly hope elsewhere to discharge myself' (*AN* 306).

CHAPTER FIVE

Queer plotting: The Princess Casamassima *and* The Bostonians

Instead of the old, familiar predicament of one heroine and two heroes, one of whom must get and one lose the prize, the two heroes are a man and woman, but the struggle is of the same general character. Who is to have Verena? Shall it be Olive or Basil? That is the question which is asked with great particularity and at great length.

Horace E. Scudder, review of *The Bostonians, Atlantic Monthly*, 1886[1]

I QUEER RIVALRIES

The standard Jamesian queer plot – a plot to which James returns again and again – involves a struggle for possession, and ends in a tragic, violent dénouement. Rivalry is of course one of fiction's core ingredients, but James consistently turns the screw of the classic rivalry plot, involving a struggle between two men for a woman.[2] In James's first (disowned) novel, *Watch and Ward*, of 1870, the male rivals, Roger and Hubert Lawrence, are cousins, and the woman for whom they compete, Nora Lambert, is a young girl, the 'ward' of one of the rivals. Here James already anticipates *The Bostonians*. *The Bostonians* also puts two cousins in competition with one another for a young girl who is one cousin's protégée. In the later novel the two rivals are a woman and a man, so the struggle is one in which the privileging of heterosexual bonds over homosexual bonds plays a crucial role. In James's queer plots, it is frequently this privileging which precipitates the tragedy.

When James, in *Roderick Hudson*, describes the rivalry of a woman (Mary Garland) and a man (Rowland Mallet) for the affections of another man (Hudson), he is exploring territory to which he will return several times throughout his career. James's queer rivalry plots are possessive struggles in which the competitors are given different handicaps; these struggles contrast the legitimation of heterosexual affection with the lack of recognition accorded to same-sex unions.

James's two major novels of the mid 1880s – he wrote *The Princess*

Casamassima immediately after he finished writing *The Bostonians*, and both novels were published in 1886 – both contain queer rivalry plots. Olive Chancellor, of *The Bostonians*, and Hyacinth Robinson, of *The Princess Casamassima*, show a marked propensity to form strong affections for members of their own sex; both choose objects of desire whose perceived working-class 'authenticity' accentuates their femininity or masculinity (Verena Tarrant and Paul Muniment[3]); both find themselves thwarted by their beloved's tendency to form heterosexual bonds.

Although the portrayal of same-sex affection is more muted in *The Princess Casamassima* than in *The Bostonians*, a queer rivalry plot plays a role in Hyacinth Robinson's suicide at the close of the novel: Hyacinth's suicide seems a logical outcome of his feelings of sexual alterity, isolation and alienation. James began writing *The Bostonians* only a few weeks after he wrote 'The Author of "Beltraffio"', in which he used his knowledge that J. A. Symonds' wife intensely disliked her husband's (homoerotic, aestheticist) writing to create the situation of a wife letting her son die in order to keep him from his father, whose books she finds unforgivably immoral.[4] Although critics have claimed that homosexuality is not relevant to the disagreement between Mr and Mrs Ambient,[5] Jonathan Freedman argues that James was more knowing when he wrote the story, and that Mrs Ambient's perception of her husband's homosexuality motivates her extreme behaviour.[6] It is indeed difficult to see another motivation – although the story suggests that Mrs Ambient thinks Ambient's 'ideas' bad for the child, it abounds in innuendo which, read in the light of J. A. Symonds's writing, suggests that James is consciously ironizing the grim situation of a woman afraid that her husband will provide an unsavoury queer tutelage for her child. In 1883 Symonds published *A Problem in Greek Ethics*, his study of Greek 'paiderastia, or boy-love', which implicitly lamented the 'undeveloped and unhonoured' state of male and female 'homosexual passions in the modern European world'.[7] James may have been unaware of *A Problem in Greek Ethics*, which was privately printed and circulated, yet he would have known Symonds's *Studies of the Greek Poets* (1873 and 1876), in which 'the ideal of Greek life' is held up to suggest the benefits of a legitimation of male same-sex affection, and been aware of Sir John Tyrwhitt's attack on Victorian homoerotic Hellenism – and on Symonds himself – in his 1877 essay 'The Greek Spirit in Modern Literature'.[8] Anxieties concerning J. A. Symonds's Hellenism are referred to in 'The Author of "Beltraffio"' when Mrs Ambient thinks her husband 'no better than an ancient Greek', 'immoral – that's the long and short of it' (*CT* 5:325, 334–5). Mark Ambient characterizes the differences between him and his wife as 'simply the opposition between two distinct ways of looking at the world, which have never succeeded in getting on together, or making any common ménage, since the beginning of time', ways which have 'borne all sorts of names, and [Mrs Ambient] would tell you it's the difference between Christian and Pagan' (334). Here the tale suggests that something more than differing views on late nineteenth-century aesthetic principles separates the couple. Mrs Ambient's anxieties concerning her husband's suitability as a father centre on a scene of pedagogic seduction; 'she has a dread of [her husband's] influence on the child – on the formation of his character, of his principles. It is as if it were a subtle poison, or a contagion, or something that would rub off on Dolcino when his father kisses him or holds him on his knee' (329). As Leon Edel writes, '[t]his tale . . . heralded the struggle in *The Bostonians*.[9] (Having made this assertion, it is odd that Edel is at pains to deny the importance of homosexuality in both narratives.) Like Mrs Ambient, Basil Ransom is obsessively driven in his quest to disrupt a scene of queer tutelage.

II *THE BOSTONIANS* AND THE ENIGMA OF OLIVE CHANCELLOR

As Terry Castle argues, literary criticism has been somewhat duplicitous in arguing that it is foolish to regard *The Bostonians* as a 'lesbian novel', or even, more modestly, as 'a novel about lesbianism', while showing no hesitation in regarding Olive Chancellor as a pathological, morbid, hysterical lesbian. How, Castle asks, 'can James's novel *not* be "a study of lesbianism" if its central character . . . is in fact a "horrid" lesbian?'[10] The question is pertinent, because *The Bostonians*, more than any other Jamesian text, has incited a huge outpouring of homophobic literary criticism.

Judith Fetterley has discussed such responses at length in her pioneering book *The Resisting Reader* (1978). As Fetterley shows, some critics simply dismiss the lesbian question as irrelevant: such a surprising dismissal is usually blithe and unsubstantiated.[11] More frequently, however, critics engage in a full character assassination of Olive Chancellor, who emerges as 'unnatural' as opposed to the healthy, life-affirming Basil Ransom. The common thread of such a response is the claim that the reader should rejoice that Basil Ransom manages to win Verena Tarrant from Olive Chancellor, whether or not Olive is lesbian, and whether or not the novel, or James, portray Basil's victory as a positive outcome.[12] This critical line has continued to be advanced after the appearance of Fetterley's study. In 1984, R. D. Gooder wrote that 'we don't at first think of Basil Ransom as a threat to Verena's liberty no less dangerous than Olive . . . because we are so anxious for Ransom to win the struggle', and that 'Verena's relations with Olive are founded on will and can only be kept up by continued application of will; her attraction to Ransom is inspired by all the forces of nature and underwritten by all the romantic conventions'.[13]

'Without encumbering the story with lesbianism, one can still recognize in Olive's obsession a serious evil',[14] Walter F. Wright wrote in 1962: this quote dramatically illustrates Castle's point that criticism of *The Bostonians* wants both to decry and deny the novel's 'lesbianism'. Yet in advancing a lesbian reading of the novel, one needs to counter a naive historicist argument, which would have it that Olive Chancellor cannot be a 'lesbian' because lesbians did not exist in Boston in the 1880s. As Lilian Faderman points out, Olive's relationship with Verena can be viewed as a 'Boston marriage', a late nineteenth-century term for 'a long-term monogamous relationship between two otherwise unmarried women'.[15] This observation can aid but not contain our understanding of the novel. It shows that much twentieth-century criticism of the novel is anachronistic, in applying a vocabulary derived from sexology and psychoanalysis to a relationship conceived in terms preceding the popularization of such sciences.[16] However, the novel is by no means content merely to present a 'Boston marriage'; rather, it actively questions the terms governing human relationships, whether same-sex or heterosexual, whether married or (to use Verena Tarrant's term) 'free'. To do justice to the subversive force of this questioning is to render the relationship between novel and historical context as fluid and dynamic, rather than merely static.

If Olive's relationship with Verena is not 'underwritten by all the romantic conventions', as Gooder claims, *The Bostonians* does its own work in creating such conventions. Olive herself feverishly romanticizes their union. She sees her relationship with Verena as a heroic servitude to the women's movement; if history does not provide a large number of obvious precedents for the relationship, it should be remembered that Olive and Verena 'insisted so much ... on the historic unhappiness of women'.[17] Certainly, the novel can be read more richly if we can think of Olive as (some kind of) a lesbian. Her views on history – her sense that her sex 'had suffered inexpressibly' (153) – and her uncompromising scorn for marriage, could be read as showing her awareness that 'history' and 'marriage' do not offer much to a woman who is drawn, romantically, to other women. Hence Fetterley argues that 'we may see [Olive's] morbidity not as the result of her lesbianism but as the result of her powerlessness to act it out',[18] and Terry Castle argues not only that Olive is seen by James as 'essentially tragic', as F. O. Matthiessen claimed,[19] but that Olive is 'English and American literature's first lesbian tragic heroine', and James 'is the first major modern writer . . . to open a space for a sympathetic reading of a lesbian character.'[20] Just as Olive and Verena want to introduce 'certain aesthetic, romantic elements' into the women's movement, Olive sees these aesthetic and romantic elements as present in relationships between women.

What is remarkable is the great imaginative projection in James's portrayal of intimacy between the two women. Consider the following exchange, which takes place after Verena has asked Olive whether she always feels 'the want of a vote':

'I always feel it – everywhere – night and day. I feel it *here*;' and Olive laid her hand solemnly on her heart. 'I feel it as deep, unforgettable wrong. I feel it as one feels a stain that is on one's honour.'

Verena gave a clear laugh, and after that a soft sigh, and then said, 'Do you know, Olive, I sometimes wonder whether, if it wasn't for you, I should feel it so very much!'

'My own friend,' Olive replied, 'you have never yet said anything to me which expressed so clearly the closeness and sanctity of our union.' (136)

Here the tenderness in the two women's 'union' is clear. Olive's choice of words suggests an awareness that their 'union' is an acceptable social form; according to Mark DeWolfe Howe, the nineteenth-century editor of the *Atlantic Monthly*, Boston marriages constituted 'a union – there is no other word for it'.[21] Olive's desires have then a certain historical specificity; a particular social context frames her consideration 'that she found [in Verena] what she had been looking for so long – a friend of her own sex with whom she might have a union of soul' (70). Nor, it should be added, was James short of material on which to model the relationship. Critics have identified the importance of his sister Alice's relationship – or 'Boston marriage' – with Katharine Loring as an important source for his portrayal of Olive and Verena.[22]

Such a context is important for several reasons. The fact that the novel predates the popularization of a sexological discourse on lesbianism does not make a 'lesbian reading' of the text implausible. (As Castle argues, James, familiar with representations of lesbian desire in French literature, didn't need sexology to help him create a lesbian plot.) On the contrary, the *absence* of sexological discourse allows the very boldness and freedom of the novel's representations. Because the 1880s reader did not have a reflex reaction to the text identifying Olive as perverse in sexological terms, James had a relatively free hand in her creation. *The Bostonians* avoids a pathologizing discourse on lesbianism because it treats same-sex desire in the absence of a defined lesbian identity: it is only in twentieth-century criticism of the novel (and in at least one twentieth-century rewriting of the novel, D. H. Lawrence's 'The Fox'[23]) that this pathologizing discourse emerges.

The identification of Olive as in some way abnormal was largely (not wholly) absent from contemporary reviews of the novel, which noted the novel's radicalism, but were quite varied in their view of Olive. Reviewing the novel in the *Atlantic Monthly*, Horace E. Scudder noticed that *The Bostonians* represents a departure from a traditional novelistic scenario, that of 'one heroine and two heroes, one of whom must get and one lose the prize'; in *The Bostonians* 'the two heroes are a man and woman, but the struggle is of the same general character'.[24] Here Scudder – like many of the novel's first reviewers – describes the central situation of the novel with ease. It was obviously easy enough to assume that the friendship was intense but chaste, and to understand it as a bond of shared political devotion. Two reviewers stated straightforwardly that both Basil and Olive 'fall in love' with Verena, although the reviewer in the *Republican*, of Springfield, Massachusetts, went on to write that 'the effect of contemplating [Olive Chancellor] is identical with that produced by any examination of insanity, – depressing in the last degree.'[25] The New York *Sun* used rather typical antifeminist humour to dismiss Olive, writing that it would be 'inapposite' to say that Olive might 'unbosom herself ... for, as Mr James allows us to discern, she is not so much unsexed as sexless'.[26] (This echoes Basil Ransom in the novel: 'what sex was it, great heaven? he used profanely to ask himself' (287).) R. H. Hutton, in the *Spectator*, however, calls her 'a refined, passionate, reserved woman', and writes with obvious sympathy of '[h]er consuming desire for a friendship that should amount to a passion, her steadfast and self-forgetting devotion when she finds such a friendship, her deep and fierce jealousy when it is threatened by her friend's liability to a stronger passion, and the tragic collapse both of the tie and of the great mission on which the two friends had embarked'.[27] Here Hutton treats the 'passion' with great respect.

Yet at least one reviewer thought the friendship unnatural. Disapproval of the bond between Olive and Verena is at its most knowing when Scudder writes that

when ... Mr. James ... push[es] his characters too near the brink of nature we step back and decline to follow. For instance, the details of the first interview between Olive and Verena in Olive's house carry these young women to dangerous lengths, and we hesitate about accepting the relation between them as either natural or reasonable.[28]

Here the codes of discretion governing not only writing but reading are fairly explicitly spelt out, even as the exact nature of the relation between Olive and Verena is not. James appears to be suggesting something 'dangerous', unnatural and unreasonable, but the reader is free not to follow him, even if this decision not to follow can only be made after some degree of cognitive tracking has made the danger recognizable. Such a commentary shows how far one can go under the protection of the 'open secret'. However, in placing the burden of the open secret in the reader's hands, it shows that the other option – the option of not stepping back, the option of following – is always there. (Reviewers of *The Author of Beltraffio*, the short story collection published one year earlier, showed similar anxieties: their virulent declamations of the title story seem to carry some awareness of its homoerotic undertones. The *Critic*'s reviewer wrote that '"The Author of Beltraffio" is a painful and repulsive story . . . Shine on putrescence as genius may, it cannot glorify it',[29] whereas the *Nation*'s reviewer approved of Mrs Ambient's decision to let the child die rather than let him grow up contaminated by his father with the following words: 'ninety-nine out of a hundred English or American readers will have less sympathy for the author of "Beltraffio" than for his wife.')[30]

Readers then could choose to regard the relationship of Olive and Verena as an acceptable friendship, or hesitate whether to accept its naturalness. Such a skewed response reflects tensions within the novel. If James describes a 'Boston marriage', he knowingly foregrounds the eroticism of such a marriage, and reveals its subversive force by subjecting it to a battle for possession – a struggle between the terms of conventional and 'Boston' marriage. James has no need of a sexological vocabulary to characterize Olive, Verena and Basil: the erotic tensions are clearly thought out, and vividly depicted. The novel is remarkably bold, and this boldness should be emphasized because it seems fairly clear that physical contact between Olive Chancellor and Verena Tarrant does not go beyond tender (if passionate) kisses and embraces. It might seem odd to ask after such details in a novel by James, but the relationship between the two women is so striking that critical reticence needs to be abandoned if its dynamics are to be fully explored. The novel just drips with desire – Olive's desire for Verena – and the centrality of this desire to the text forces us to consider the *form* of their relationship. Here I am not asking after a 'true' form of the relationship which might differ from its 'textual realization', because of censorship – whether the censorship of publishing conventions, or that imposed by the author on himself. Rather the question is: how does *The Bostonians* portray the relationship between the two women?

What, according to the novel itself, occurs between them: what behaviour is allowed, what is avoided?

That James wants his reader to understand both that Olive Chancellor is passionately – and *erotically* – attracted to Verena, but that there is no sexual relationship between the two women, is made clear above all in the way that Olive constitutes their union as a feverish cult of virginity, a virginity preserved for political ends. Thus Olive, wondering whether Verena might marry Mr Burrage, reasons that Verena would remain '[s]acredly, brightly single . . . her only espousals would be at the altar of a great cause' (147). Olive's reasoning here shows how the two women can be both 'virginal' and 'married'; she uses a marriage metaphor to indicate that her and Verena's devotion will be anything but sterile. Like brides of Christ, they will be married to the cause; Olive tells Verena 'that there is something noble done when one makes a sacrifice for a great good. Priests – when they were real priests – never married, and what you and I dream of doing demands of us a kind of priesthood' (119).

One feels that if Verena had been a different kind of girl, and responded more physically to Olive's embraces and kisses, marriage might not have been opposed to chaste devotion but to (let's not be coy) a sexual relation between women. It is ironic that Olive 'hated the writing of the French' (76), given that, as Terry Castle has shown, her relationship with Verena is replete with intertextual echoes of depictions of lesbian desire in French fiction, such as Gautier's *Mademoiselle de Maupin* and in particular Zola's *Nana*.[31] Yet this dislike is wholly appropriate: as Olive chooses to fashion herself according to a model of heroic, passionate renunciation drawn from German romanticism, her dislike of the overt eroticism of French fiction may be defensive. Goethe is 'almost the only foreign author she cared about', and a line from *Faust* – '*Entsagen sollst du, sollst entsagen!*' – is to represent, for Olive, the creed of her and Verena's friendship (75–6). Verena's lack of German is a mere detail; it cannot get in the way of Olive's vision of Winter evenings spent producing 'successful renderings, with a chosen companion, of Goethe'. Indeed, her companion's monolingualism will enable Olive to enjoy to the full her beloved tutelary role. (Olive 'almost panted' at this vision.) Thus she can translate the Goethe quote for Verena – '"Thou shalt renounce, refrain, abstain!" That's the way Bayard Taylor has translated them," Olive answered' (76) – while enjoying a private reference ('few books had passed through Verena's hands' before her acquaintance with Olive (153)) to the author of *Joseph and His Friend*, a novel which, in its description of same-sex partnership threatened by marriage, would have interested a reader like Olive.[32] Hence Olive's highly individual interpretation of Goethe's lines: what Verena and Olive must renounce is not their own passionate friendship, but marriage, and this renunciation will allow the uninterrupted enjoyment of each other's company. A catty but perceptive remark by Mrs Luna sums up this mode of virginal partnership: Olive 'wants to keep [Verena] in the single sisterhood; to keep her, above all, for herself' (224).

No single sister inspires the two young women so much as Joan of Arc, burnt at the stake in 1431, aged less than twenty. Visiting Olive and Verena's summer retreat in Monadnoc, Basil notices 'that his cousin Olive had as many German books as ever lying about' (309). It seems likely that one of the German books James had in mind, and which the fictional Olive would have read and admired, is Schiller's epic drama of 1801, *Die Jungfrau von Orleans* (*The Maid of Orleans*). Marina Warner remarks that Schiller was the 'first person to create Joan of Arc in the image of a romantic heroine',[33] and both Olive and Verena like to compare their role in the emancipation of women to that of Joan. (In this analysis, Basil would be Joan's judge and executioner.) When Olive asks Verena 'where she had got her "intense realization" of the suffering of women', Verena 'inquired ... where Joan of Arc had got her idea of the suffering of France. This was so prettily said that Olive could scarcely keep from kissing her; she looked at the moment as if, like Joan, she might have had visits from the saints' (74). Here James captures the peculiar combination of fervid – or feverish – sexuality and virginity that so frequently characterized nineteenth-century visions of Joan. Commenting on nineteenth-century descriptions of Joan's amenorrhea, Marina Warner writes: '[o]n the one hand, Joan is all woman, seductive, even beautiful, with the full complement of sexual characteristics; on the other, she annuls the usual consequences of these characteristics, remaining in the virginal state of prepubescence.'[34] In this cult of the virginal young woman, we recognize Olive's vision of Verena. Olive, while fully appreciating Verena's physical attractiveness, is anxious to ensure that Verena remain chaste. Not only does she ask Verena to promise not to marry; one of her principal occupations throughout the novel is to worry, on Verena's behalf, about the threat, the 'insult to one's womanhood' and 'the dangers that might arise from encounters with young men in search of sensations' (106). Olive knows she is right in doing this, because 'a "gifted being" is sent into the world for a very different purpose, and ... making the time pass pleasantly for conceited young men is the last duty you are bound to think of if you happen to have a talent for embodying a cause' (104–5). The narrator hints that Olive's vision of Verena might be more hagiography than accurate representation of reality by telling us, 'she reflected that Verena was not in the smallest degree a flirt ... it shall be confided to the reader that in reality she never knew, by any sense of her own, whether Verena were a flirt or not' (105).

Like Schiller's maid of Orleans (and also like his Elizabeth I in *Maria Stuart*), Olive appears to believe:

> A virgin without stain
> can accomplish all the good deeds in the world
> if she withstands the love that's of the world.[35]

The analogy of the chaste service of the two women with Joan of Arc 'had lodged itself in Olive's imagination' (126). Olive would be aware that, as Schiller's play suggests, Joan's power is fully dependent on her virginity. Joan specifically protests that the servitude of a wife is incompatible with her political vocation – 'I am a soldier of the Lord of Hosts: / I cannot be the wife of any man' – and repudiates the marriage proposal of the Dauphin with a fury worthy of a lesbian icon: 'Any man who looks / at me with longing is a horror to me, / a sacrilege.'[36] (One might easily imagine Olive uttering these lines.) Yet, just as Schiller's Joan becomes quite powerless when she falls in love with Lionel, an English soldier whom she meets in battle, Verena loses her commitment to Olive's feminist vision (and to Olive) when she falls in love with Basil, a man from the enemy camp.

Verena represents a Joan of Arc distracted from her purpose by an attractive and politically unsound man; it is Olive who embodies a 'truer', unswayed Joan, physically virginal yet passionate in her emotions and in her dedication to a public cause. When Olive eventually addresses the Boston public, she 'might have suggested ... some feminine firebrand of Paris revolutions, erect on a barricade, or even the sacrificial figure of Hypatia, whirled through the furious mob of Alexandria' (388). Basil might speak scornfully of Olive as 'a morbid old maid' (337), yet, in the tradition in which Olive places herself, described by Warner as 'the history of virginity as an expression of female independence and ambition',[37] virginity is noble and empowering.

The novel, then, makes it more than clear that Olive Chancellor – the fictional character – is a virgin. Having reported this, much as the Queen of Sicily and the Duchess of Bedford (and countless others) reported on the virginity of Joan,[38] I need to ask another question: how convincing is Olive as a lesbian character, if her virginity is not just casually mentioned but heroically insisted on? The answer is, of course, extremely convincing indeed, given that Olive, more fully than Rowland Mallet or Hyacinth Robinson, embodies the tragic concept of the queer hero or heroine unable to find a person of the same sex to return his or her devotion.

(Stephen Gordon, in Radclyffe Hall's *The Well of Loneliness*, occupies this role somewhat insistently, whereas James's protagonists occupy it unwillingly.)[39]

The remark of Mrs Luna's I have quoted shows how free the novel's characters are in indulging in a mode of double-reading, thinking of Olive and Verena both as virginal friends and as sharing a relationship which exceeds the terms of conventional friendship. Such interpretive duplicity is evident throughout the novel, which is extraordinarily knowing – even cynical – about desire and identity, about discrepancies between hidden motives and professed purposes. Moreover, the privilege of knowing is not restricted to the narrator; it is often conveyed through access to what the characters are thinking about each other, or by what they say to each other. In the novel's opening scene, for instance, when Basil Ransom thinks to himself that '[t]here are women who are unmarried by accident, and others who are unmarried by option; but Olive Chancellor was unmarried by every implication of her being' (17), the novel is already flashing campy signals that this 'sexless' person, 'a spinster as Shelley was a lyric poet' (17), might very well be sexual enough. When James tells us, also near the beginning of the novel, that Olive 'had an immense desire to know intimately some *very* poor girl' (31), he appears to be mocking the genteel conventions by which the reader should have an innocent understanding of 'know intimately'. Again and again the novel embarrasses the reader who would, in the words of Horace E. Scudder's review, 'step back and decline to follow'.

The novel shows a number of resigned responses to the situation. The worldly Mrs Burrage shows no embarrassment or hesitation in using her perceptions of the bond between Olive and Verena for her own ends. Attempting to persuade Olive of her son's suitability as a husband for Verena, she goes straight to the point, arguing that 'young, pretty, attractive, clever, charming' Verena will be 'safer with my son . . . than as a possible prey to adventurers, to exploiters', and that Olive will not 'be able to keep her always, to exclude other affections' (271). Here we see a genteel knowingness – a knowingness which Olive (understandably) 'couldn't endure', with its 'look of worldly cleverness, of a confidence born of much experience' (271). In other words, Olive has to endure Mrs Burrage's deprecating insinuations of knowledge about her relationship with Verena, and allow Mrs Burrage to inform her that the relationship has no status which can make it secure for Olive; while she herself can make no special claim for the relationship which would allow her to tell Mrs Burrage where to go. (She cannot say, 'your darling son simply cannot marry Verena, don't you see, because we're lovers'.) It is astonishing that many critics should claim that James is unsympathetic to Olive, when he imagines the painful intricacies of her situation so intimately. Read with 'worldly cleverness', the novel spells out the tension between same-sex friendship and marriage in black and white, and does so through a thorough exploration of the terms of sexual identity.

Mrs Burrage's advice is remarkable, in that she appears to be urging Olive to maintain precisely the kind of intimacy enjoyed by many upper middle-class women in nineteenth-century America. If Verena is to marry her son, she tells Olive, the women's friendship will not be threatened. Olive should avoid letting Verena fall into the hands of the wrong kind of person, who 'would shut her up altogether' (271). The question of whether such close friendships between women were compatible with heterosexual marriage becomes extremely important towards the end of the nineteenth century. Carroll Smith-Rosenberg has shown that in nineteenth-century America such erotic, intimate and long-lasting friendships were indeed common between women and continued through marriage[40]; Sheila Jeffreys has argued that at the turn of the century sexological literature created 'a distinction ... between an acceptable level of friendship and lesbianism'.[41] Yet it appears that this distinction remained, to a certain extent, negotiable. Suzanne Raitt, in writing about the friendship of Virginia Woolf and Vita Sackville-West, writes that 'women active in the 1920s did not *have* to drop all other allegiances ... Lesbianism was not a political identity ... Conceived as an intermittent sexual or emotional orientation, it could flourish happily in the interstices of heterosexual existence, hardly threatening it at all.'[42] In this context, it can be seen how strongly the virginal Olive is marked as a lesbian. Even if she would and could not describe her identity as 'lesbian', Olive's rejection of and distaste for heterosexual marriage, conceived of as a form which subordinates and degrades women, does constitute a political identity. The kind of friend-ship Olive wants is *not* compatible with marriage; in this sense, to the extent that we can call her a 'lesbian', her lesbianism is distinctly modern, not to be enjoyed alongside the demands of marriage. If we are told that Olive Chancellor is 'unmarried *by every implication of her being*', we must deal with the paradox that her incipient 'lesbianism' has a peculiar ontological density, even if there is no available language by which she can constitute herself as lesbian.

Unlike Stephen Gordon in Hall's *The Well of Loneliness*, Olive cannot discover an annotated sexological text in her father's library. (Yet we should remember that Stephen Gordon has a marked sense of alterity

even before she has heard of Krafft-Ebing.) Olive's 'incipient lesbianism' –
her 'protoqueerness' – is constituted in terms of persistent negation. If the
heroic side of such negation is Olive's virginity cult, its more prosaic face
is, quite simply, her dislike of men. Should Olive reflect that a young man
is 'very handsome', she has at hand 'a moral resource ... it had already
been a comfort to her, on occasions of acute feeling, that she hated men, as
a class, anyway' (21). Here the qualification, 'as a class', is typical of the
novel's ironies and control of tone. A perfectly simple vocabulary is all that
is needed to explain why Verena just isn't the right young girl for Olive's
purposes: Verena just likes men too much. 'It might have been fancied',
the narrator tells us, describing Verena with a group of male admirers,
'that Verena's vocation was to smile and talk with young men who bent
towards her' (104). Olive Chancellor will eventually describe this vocation
as a weakness: 'the great trouble was that weak spot of Verena's, that sole
infirmity and subtle flaw, which she had expressed to her very soon after
they began to live together, in saying ... "I'll tell you what is the matter
with you – you don't dislike men as a class!"' (249). Here the repetition of
the phrase 'as a class' accentuates its irony. 'The matter with you', we
might understand Olive as telling Verena, 'is that you like men, whereas I
want you to like women!'

Olive's virginity cult and Verena's fondness for men have little restrain-
ing influence on the erotic ardour of their friendship, however. Fired by
her passion for Verena, the nervous and inexperienced Olive is a remarkably bold and skilled strategist. On first meeting the girl, she issues an
invitation and takes care to see that her cousin Basil is not introduced to
her; Olive is always aware of Basil as her principal rival. When Verena
accepts the invitation the very next day, the erotic momentum of the
friendship is unstoppable. As Terry Castle points out,[43] Olive is Zeus to
Verena's Ganymede: 'Olive had taken her up, in the literal sense of the
phrase, like a bird of the air, had spread an extraordinary pair of wings,
and carried her through the dizzying void of space. ... From this first
interview [Verena] felt that she was seized, and she gave herself up' (69).
Verena's visit confirms for Olive 'that she found here what she had been
looking for so long – a friend of her own sex with whom she might have a
union of soul' (70). Verena has not been in the room 'five minutes' before
Olive asks her: 'Will you be my friend, my friend of friends, forever and
forever?' (71). Nor is the friendship one-sided: as the acquaintance grows,
Olive can reflect that Verena's 'share in the union of the two young women
was no longer passive, purely appreciative; it was passionate, too, and it
put forth a beautiful energy' (146).

Whereas *The Bostonians* resembles *Roderick Hudson* and *The Princess Casamassima* in its concern with same-sex relationships which exceed the terms of 'friendship', it is unique in its exploration of reciprocated affection within a same-sex union. The novel shows consistent respect for the friendship; Verena's reflection that '[i]t was a very peculiar thing, their friendship; it had elements which made it probably as complete as any (between women) that had ever existed' (334) is uncompromised by Jamesian irony.

If the triangular plot of *The Well of Loneliness* is influenced by *The Bostonians*, then Olive differs from Stephen Gordon in her heroic resistance of her male rival. (Stephen Gordon actively encourages Martin Hallam's rivalrous bid for Mary Llewellyn, in what seems to be an attachment to the ontological clarity of punishment.) Olive resembles Stephen, however, in her unassuaged suffering. The day she realizes Verena will leave her for Ransom is the 'day she was destined never to forget; she felt it to be the saddest, the most wounding of her life ... [A]n immeasurable load of misery seemed to sit upon her soul; she ached with the bitterness of her melancholy, she was dumb and cold with despair' (351). Nothing in *The Bostonians* is presented as forcefully, and with such tangible narrative sympathy, as the tragic spectacle of lesbian loss.

III THE CRUEL TRIANGLE OF *THE PRINCESS CASAMASSIMA*

The quadrangle of *Roderick Hudson*, made up of Christina Light, Roderick, Mary Garland and Rowland Mallet, finds an echo in the triangle of Hyacinth, 'the Princess' and Paul Muniment of James's novel *The Princess Casamassima*. Both Joseph Litvak[44] and Wendy Graham have pointed to the importance of this novel's homoerotic thematics. Graham gives the more detailed reading, arguing that James's portrayals of Hyacinth, Muniment and Sholto show his 'familiarity with the medico-psychiatric literature on homosexuality', with Hyacinth resembling 'Ulrich's congenital invert', Muniment representing 'the straight-man for hire, who lends himself to, rather than shares, the passions of others', and Sholto being 'the extreme sensualist, the case of acquired inversion'.[45] Such a degree of specificity, however, seems to misrepresent the novel's (often frustrating) epistemological vagueness, and has James familiar with a very particular scientific literature before its translation into English, as Graham's own careful account shows (55–6). (Early in 1893 James read J. A. Symonds's *A Problem in Modern Ethics* (1891), which contains a survey of sexological literature on 'sexual inversion';[46] it is difficult to say whether

James was familiar with such literature before this date, even if it is likely that his acquaintance with late Victorian intellectual élite circles would have given him some knowledge of it.) The similarity between the erotic dynamics described in the novel and the sexual scenarios described in sexological literature may be coincidental rather than knowing.

The Princess Casamassima confronts us with the *difficulty* of reading, and this difficulty is one which arises through a misfit between the terms of desire and the terms of identity. The novel follows *Roderick Hudson* in registering the discrepancies resulting from the circulation of same-sex desires in a social space in which such desires have no recognition. Hyacinth's strong feelings for Paul Muniment are rather baldly stated, and take the form of an unstable cross-class attraction: Hyacinth's indeterminate class status is opposed to Paul's working-class solidity, yet Hyacinth also feels a desire to serve Paul, who is figured as a natural master and ruler, whose majestic stature sets off Hyacinth's tininess (Muniment is 'tall and fair and good-natured looking', possesses a 'rude, manly strength'; indeed, the novel cannot do enough to emphasise the 'powers of body' of this young man 'as strong as a horse').[47] James indicates all this in the first meeting of the two men, telling us that '[o]ur little hero had a great desire to know superior people, and he interested himself on the spot in this strong, humorous fellow, who had the complexion of a ploughboy and the glance of a commander-in-chief' (128). Hyacinth resembles Rowland Mallet in the swiftness with which he takes a fancy for Muniment, 'something in [whose] face', on their first meeting, gives Hyacinth 'the desire to go with him till he dropped'; after this, it seems scarcely necessary for James to add that Hyacinth 'had taken so great a fancy to Muniment' (131).

The novel's emphasis on unreciprocated affections also recalls *Roderick Hudson*. Whether or not the novel as a whole successfully merges anarchist plot with a homosexual subplot, the two do come together with great intensity in the figure of Hyacinth, as it is left unclear whether the motivation behind Hyacinth's pledge to assassinate an English aristocrat consists of a genuine, if confused, political feeling, which is lent intensity by his own confused class identity, or a desire to serve Paul Muniment, or 'Mr Monument', as Millicent Henning so aptly calls him (181). Hyacinth likes to think that he 'would never beg for a favour; but . . . in any relation he might have with Paul Muniment such a law would be suspended. This man he could entreat, pray to, go on his knees to, without a sense of humiliation' (151). Here we are given a stunning picture of the physical relation between the two men's bodies which Hyacinth feels might aptly express his feelings for his new friend.

This sentimental eroticism is, at crucial moments in the text, shown to exceed Hyacinth's political conviction, as when, towards the end of the novel,

> our hero felt the simple inrush of his old, frequent pride at having a person of that promise, a nature of that capacity, for a friend. He passed his hand into Muniment's arm and said, with an imperceptible tremor in his voice, 'It's no use your saying I'm not to go by what you tell me. I would go by what you tell me, anywhere . . . I don't know that I believe exactly what you believe, but I believe in you, and doesn't that come to the same thing?' (446)

Hyacinth's passionate servitude – whether to the revolutionary movement or to Muniment himself – is said by James to have

> a strain of heroism . . . of which the sense was not conveyed to Muniment by a vibration in their interlocked arms. Hyacinth did not make the reflection that he was infernally literal; he dismissed the sentimental problem that had bothered him; . . . resting happy for the time in the consciousness that Paul was a grand fellow, that friendship was a purer feeling than love, and that there was an immense deal of affection between them. He did not even observe at that moment that it was preponderantly on his own side. (447)

If the narrative of *The Princess Casamassima* is characteristically murky, James writes here with surprising clarity. However, these clear emotional dynamics have an unresolved status – Hyacinth has to ask after the meaning of this intensity, an intensity of Jamesian 'tremors' and 'vibrations'. When Hyacinth reasons 'that friendship was a purer feeling than love', is he contemplating his own feeling for Paul or is he attempting to console himself with the reflection that Paul's 'friendship' might be worth more than the 'love', that less pure feeling, he appears (despite this disavowal) to crave? This definitional instability has two principle functions. Firstly, it situates the text in a context *preceding* the formation of recognizable 'homosexual' identities – there is no 'panic' in evidence here as there is no 'homosexual' possibility from which Hyacinth can recoil; rather he can only think of his relationship with Paul as friendship. Secondly, it lays the foundation for another possible reading of the novel's ending. Whereas Hyacinth's suicide appears to reflect his growing doubts in the revolutionary cause, it is also a consequence of his sense of being doubly rejected. If the instability of his sexual identity has been played out through the tensions between his attraction for the Princess and for Muniment, he is naturally shattered when he feels that the Princess both deserts him and carries Paul away at the same time. (The Princess is, of course, a revival of Christina Light from *Roderick Hudson*, and in both novels she is close to sexually ambiguous men, for whom she plays the role of cruel lady.) Hyacinth kills himself almost directly after his final meeting with the Princess, when she 'expressed an indifference to what it might interest him to think about her to-day, and even a contempt for it, which brought tears to his eyes' (574), and it becomes 'perfectly clear' to Hyacinth that he has been 'superseded' in the Princess's affections by Muniment 'so completely . . . that it did not even occur to her . . . that the sense of supersession might be cruel to the young man' (570).

Here the novel resembles the sentimental masochism of Masoch's *Venus in Furs* (1870) more than any sexological literature.[48] If Hyacinth 'could entreat, pray to, go on his knees' to Paul (151), Vetch remarks that Hyacinth has become the Princess's 'slave' (465). Like Masoch's hero, Severin, Hyacinth can figure his relationship with his mistress in erotic terms, but such terms are not available to express the relationship with his master, which is mediated through the mistress; Hyacinth also resembles Severin in that his erotic investment in his master is tangible in his ecstatic distress when master unites with mistress. A Freudian interpretation would emphasise that this erotic tableau recreates a primal scene, with the sexual subject repeating the childhood experience of spectatorship.[49] Yet such a reading should not discount the strong sense conveyed of an adult sexual subject unable to find a sexual identity. The liminal erotic subject observes a scene of heterosexual coupling which emphasises his – or her – own alterity; such a scene is to become a classic in lesbian and gay writing, made most memorable, of course, in Radclyffe Hall's *The Well of Loneliness* (1929).[50]

At the climax of *The Princess Casamassima* the structural echoes of *Roderick Hudson* become poignantly clear: Hyacinth, like Rowland Mallet, has to confront the erotic conjunction of the man to whom he has been sentimentally attached and Christina Light. In both novels the confusion between 'straight' and 'gay' readings of the triangle relates intimately to the ontological instability of the male protagonist (Rowland and Hyacinth respectively). The relationship between the novel's anarchist plot with its homosexual subplot remains difficult, however. Does the one displace the other? Graham writes that 'the anarchist fraternities' of the novel 'serve a further function . . . as a homosexual underground', yet to claim that James, in 1886, wants the predominantly working-class and lower middle-class anarchists of the novel to represent emergent homosexual identities when such identities were predominantly still the domain of the Victorian upper middle classes, is somewhat implausible, even if Graham's comparison of the linguistic and psychic conditions of secret identities among anarchist and homosexual communities is convincing. Certainly, as Graham shows, James creates a web of homoerotic signifiers which exceeds and destabilizes the novel's ostensible anarchist plot. Graham compares the language with which James figures the anarchist underworld to that used in late nineteenth-century texts to describe a secretive homosexual subculture.

Consider one instance of such language. ' "Why do you want to poke your head into black holes?" ' Muniment asks Hyacinth in one of their early discussions (151). The novel would seem to exclude the possibility that the petty bourgeois Muniment (as a chemist's assistant, his working-class status seems less than genuine) is taunting Hyacinth for having homoerotic desires (even if he does go on to call Hyacinth an 'infatuated, deluded youth' (151)). However, these repeated suggestive *double entendres*,[51] in which the secret holes of anarchist activity suggest both the furtiveness of homoerotic encounters and the more hidden apertures of the human body, appear to make knowing asides to the reader which are embarrassing to the perpetually compromised Hyacinth.

Graham's discussion of Hyacinth's embarrassment at his name,[52] which he feels is too tonsorial, is telling, and demonstrates the hierarchical structuring of knowledge between reader, text and fictional character. James repeatedly suggests that Hyacinth needs to refute embarrassing imputations, but is reticent in describing these embarrassments in detail. We as readers can imagine ourselves as sharing a knowledge with the sophisticated narrator, or, alternatively, we can claim that the narrator is innocent of such implications. However, an innocence on the part of the fictional speakers is a necessary precondition for the circulation of such homoerotic innuendos, given that they are not circulating *between homosexuals*. Hence the importance of Hyacinth's homoeroticism in the novel seems to lie ultimately in the fact that there are no socially defined relationships in which it can be adequately expressed. If, as Graham points out, Hyacinth 'is cast in the mold of the *fin de siècle* aesthete' (63), this casting takes place in a decade when the connection between the aesthete and the homosexual was still vague, rather than incriminating. In Hyacinth, James portrays the passionate tremors and vibrations of a nervous and delicate young protoqueer.

IV JAMES'S LEGACY: EARLY TWENTIETH-CENTURY QUEER FICTION

Even if *Roderick Hudson*, *The Bostonians* and *The Princess Casamassima* predate the consolidation of modern queer identities in the 1890s, they establish dominant motifs and narrative patterns in twentieth-century cultural representations of same-sex love. Before Stonewall made affirmative endings possible, twentienth-century bourgeois queer fiction and film predominantly adhered to melodramatic plotlines, in which queer characters either met with disastrous fates, or ended up feeling sad.[53] Same-sex unions routinely collapse, whether through defection to heterosexuality, death (murder or suicide), failure of nerve, or a combination of these factors. (Djuna Barnes's *Nightwood* stands out in that Nora Flood loses Robin Vote not to a man but to another woman.) The misery of Rowland Mallet and Olive Chancellor, and the suicide of Hyacinth Robinson, are echoed in various twentieth-century novels, which abound in intertextual echoes of James's writing. Such a lineage may be traced through members of the generation of writers after James like Howard Sturgis, E. M. Forster and D. H. Lawrence.

Just as Djuna Barnes and Radclyffe Hall's fiction interacts with *The Bostonians*, the fiction of Lawrence and Forster establishes its queerness partly through a rich engagement with James's tales of thwarted desire. Lawrence's novella 'The Fox', first published in 1919, reworks *The Bostonians*, with Henry Grenfel as the Basil Ransom figure who breaks up the friendship of Jill Banford and Nellie March, marrying one woman and causing the death of the other. Banford here is the 'true' lesbian who dies, whereas March is the woman with the ambiguous identity, the Verena-like figure whose heterosexuality can be awakened by the right man.[54] Lawrence's rewrite of *The Bostonians* is both misogynist and homophobic, and Banford, unlike Olive Chancellor, can be identified as a 'sexual invert'; the novella's negative presentation of lesbianism mobilizes stereotypes derived from sexological literature. However, *Women in Love* (1920) shows a much more positive rewriting of James's fiction, working through and making more explicit the tensions James explores in Rowland Mallet, the protagonist of *Roderick Hudson*.

Women in Love and *Roderick Hudson* are both constructed around unstable quadrangles. The four principle characters of Lawrence's novel resemble their Jamesian precedents in the way that heterosexual bonds between them are compromised by same-sex desire. The title of *Women in Love* might suggest that the exploration of female sexual identity will be central to the novel, but for all its candour and daring, Ursula and Gudrun's choices are fairly restricted. To marry or not to marry, to have a man or not to have a man, to have a man for life or to enjoy more casual liaisons: these are the possibilities explored by the two sisters. If the problem of marriage is the man – 'The man makes it impossible', as Gudrun succinctly remarks[55] – then the obvious solution, that of finding a lovely woman, isn't considered by the two sisters, and their status as siblings seems to preclude them finding each other. The relationship between Gudrun and Ursula is, however, one of the strongest in the book, replete with kisses and intimate chats and 'exclamations inarticulate and stirring' (392) and shared stocking moments. 'What was it, after all, that a woman wanted?' muses the narrator (451); it would be surprising that Lawrence does not explore lesbian answers to this question more fully, if he had not, in *The Rainbow*, already demonstrated the futility of such solutions. In the earlier novel, Ursula Brangwen, as any early twentieth-century schoolgirl might, ends her affair with her lesbian schoolmistress by marrying her off to her homosexual Uncle Tom (who is perfectly described as a homosexual Uncle Tom); she is 'glad' at this solution because, of course, '[t]heir marshy, bittersweet corruption came sick and unwholesome in her nostrils. Anything, to get out of the foetid air'.[56]

Yet the men in *Women in Love* certainly go far in exploring 'other possibilities', what Rupert Birkin calls 'eternal union with a man too: another kind of love' (481). (Rupert follows Olive Chancellor in using the word 'union'.) Rupert's difficulty, however, lies in his failure to recognize that nothing so much as his own phobia prevents him from finding this love: whenever he meets 'another kind of man', with whom such a love might be possible, he recoils in disgust. Rupert, like Forster's Maurice, wants a man who is not recognizable as a 'homosexual': his unchecked eloquence should not mask the fact that the word 'homosexual' is one he carefully avoids. These difficulties are apparent when he tries to persuade Gerald of the necessity of such a bond in the chapter named 'Man to Man': having just said that 'We will swear to stand by each other – be true to each other – ultimately – infallibly – given to each other, organically – without possibility of taking back', he goes on to say that the bond will not involve 'sloppy emotionalism', but will be '[a]n impersonal union that leaves one free' (207).

The problem for Rupert is not that such a love cannot be articulated, but its articulation risks summoning up the spectacle of the homosexual, which for Rupert (or for Lawrence) is overloaded with the abject, or, to use a Lawrentian term, the inorganic. Hence erotic and romantic possibilities between Rupert and Gerald are circumscribed, with the semantically overloaded Herr Loerke, the Austro-Polish Jewish homosexual bastard artist attracted to teenage girls ('they are beautiful, at sixteen, seventeen, eighteen – after that, they are no use to me' (433)) and men 'at all ages' as long as they are 'big and powerful' (434), embodying the absolute, verminous abjection that homosexuality represents. Given Rupert's more than phobic response (indistinguishable from that of Lawrence, or the

narrator) to Loerke, it is not surprising that Rupert should avoid genital
contact and make do with a 'Blutbrüderschaft' (277) and nude Japanese
wrestling. (The planned initial chapter of the novel, left out of the published
text, describes Rupert's frequent erotic infatuations with other men, but
insists that 'though he admitted everything, he never really faced the question. He never accepted the desire, and received it as part of himself.'[57]
Which is to say: he recognized his homoerotic *desire*, but not his homosexual *identity*.)

Loerke's multifarious appetites are associated with a dissolution of categories. Rupert thinks of him as 'a Jew – or part Jewish', as 'the wizard rat
that swims ahead' (428). The narrator is even more unable to decide how
to figure Loerke: he is 'a mag-pie', 'a lop-eared rabbit, or a troll', 'a rabbit
or a bat or a brown seal', 'a mud-child', 'a lost being', with the 'figure of a
boy' and 'the nostrils of a pure-bred street arab' (422–3, 427). Just as Winifred
Inger and Uncle Tom Brangwen warn Ursula of homosexuality's sterility,
its 'nauseating effect of a marsh, where life and decaying are one',[58] Loerke
serves to illustrate the 'black look of inorganic misery' of perversion for
Rupert and Gerald (422). Whereas *Roderick Hudson* shows a centrifugal
movement around the love that cannot find its name, *Women in Love* hesi-
tates before the spectacle of the love that has too many names altogether. If
'homosexual' is not a word used in the novel, Lawrence hovers interminably
around this absence, deploying any number of tropes which suggest the
'homosexual' even as they do not name it. The fact that love between men
is no longer nameless does not make it any more possible, at least for a hero
who wants to hang on to his organic English masculinity. That ethnic
integrity is at stake for Lawrence in warding off homosexual spectres is
made evident by the fact that Loerke is not the first but the third ethnically
compromised abject homosexual of *Women in Love*, the first two being
Julius Halliday and the Russian Jew Maxim Libidnikov. Although these
two men are ambiguously involved with the woman they call 'Pussum' or
'the Pussum', a name with a more than faintly misogynist ring, they share a
room, wander round their flat naked, and have a rather puzzling relationship with their Hindu servant, Hasan, who is always demanding money,
apparently for underclothes (73–75). Pussum complains that Libidnikov
has 'such an influence over Julius', and that '[h]e's a Jew, really. I can't bear
him' (71). Rupert writes Julius a letter urging him to transcend 'this process
of active corruption, with all its flowers of mud' (383). The novel relentlessly associates sexual irregularities with an ethnic stew.

Both *Roderick Hudson* and *Women in Love* end in an overpowering, romantic
serving-up of the unavailable erotic object – the plot of Salome, made

more explicit by James when he revised his novel, or the plot of Sebastian. Moreover, in both novels the loved man dies after a lone excursion in the Alps, which supply the sublime landscape necessary for the tragic death which will separate the same-sex lovers, even as it eroticizes the dead man, who becomes an unavailable homoerotic icon. Rupert, looking at Gerald, 'remembered also the dead face of one whom he had loved . . . That dead face was beautiful, no one could call it cold, mute, material' (480). Similarly, Rowland, gazing at the dead Roderick, thinks that his 'eyes were those of a dead man, but in a short time, when Rowland had closed them, the whole face seemed to awake. The rain had washed away all blood; it was as if Violence, having done her work, had stolen away in shame. Roderick's face might have shamed her; it looked admirably handsome' (386). In both novels death elevates the lost beloved into an idealized beauty; both novels show, at their close, the surviving lover realizing the fullness of his affection only in a rhetorically expansive outpouring of grief. 'The most rational of men [Rowland Mallet] was for an hour the most passionate', James tells us. Rupert in *Women in Love* gives 'a strange whimpering cry' at the sight of Gerald's corpse (479), whereas Rowland Mallet is left with the persistent memory of the 'loud tremendous cry' uttered by Mary Garland. *Women in Love* might be slightly bolder, but the essentials of its poetic figuration of the impossibility of same-sex love are already present in *Roderick Hudson*, which lacks, however, Lawrence's fuller, and phobic, imagining of an embodied homosexual identity. The earlier novel has the melancholia of an unrealized homoeroticism; the later novel has the tortured self-loathing arising from the simultaneous craving and fear of homoerotic possibility.

An unmistakable Jamesian influence is also discernable in E. M. Forster's *The Longest Journey* (1907), a novel concerned both with the legitimation of same-sex unions and with rivalrous heterosexual and homosexual claims. Joseph Bristow has recently summarized the plot as 'an erotic triangle where the woman and the scholarly young man are tragic competitors in their shared desire for the same athletic male' – hence a neat, diagrammatic male homosexual version of the lesbian plot of *The Bostonians*.[59] Forster's novel repeats the question often posed in James's fiction: can same-sex friendship last if one of the friends should marry? Stewart Ansell, the closest friend of the novel's protagonist, Rickie Elliot, behaves quite desperately when Rickie becomes engaged to Agnes Pembroke. He tries to dissuade Rickie from marrying by writing him vicious letters denouncing Agnes; the second of such letters claims bluntly: '(1) She is not serious. (2) She is not truthful.'[60] Tilliard, a mutual

friend, has argued that Ansell has no right to be so upset, pointing to a hierarchy of values which the novel does its best to upset: ' "Wife first, friends
some way after. You may resent the order, but it is ordained by nature" '
(80). Before marrying, Rickie also has pondered 'the irony of friendship –
so strong it is, and so fragile ... Nature has no use for us: she has cut her
stuff differently' (64). Here the use of 'us' accentuates the band of 'friends'
unrecognized by nature; such 'friends' become a constituency bound by a
shared identity. 'Friendship', in *The Longest Journey*, is nevertheless an
unstable concept. Tilliard's resigned view of friendship as a casual and
ephemeral association is contrasted with that of Rickie and Stewart, who
consider friendship incompatible with marriage.

Even as *The Longest Journey* advances an apologia for homoerotic relationships between men, it can only conceive of such relationships as ancillary
to heterosexual relationships; homoerotic bonds are characterized as lacking qualities found in heterosexual couplings, in particular legitimation
through marriage and reproduction. Rickie uses a Biblical opposition to
emphasize the lack of these qualities:

Abram and Sarai were sorrowful, yet their seed becomes as sand of the sea, and
distracts the politics of Europe at this moment. But a few verses of poetry is all
that survives of David and Jonathan.

'I wish we were labelled,' said Rickie ... [M]an is so made that he cannot
remember long without a symbol; he wished there was a society, a kind of friendship office, where the marriage of true minds could be registered. (64)

Here the positive, almost definitive, image of gay friendship – the friendship of David and Jonathan – is seen as flawed and impermanent beside
the patriarchal solidity embodied by Sarah and Abraham; here also, as in
Bayard Taylor's *Joseph and His Friend*, Shakespeare's sonnets serve as a
crucial intertext to the gay legitimation plot. (It is interesting that this
meditation, which dwells implicitly on the treatment of homosexuals,
refers explicitly to contemporary anti-Semitism.) Such cries, made at
strategic, isolated points in *The Longest Journey*, constitute a leitmotif in
Hall's *The Well of Loneliness*, building up to the novel's famous ending:
'Acknowledge us, oh God, before the whole world. Give us also the right to
our existence!'[61]

The Longest Journey uses the trio of central male characters – Stewart
Ansell, Rickie Elliott and Rickie's illegitimate half-brother Stephen
Wonham – to go through a number of major variations of gay plotting.
The novel differs from its nineteenth-century precedents, however, in that
it has a more explicit body of doctrine underpinning its anxieties about the
legitimacy of same-sex intimacy. In making its protoqueer protagonist not

only effeminate, like Hyacinth Robinson, but also lame, it covertly draws on sexology, theories of degeneration and eugenics.[62] We should not be surprised that a hero suffering under the triple whammy of homoerotic desire, lameness and effeminacy should end his novelistic life crushed by a train. The echoes of Howard Sturgis's *Tim* (1891) and *Belchamber* (1904) are striking. The effeminate Tim dies not from any 'organic disease' but from 'sheer weakness', his frail constitution unable to recover from the blow induced by the marriage of his beloved and beautiful Carol Darley, an 'angel' of a boy who has grown into a no less beautiful, athletic man – notwithstanding his compromising name (26, 293). Tim's favourite text, and the novel's epigraph, is 'David's lament over his dead friend Jonathan' (158): 'Thy love to me was wonderful, passing the love of woman'. 'Sainty', Earl and Marquis of Belchamber, Sturgis's second effeminate eponymous hero, while unhappy at Eton – not only do his schoolfellows called him 'Belcher', he also plays no part in the 'massacre of the innocents' in which his handsome brother Arthur and his handsome cousin Claude Morland are implicated (40–1) – goes on to experience the happiest years of his life at Cambridge, where he forms a strong attachment to a don, Gerald Newby. Sainty eventually marries Cissy Eccleston, who agrees to marry him only when she finds herself impregnated by his cousin Claude. Just as Rickie Elliot's marriage to Agnes Pembroke seems an attempt to capture the virility of Agnes's dead fiancé Gerald Dawes, the 'cruel and brutal' (37) handsome athlete whose erotic hold over Rickie is intensified by bullying, Sainty's feeble attempt at heterosexual union with Cissy is also an attempt to capture some of infamous Claude's erotic allure. Even if Rickie Elliott does not require the assistance of his more virile beloved to sire offspring, he remains essentially as 'innocent' as Sainty, and unable to verify his virility through paternity; his lame daughter dies not long after birth. (This is a curious echo of *Belchamber*, in which Sainty's son dies, despite his biologically healthy parentage; the poor young boy inherits the degeneracy of his legal father.)

Sainty anticipates Rickie Elliot in his effeminacy, his inability to breed successfully, and in his unhappy marriage; both men are successful neither in the heterosexual unions that are forced on them, nor in securing the homosexual unions they crave. Rickie's marriage is doomed to failure: he abandons it to look after Stephen, whose erratic behaviour enables Rickie's clearly homoerotic feelings to be thought of as legitimate fraternal care and affection. Rickie's eventual death, or martyrdom (he dies pulling Stephen Wonham from a railway track), is a perfect example of the 'tragic' homosexual plot, in which either the lover or the loved one must be killed. *The Longest Journey* combines both forms of this plot, as Stewart sees his friend die, and Rickie dies while saving his beloved.

Stewart Ansell joins Rickie in falling under the spell of Stephen Wonham, but Forster offers Stewart a less tragic, if still rather pathetic, resolution. In the course of his obsessive attempt to destroy Rickie's marriage to Agnes, Stewart finds himself crushed into a bed of lobelias by Stephen Wonham; after this experience (a sentimental and masochistic coupling of effete middle-class man with working-class brute which is quite typical of Forster), he becomes Stephen's champion. At the end of the novel Stewart is living in Stephen's family home, thus defying the order 'ordained by nature' of 'Wife first, friends some way after'. Stephen's masculinity has been authenticated through marriage and paternity, both areas in which Rickie fails dismally (Rickie and Agnes's daughter dies as a young baby, having inherited her father's frail disposition). The ending of *The Longest Journey* echoes that of *Joseph and His Friend*, with the lover playing the role of involved spectator and vicarious participant in the loved one's marriage. Here again the plot is both bold and timid: bold in letting the two men stay together, timid in allowing them to do so only within the legitimized frame of a heterosexual marriage. It is timid also in leaving it to the reader to work out the implications of the presence of 'Stewart' in Stephen Wonham's household. When Stephen Wonham reassures his (unnamed and uncharacterized) wife that ' "Stewart's in the house" ' (288) we can assume that Stewart Ansell, the Cambridge intellectual who has failed to get a fellowship, finds solace in the companionship of a working-class man who embodies an authentic masculinity. The rather improbable circumstances in which this homoerotic friendship endures anticipates Forster's fascination with Carpenter and the plot of *Maurice*. Although *Maurice*, more boldly, dispenses with the legitimating props of wife and family, it was of course not published within Forster's lifetime.

James's early conquering of the terrain of modern queer narratives raises several important questions. In trying to understand the enigma of a woman like Olive Chancellor – a lesbian who exists before lesbians existed – or of characters like Hyacinth Robinson and Rowland Mallet, homosexuals without a homosexual culture – one comes up against the limitations of the extensive debate which attempts to decide whether sexual identity is 'essential' or 'constructed'.[63] According to the constructionist argument, 'homosexuality' cannot exist without a social context and a discourse which defines, or constitutes, homosexuality. (In Alan Sinfield's words: 'Constructionism means that it is hard to be gay until you have some kind of slot, however ambiguously defined, in the current framework of ideas.[64]) Yet James, in novels like *Roderick Hudson*, *The Princess Casamassima* and *The Bostonians*, imagines the pathetic situation of the only homosexual, the only lesbian, in the world. Rowland Mallet, Hyacinth Robinson and Olive Chancellor all feel the pull of same-sex desires, yet there is nothing in their cognitive horizons which can enable them to constitute themselves as 'homosexual', or to construct an identity in which same-sex desire is acknowledged as important. Much recent queer theory valorizes the resistance of fixed notions of identity, and James's late nonfiction has recently been read (by Ross Posnock) as representing 'experience unburdened by the cultural imperative of "prime identity"', resisting the 'compulsion to identity' in a manner exemplary of 'nonidentity thinking'.[65] *Roderick Hudson*, *The Princess Casamassima* and *The Bostonians*, however, foreground the prohibitions which halt the formation of lesbian or homosexual identities, let alone resistance of such identities. 'Nonidentity' in James, then, should not be thought of as an amorphous resistance to all forms of identity; rather, his fiction appears to resist those constructions of identity which would explicitly refuse certain possibilities. In novels like *The Bostonians*, James presents the unavailability of lesbian and gay identities as a situation prone to tragic outcome.

My argument implies that James, as writer of such novels, has an epistemological advantage over his characters; namely, if he creates the tragic situation of characters who cannot find a space in which to articulate aspects of their identity, then James himself is articulating this space. Yet James is identified with his characters as well: even if he imagines this space more fully, it does not exist for him any more than it does for them. However, in creating a gallery of characters whose same-sex desires are more than accidental, James is working at the vanguard of his culture; possibilities within that culture are not static, but can be enlarged by the workings of his own imagination. My readings of these three novels make a particular claim: not the biographical claim that the younger Henry James was a novelist who was gay, but the literary claim that the early Henry James was already a *gay novelist*, who created lasting fictions which, ahead of their time, explore the workings of same-sex desire, and the difficulties of admitting such desires, within a cultural formation marked by homosexual prohibition. It is unclear why James did not revise *The Bostonians* for the New York Edition of his fiction. However, by 1908 such a novel could certainly have attracted more explicit comments on its lesbian scenario, whether or not this was James's reason to leave it unrevised. (If this were his reason, he is hardly likely to have stated it.) At some point – let us say 1891, the year of 'The Altar of the Dead' – James stopped writing the tragic scenario of the queer person unaware of queer possibility. Paradoxically, even while many of the protagonists of his later works – in particular his tales – are aware of the 'homosexual', it is chiefly as something to be avoided. This later fiction is not nearly so carefree in its presentation of same-sex affections: the identifiability of homosexuality tangibly restricts such narrative freedom. In the late 1880s, before the Wilde trials, sexual scandal in Britain, and the growing circulation of sexological texts, is beginning to give homosexuality a face. 'Is that my face?', any novelist concerned with same-sex desire might reasonably ask. So might his fictional characters.

CHAPTER SIX

James's late short fiction and the spectacle of modern homosexuality

I THE PLAY AND LANGUAGE OF 'IDENTITY': 'MORA MONTRAVERS' AND OTHER TALES

In the next two chapters I will be arguing that several of James's late tales – prominently 'The Altar of the Dead', 'In the Cage', 'The Papers', 'Mora Montravers', 'Crapy Cornelia', 'The Jolly Corner' and 'A Round of Visits' – make up a sophisticated, incisive, deeply considered, heartfelt response to the emergence of 'homosexuality' as a specific form of subjectivity, as a 'sexual identity'. Many of these tales are already recognized as among James's finest work, but the persistent homoerotic thematics within them has not received any detailed commentary (because of existing readings of 'The Pupil' and 'The Beast in the Jungle', these two tales will not be considered here).[1]

In James's late short fiction there is always a tension between a silence around which the tale hovers and which lends the tale momentum, and a violent *content* which threatens to disrupt the tale, fracture its aesthetic quietude. It is in fact this *tension* which needs to be productively read; only by acknowledging its influence can criticism avoid labelling the late short fiction as aesthetically rare but vapid, or collapsing the stories into symptomatic curiosities of an over-refined, over-developed sensibility curiously lacking in self-knowledge. And attention to the historical pressures informing such a tension enables James's late short stories to be read not only as masterpieces of narrative but as fully informed responses to anxieties surrounding the construction of identities (of various sorts) in turn-of-the-century Britain and America.

It is precisely in that they attend to the *construction* of identities, rather than to the expression of identities already constituted, that the late tales are so resonant. Identity in James's late fiction is both burden and necessity, but, *even as necessity*, evanescent and intangible. The burden of Jamesian identity is the burden arising from relations which stop nowhere: if identity is predicated on the subject's placement in a chain, what James calls, in the prefaces to *The Wings of the Dove* and *The Golden Bowl*, a 'tangled web' (*AN* 302, 345), then crucial to such a construction are the relations admitted by the subject and those relations the subject repudiates, or, just as importantly, cannot admit in a given cultural context. The play of identity in James's fiction always proceeds with reference to a series of relations admitted or denied. The late narratives hover round such questions, questioning the legitimacy of any received 'map of the social relations', asking after the other ways in which relations might be configured. Thus in *The Sacred Fount* the narrator believes he can see identity characteristics flowing from one character to another according to the sexual relationship they might be enjoying. In 'Fordham Castle' (1904) new names are adopted by Abel Taker, who becomes Mr C. P. Addard, and Mrs Magaw, who becomes Mrs Vanderplank, so that they may be successfully shuffled away, respectively, by wife and daughter to whom they constitute embarrassments. Rather than suffering under the ignominy of social anonymity, Addard thinks himself and Mrs Vanderplank 'protected, indeed positively ennobled, by their loss of identity,' and relishes 'the foretaste of a kind of felicity that he hadn't in the past known enough about really to miss it.'[2] Such a feeling is also felt by the writer, George Dane, in 'The Great Good Place'. Dane is transported, on being visited by a youthful male admirer, to a blissful hydrotherapeutic dreamland, in which 'the Brothers' enjoy a bodily commingling at the breast 'of some great mild invisible mother who stretches away into space and whose lap is the whole valley'. He finds this experience 'exquisite' because in the great good place he is 'without the complication of an identity, and the greatest of all [was] doubtless the solid security, the clear confidence one could feel in the keeping of the contract' (*CT* 11:38, 32).

In 'Fordham Castle' identity – and the possibility of loss of identity – are related to verbal play. If the name 'Abel Taker' suggests something vulgar, then in this story Mr Taker has to be relegated to obscurity precisely because of this vulgarity. Taker's wife Sue considers 'that her being a thing so dreadful as Mrs Abel Taker was a stumbling-block in her social path that nothing but his real, his official, his advertised circulated demise (with "American papers please copy") would avail to dislodge' (*CT* 12:132). (Of course the name 'Addard' is not such a great improvement! – but it is not the name chosen by Mrs Taker, who reinvents herself as Mrs Sherrington Reeve.) If the pronounced sexual innuendo in the name 'Abel Taker' is responsible for its having to be relinquished, then the very polished surface of James's text depends on the foreclosure of erotic suggestions, even as the text proliferates in such suggestions. In other words, the production of 'story' and the production of 'social identity' within the story take place according to a similar process of inclusion and denial, a process which is however always incomplete.

James's late short stories are highly ironic about the laws of prohibition which govern their own production. Although they thematize respect for social decorum, they also zoom in on those parts of the body and those bodily relations their very gentility would require they should ignore. In 'Mora Montravers' (1909), for instance, Jane and Sidney Traffle, a childless, middle-aged couple living in Wimbledon, become alarmed at the open manner in which their beautiful 'niece' Mora – the daughter of Jane's dead half-sister – has taken up residence with the no less beautiful painter Walter Puddick. Although they are eager that the relation between the two young people should be regularized through marriage, they feel it a shame that the 'grand air' of the name 'Montravers' should be lost for the 'vulgar name' (as Jane Traffle calls it), the 'unfortunate name' (as Puddick himself calls it), of Walter Puddick. Wondering if this is also Mora's objection to matrimony, Jane notes that '[h]er reason – if it is her reason – is vulgarer still' (*CT* 12:278–9). Mora's name is so grand, presumably, because of its suggestion of crossing mountains, but what is so objectionable about Puddick? This question takes on considerable narrative urgency. A 'puddock' is a toad; in marrying Puddick it seems that Mora will turn into a toad, but Puddick will not become a prince.[3] Yet Puddick's name has other vulgarities. In the early eighteenth century 'pudding' was a slang term for penis; James Joyce uses the derivative 'pud' in *Finnigan's Wake*. 'Pud' is also close to 'put'. The syllable 'pud' is ambiguous, then, but certainly 'dick' was a slang term for penis at the turn of the century.[4] Hence it is understandable that Jane and Sydney should wish to avoid the combination 'Mora Puddick'. An obsolete meaning of 'walter' is 'To wallow or revel *in* (prosperity, pleasure, sin)' (*OED*); Walter Puddick's name is an assertive wallowing in mire, a phallic monstrosity.

Tales like 'Fordham Castle' and 'Mora Montravers' self-consciously create humourous scenarios around the 'vulgarity' and embarrassment of their 'rude' names; James seems fully aware of the subversive innuendo his fiction deploys. Other names in the late fiction which overflow with innuendo are Fanny Knocker, in 'The Wheel of Time' (1892); Prodmore, in 'Covering End' (1898) recalling Longmore from the early 'Madame de Mauves' (1874) and Miss Overmore from *What Maisie Knew* (1987); Sir A. B. C. Beadel-Muffet, from 'The Papers'; Murray Brush from 'Julia Bride'; Captain Roper from 'The Bench of Desolation'; Mark Monteith, Phil Bloodgood and Newton Winch, from James's last published tale, 'A Round of Visits'; and, from James's late novel *The Outcry* (1911), Pappendick and Bender. It is not only in his late fiction that James shows a liking for obscene or near-obscene names; a (conservative!) list of such names would include, for instance, Rowland Mallet, Caspar Goodwood and Henrietta Stackpole. But in James's fiction of the 1890s and 1900s such names are more frequent, and their obscenity is more likely to be foregrounded, either by explicit comment (as in 'Mora Montravers') or by their sheer exaggeration and outrageousness. 'In the Cage' shows this extremity: this tale's 'Captain Everard', a frequent user of the telegraph service at 'Mr Cocker's', who is 'very tall, very fair, and had, in spite of his thick preoccupations, a good-humour that was exquisite, particularly as it so often had the effect of keeping him on', is also known as 'Philip with his surname and sometimes Philip without it', 'merely Phil' or 'merely Captain', William, ' "the Count" ', ' "the Pink 'Un" ', and 'Mudge' (*CT* 10:151–2).

Like most novelists, James took naming seriously; the self-consciousness with which he named his characters is exceptional. In addition to the suggestive names to be found in his published fiction, James made several lists of possible names in his notebooks, and these lists attest to his fondness for erotic (even if sometimes ambiguous) double entendres. Three such lists contain the following names:

Counterpunt – Prime – Mossom – Birdle – Brash – Fresh – Flore
  Server – Yateley – Lender – Casterton – Taker – Pouncer
  Assingham – Padwick – Lutch – Marfle – Bross – Crapp – Didcock – Wichells –
  Putchin – Brind – Coxeter – Cockster – Angus – Surrey – Dickwinter[5]

Here James plays with sequences, the echoes from name to name intensifying the indecent suggestions of each individual name. The wordplay in his lists is complex, but some prominent features should be noted, even if in doing so one's critical propriety is compromised. Often the names are suggestive in more ways than one; hence in the following analysis I sometimes use the same names to illustrate different features.

James shows a liking for names and syllables ending in 'k' or 'ck', often (but not always) beginning with 'c' or 'd': 'Pook', 'Peckover', 'Brigstock', 'Carvick – 'Corvick', 'Dedrick – Emerick – Bauker – Flickerbridge – Marsock', 'Chirk', 'Treck', 'Ludovick', 'Charlick – Carrick', 'Stroker', 'Drack – Drook', 'Cherrick', 'Brocco'. 'Roderick' is such a name, merging 'rock' and 'dick'; 'Pocock', from *The Ambassadors*, is another, a name too rude for full explanation (note what the first syllable can mean, in combination with the initial consonant of the second). There is a fondness for names whose syllables can be broken down into rude homonyms, which together form even ruder combinations: 'Popkiss', 'Ledward – Bedward –

Dedward – Deadward', 'Coxon', 'Overmore – Undermore – Overend', 'Catchmere – Catchmore – Cashmore' (this is a good example of the elision of the sexual and the financial), 'Neversome – Witherfield – Withermore'. Often the names' rudeness derives purely from their phonetic rather than their lexical qualities, from unseemly consonant clusters, which force the mouth and throat to adopt indecent postures. The lips, tongue and palate need to 'popkiss' and 'mush' to utter such sequences as 'Maudling – Lillington – Wittering – Ashling – Bruss – Bress – Hillingly – Lissack – Mant'. 'Matcham – Matchlock' and 'Match' suggest the very act of punning, whereas names such as 'Pardon', 'Hush', 'Bleat', 'Wittering' and 'Wisper' suggest various modes of communication. The mouth and other parts of the body are repeatedly evoked: mouth or near synonyms for mouth crop up in 'Monmouth', 'Waymouth', 'Crawforth', 'Belgeorge' (French *gorge*, throat), 'Mundham' (German *Mund*, mouth). Other bodily names include 'Facer', 'Crevace', 'Loynsworth (Loinsworth)' and 'Brabally'. 'Water' flows suggestively in 'Waterbath', 'Waterworth', 'Waterway', and 'Leakey'. 'Wood' and hard long objects are favourite syllables (remember the name 'Vanderplank' from 'Fordham's Castle'): 'Rosewood', 'Brickwood', 'Woodwell' 'Welwood' (remember Caspar Goodwood from *The Portrait of a Lady*), 'Ledward – Bedward – Dedward – Deadward', 'Pilbeam', 'Brigstock' (German *Stock*, stick), 'Mellet', 'Chorner' (this name recalls Wycherley's Horner, of *The Country Wife* (1675)); 'long' itself features often, in 'Longhay', 'Longdon', 'Longersh', though none of these names are as suggestive as a name from one of James's tales, 'Longstaff's Marriage'. 'More', 'over' and 'end' form various compromising combinations: 'Philmor', 'Passmore', 'Billamore', 'Overmore – Undermore – Overend', 'Catchmore – Cashmore' ('Cashmore' is typical of names which fuse the financial and the sexual), 'Stilmore', 'Withermore', 'Peckover'. A number of names suggest unconventional bodies, the body in compromised postures, or various sexual engagements and relations of bodies: 'Tester', 'Carrier', 'Croucher', 'Helder', 'Gainer', 'Bender', 'Bagger', 'Stroker', 'Gasper', 'Player', 'Marcher', 'Gaymer (or Gamer)', 'Cramp', 'Round', 'Grose', 'Dyde'. Innuendo in the names is often financial as well as sexual, and a number of names suggest money, payment and exchange: 'Gift', 'Monier, or Monyer', 'Gainer' and 'Cashmore' again, 'Dyme', 'Coyne', 'Casher', 'Budgett'. James came up with many wonderful combinations in notes he made for the unfinished novel *The Ivory Tower*: at various stages he considered 'Haughty Crimper' (or 'Horton Crimple'), 'Graham Riser', 'Clencham', 'Grabham', 'Wrencher', 'Bright Riser', 'Wenty Hench', 'Romper', and 'Finder'.[6]

While names such as Haughty Crimper have a Dickensian ring, they recall the vulgar names of Restoration drama. Often it seems that a vulgar original undergoes a slight permutation, to edge it towards respectability – 'Wench', 'Gross' 'Leaky' and 'Smudge' become 'Wenty Hench', 'Grose', 'Leakey' and 'Mudge'. Yet this vain disguise only accentuates the vulgarity. The name's ill-concealed secret gives it a shameful quality, which makes one linger on its dirtiness. More brash names, advertising their bodily qualities more loudly, would not create such a *frisson* – the frisson arising from the meeting of the genteel and the coarse. (One of James's names is 'Properly', and many of his names have the effect of a very proper person farting.) Often a feeling of unease attaches to names which have the air of a secret, which sound vaguely obscene, but whose obscenity cannot be pinned down: consider 'Windle', 'Chiddle', 'Buddle', Pugsley', 'Parm'.

These Jamesian puns are condensed jokes, yet the joke, according to Freud, is already a product of 'condensation, displacement and indirect representation'.[7] Freud's analysis of jokes links the 'pleasurable condens-tions' of 'joke-work' – analagous to the 'dream-work' – to 'the unconscious thought-processes ... produced in early childhood'. A reversion to an infantile state aims at recapturing a 'childish source of pleasure'; the joke's ambiguity enables forbidden childish play – 'the ancient dwelling place' of the subject's 'former play with words' – to inhabit adult life. Jokes, how-ever, differ from dreams in the way they deal with inhibitions:

For jokes do not, like dreams, create compromises; they do not evade the inhibition, but they insist on maintaining play with words or with nonsense unaltered. They restrict themselves, however, to a choice of occasions in which this play or this nonsense can at the same time appear allowable (in jests) or sensible (in jokes), thanks to the ambiguity of words and the multiplicity of conceptual relations. Nothing distinguishes jokes more clearly from other psychical structures than this double-sidedness and duplicity.[8]

Certainly James's wordplay seems to recover a joyish sense of childish defilement. His names, considered as jokes, do not 'evade the inhibition', yet ambiguity makes them 'allowable'. The 'double-sidedness and duplicity' Freud identifies describe the jarring discrepancies of James's obscene puns, the way they both adhere to and mock the demands of polite discourse. James's obscene language shows affinities to the modes of revolutionary poetic practice analysed by Julia Kristeva, which 'underscore the limits of socially useful discourse and attest to what it represses: the *process* that exceeds the subject and his communicative structures'. Kristeva talks of the 'semiotic violence [which] breaks through the symbolic border, and tends to dissolve the logical order, which is, in short, the outer limit founding the human and the social'.[9] Such '[c]arnivalesque discourse breaks through the laws of a language censored by grammar and semantics and, at the same time, is a social and political protest'. For Kristeva '[t]here is no equivalence, but rather identity between challenging official linguistic codes and challenging official law'.[10] As Peter Stallybrass and Allon White have shown, the carnivalesque does not only cut across the temporal boundary of the infantile and the adult; following Bakhtin, Stallybrass and White emphasize how the carnivalesque crosses spatial boundaries, mixing high and low, summoning up the grotesque and vulgar lower body, displaying the body's orifices and genitalia. Punning, they write, is one form of the *grammatica jocosa*, in which 'grammatical order is transgressed to reveal erotic and obscene or merely materially satisfying counter-meaning'.[11]

When Lucky, in Beckett's *Waiting for Godot*, talks of the 'Acacacacademy of Anthropopopometry in Essy-in-Possy of Testew and Cunard' or of 'the labours of Fartov and Belcher',[12] critics do not usually assume that Samuel Beckett has unwittingly introduced obscenities onto the stage. They have been less willing to grant that Henry James might have a similar awareness of the subversive power of obscenities. Yet James's deployment of obscenities in his fictions seems precisely calculated to maximise their disruptive, embarrassing potential. Psychoanalytic interpretation typically allows the commentator more knowledge than the creative artist, yet James seems all the time to be aware of the erotic undertones of his language, so that he both takes pleasure in its defiant, taboo-breaking status, and mocks the social formations which would repudiate such bodily modes of expression.

In James's fiction the sexual connotations of such names pass comment on the erotic scenarios the stories describe, or hint at. The names create an erotic register which subverts the genteel veneer of James's text, yet their resonances are amplified by their context. Let us return to our consideration of 'Mora Montravers'. In this tale Walter Puddick, faced with Jane Traffle's insistence that he should marry Mora, an act which Jane promises to remunerate with four hundred and fifty pounds a year, 'repudiate[s] absolutely' Mrs Traffle's charge that his relationship with Mora is not innocent (293), and breaks down into tears. These tears provide a pretext for Sidney to comfort Puddick: 'Into the hall he ushered him, and there – absurd, incoherent person as he had again to know himself for – vaguely yet reassuringly, with an arm about him, patted him on the back' (296). Sidney's comforting gesture ushers the two men into intimacy: 'while the closed door of the drawing-room and the shelter of the porch kept them unseen and unheard from within, they faced each other for the embarrassment that, as Traffle would have been quite ready to put it, they had in common' (296). This hint that Traffle's interest in the young man might be more than platonic is reinforced later in the story by an incident at Traffle's club, with which, as a result of 'the state of his own nerves', he is on 'fidgety terms':

his suspicion of his not remarkably carrying it off there was confirmed to him, disconcertingly, . . . by the free address of a fellow-member prone always to over-doing fellowship . . . – 'I say, Traff, old man, what in the world, this time, have you got "on"?' It had never been anything but easy to answer the ass, and was easier than anything now – ' "On"? You don't suppose I dress, do you, to come to meet *you?*' – yet the effect of the nasty little mirror of his unsatisfied state so flashed before him was to make him afresh wander wide . . . (303)

Portraying with ease the intervention of homosexual panic into male clubland, James foregrounds the anxiety of legibility. Fearing that his own 'unsatisfied state' is visible to the 'fellow-member prone always to over-doing fellowship', Traffle's repudiation of this approach accompanies a recognition of himself in what he is rejecting.

Surprisingly Jane Traffle, who has been figured as morally stern, eager to adhere and see that others adhere to rigid standards of decency, takes up an interest in Puddick, after a discussion with him during which she discovers much about the young man, who 'likes to talk to me, poor dear' (323). Later she explains her interest to her baffled husband:

'And you like to talk with *him*, obviously – since he appears so beautifully and quickly to have brought you round from your view of him as merely low.'
 . . . 'I never thought him low' – she made no more of it than that; 'but I admit . . . that I did think him wicked.'
 'And it's now your opinion that people can be wicked without being low?'
 . . . 'It depends,' she complacently brought out, 'on the kind.'
 'On the kind of wickedness?'
'Yes, perhaps. And' – it didn't at all baffle her – 'on the kind of people.' (323)

As a result of the 'kind of wickedness' Puddick exhibits, and the 'kind of person' he represents, Jane comes to think of Puddick as 'my poor ravaged, lacerated, pathetic nephew', and her newfound interest 'made her distinguishably happier . . . than she had been for so many months' (319–20, 327). Jane is re-vitalized by her fascination with her originally wicked nephew, although she is by no means reconciled with Mora, who decides to leave Puddick one month after having married him in a registry office. Jane is also sure that her interest in Puddick will be shared by her husband. And Sidney does derive pleasure from Jane's entrée into what he had previously thought of as 'the essential impenetrability . . . of an acutest young artist's *vie intime*' (299). 'Lord, the fun some people did have!' he thinks as the story closes. 'Even Jane, with her conscientious new care – even Jane, unmistakably, was in for such a lot' (333).

Read without what Sedgwick calls 'the easy assumption . . . that sexuality and heterosexuality are always exactly translatable into one another',[13] 'Mora Montravers' emerges as a pithy comedy in which a middle-aged couple project themselves with vigour, imagination and sympathy into the life of a young bohemian artist, whose work and modes of erotic expression offer them an excitement they had found lacking in their suburban existence – an existence which is figured as being quartered in ' "spare" rooms, dreary and unapplied, . . . even year after year, quite as on some dull interminable visit' (267–8). The story shows the extent of what was and was not possible for the late James.

In asking what James avoids in his fiction, reticence should not be equated with timidity. It is true that none of James's stories makes a direct characterisation of any character's '(homo)sexuality', or assumes that 'sexuality' can be adequately described by a particular label. Further, the fiction consistently refrains from describing any genital activity. These two (seemingly obvious) absences are important for the *freedom* of interpretation they allow, rather than for the way they restrict interpretation. It should not be assumed that James's avoidance of those reductive epithets 'homosexual' and 'heterosexual' is merely a consequence of the conditions in which he published his fiction. Rather the very spirit of his fiction repeatedly questions whether 'sexuality' can be reduced to two such circumscribed concepts. If James's late fiction registers that such a homo/heterosexual definitional frame has in fact come to predominate perceptions of 'sexuality', his interrogations of such definitional mechanisms focus on the violence and psychic difficulties such a frame can precipitate.

It is as important to ask what modes of representation *were* possible for James. The late James, famous for his timidity, was in fact exploring new possibilities for eroticism in fiction. In his late tales, James develops and takes advantage of an erotic lexicon, invents a discursive eroticism in which erotic tensions and connections between fictional characters are not contained by a heterosexual frame. If the stories avoid description of sexual activity, the genitality of their language and of the erotic spaces they describe ironize and critique the standards of literary gentility to which they ostensibly conform. Moreover, through a series of well-honed puns, double entendres, and references to the spectres of homosexual blackmail, scandal and suicide, the late tales nevertheless manage to thematize homoerotic desire and the fate of the 'homosexual'. In particular, both the life and writings of Wilde – who, more than anyone else, made the 'homosexual' a visible feature in late Victorian and Edwardian social life – provide James with opportunities to stretch and extend the visibility of homoeroticism. If James is developing the potential of narrative fiction to represent homoerotic pleasures, and interrogating the (psychic and physical) violence accompanying visible expressions of delight in such pleasures, he is partly able to do so because of the development, in late nineteenth-century Britain, of a language in which a lack of specificity accompanied an excess of suggestion, of connotation.[14] James takes full advantage of such a set of reference points, which enable him to portray indecency without any threat to decency.

The thematization of homoeroticism in James's late short fiction is neither sporadic nor incidental. The anxieties arising from the violent repudiation of homoerotic bonds in the wake of the Wilde trials, and the pressures put on male friendship and constructions of masculinity arising from the more fully defined contours of that abject figure, the 'homosexual', fully inform James's attention to the minutiae of late Victorian and Edwardian social transactions. Further, James's response to such tensions is so sophisticated, that reading such a response cannot merely note the presence of homoeroticism or of figures who may or may not be identifiable as 'homosexual' (that old question, 'Is there a homosexual in the text?'). Rather the terms of the construction of the 'homosexual' are always actively questioned. If James's late fiction expresses no optimism about an identity construction predicated on (homo)sexuality, it is attentive to the costs of a structure in which homoerotic bonds are necessarily subject to censure. For many masculine subjects in James's late fiction, called by James his 'poor sensitive gentlemen' (*AN* 246), homosexual identity is a difficulty, even an impossibility. However, for these poor gentlemen, an 'identity' foreclosing the homoerotic is equally difficult, equally problematic. For them, to ignore or to acknowledge the homoerotic is a 'rum' choice, for both choices mean exposure to various forms of violence.

II SPECTRES OF WILDE

'I went last night to the Loring's . . . and found there the repulsive and fatuous Oscar Wilde' 'Oscar Wilde is here – an unclean beast.'

Henry James to Isabella Stewart Gardner
and E. L. Godkin, January 1882[15]

Since Michel Foucault's and Jeffrey Weeks' pioneering work on homosexuality, queer historiography has argued both that the second half of the nineteenth century saw the development of 'scientific' modes of understanding sexuality according to a binary model of 'sexual orientation', and that the 1890s in particular saw the development of modern notions of homosexual identity and homosexual communities in Britain and America.[16] Such a picture allows for the existence of local homosexual communities, such as existed in Victorian Oxford,[17] and does not deny the existence of the city as a homoerotic location before the late nineteenth century. Yet it appears that the 1890s saw the development of universalizing understandings of homosexuality in the West. It is in the 1890s that the homoerotic scenarios of James's fiction turn from tragedy – the love that cannot find its name – to anxiety – the love that dare not speak its name.

Perhaps the most-quoted words of Foucault are his claim, in *La Volonté de Savoir*, that 'the psychological, psychiatric, medical category of homosexuality was constituted from the moment it was characterized – Westphal's famous article of 1870 on "contrary sexual sensations" can stand as its date of birth – less by a type of sexual relations than by a certain quality of sexual sensibility ... Homosexuality appeared as one of the forms of sexuality when it was transposed from the practice of sodomy onto a kind of interior androgyny, a hermaphrodism of the soul. The sodomite had been a temporary aberration; the homosexual was now a species.'[18] While the shift Foucault identifies is upheld in more recent scholarship, his metaphor, the 'date of birth', is perhaps unfortunate, as it suggests a sudden transformation rather than a gradual development, and does not allow for local differences between European nations and between Europe and America, or, indeed, between metropolis, large town and country. Modern scholarship seems to agree, however, that 1895 was a year of profound significance for understandings of homosexuality throughout the Western world. Around May 1895, when Oscar Wilde was found guilty of committing 'acts of gross indecency with another person', modern homosexuality found a face. As Ed Cohen has argued, the trials (both in the courtroom and in the newspaper accounts) were effective in 'designating Wilde as a kind of sexual actor without explicitly referring to the specificity of his sexual acts, and thereby crystallized a new constellation of sexual meanings predicated upon "personality" and not practices.'[19] Alan Sinfield agrees, writing that 'our stereotypical notion of male homosexuality derives from Wilde, and our ideas about him'.[20] However many homosexuals there might be, Oscar Wilde was *the homosexual*.

In E. M. Forster's *Maurice*, written in 1913 and 1914, homosexuals are referred to as 'unspeakables of the Oscar Wilde sort'.[21]

1895: even this birthdate might not be entirely authentic, however. (Can authenticity ever attach itself to Oscar Wilde?) The trials were responsible for cementing the image of Wilde as queer, and the image of the queer as Wilde, in the public mind. Sinfield argues that it is only a year or so before the trials that a 'consolidation of a queer identity begins to take shape around Wilde in Robert Hichens's novel, *The Green Carnation*'. Before the trials 'Wilde was regarded by society, the press and the public as rather wicked, but by no means as a pariah', and that 'well-informed people were surprised when his queer practices came to light.'[22]

The association of Wilde with homosexual practices and a nascent queer identity might not have been universal, then; yet one wonders how much currency this association enjoyed before the trial among *savants*. As early as 1881, Bunthorne, the mock-aesthete hero of Gilbert and Sullivan's comic opera *Patience*, who has, as Richard Ellmann points out, 'aspects that come unmistakably from Wilde as the most articulate standard bearer of aestheticism at the time',[23] can sing that, in order to be a successful aesthete,

> a sentimental passion of a vegetable fashion must
>   excite your languid spleen,
> An attachment *à la Plato* for a bashful young
>   potato, or a not-too-French french bean!
> Though the Philistines may jostle, you will rank
>   as an apostle in the high aesthetic band,
> If you walk down Piccadilly with a poppy or a lily
>   in your mediaeval hand
>   And everyone will say,
>   As you walk your flowery way,
> 'If he's content with a vegetable love which would
>   certainly not suit *me*,
> Why, what a most particularly pure young man this
>   pure young man must be!'[24]

It was widely alleged that Wilde had 'walked down Piccadilly with a poppy or a lily' in his hand;[25] here the libretto is not fully transparent, but certainly not wholly opaque, in associating Wilde with suspect 'passions' ('*à la Plato*') which meet with distaste in the normative response of 'everyone'.

One wonders then what informs James's hostile response to Wilde, which can be seen clearly as early as 1882. In January of that year both men were in Washington, and the young Wilde, whose literary output was then small, was enjoying the status of a celebrity. His fame was partly helped by Gilbert and Sullivan's satire: Edel writes that '[t]he press talked largely of Bunthorne-Wilde'.[26] Douglass Shand-Tucci has recently shown that Wilde's presence in Boston was responsible for 'setting in motion cultural developments ... that made the New England capital the center of aestheticism in America'; Shand-Tucci shows that Boston aestheticist circles functioned as a kind of early urban gay subculture, so it is possible that Wilde was enjoying local fame as a 'gay icon' before the trials made this status universal.[27]

James visited Wilde when he was in Washington, but told his host Mrs Henry Adams that he was a 'fatuous cad', and wrote to E. L. Godkin, editor of the *Nation*, that 'Oscar Wilde is here – an unclean beast'.[28] His loathing was then already intense. Professional jealousy may have contributed to James's dislike – although in the 1880s James did not have nearly so much cause for envy as he would in the 1890s. More than rivalry seems to feed James's antagonism. In a revealing letter to Isabella Stewart Gardner, who was to become the presiding hostess of Boston's *fin-de-siècle* male gay circles,[29] James wrote:

I went last night to the Loring's where you told me you had flung down your *sortie de bal* in the dusky entry, where it looked like a bunch of hyacinths, – and found there the repulsive and fatuous Oscar Wilde, whom, I am happy to say, no one was looking at.[30]

What does James recognize in Wilde that is 'repulsive and fatuous'? Is the coupling of Wilde and hyacinths coincidental? (Only four years later James is to give the name Hyacinth to the troubled protoqueer hero of *The Princess Casamassima*.[31]) Why should Wilde be an 'unclean beast'? In short, what does James know about Wilde in 1882? The next major novel James publishes after *The Princess Casamassima* is *The Tragic Muse* (1890), with the aesthete Gabriel Nash, whom, as several scholars have shown, James clearly based on Wilde – if Wilde is 'repulsive and fatuous', he is clearly also fascinating to James.[32]

Ten years later, in 1892, James was present at the opening of *Lady Windermere's Fan*, at which Wilde and a number of other men were wearing, at Wilde's request, green carnations. Regenia Gagnier writes that Wilde wanted to 'annoy the public':

... they will look round the house and see every here and there more and more little specks of mystic green. 'This must be some secret symbol,' they will say. 'What on earth can it mean?'[33]

Gagnier adds that although Wilde claimed it meant '[n]othing whatever', he was being 'disingenuous'. Wilde 'knew that the distinctive green carnation was the emblem worn by homosexuals in Paris'. Wilde was certainly enjoying a dangerous joke at his audience's expense, then, when he walked on stage after the performance to address the audience: 'I congratulate you on the *great* success of your performance.'[34]

James wrote (to the dramatist Florence Bell) about the spectacle with the same disgust (and the same fine cadences) he had shown in 1882:

The 'impudent' speech at the end was simply inevitable mechanical Oscar – I mean the usual trick of saying the unusual – complimenting himself and his play ... Everything Oscar does is a delicate trap for the literalist, and to see the literalist walk straight up to it, look straight at it and step straight into it, makes one freshly avert a discouraged gaze from this unspeakable animal.[35]

The vehemence and violence of this reaction suggests that some raw nerve – more than that of professional jealousy[36] – is being touched here. Indeed, James piles queer trope upon queer trope. As well as suggesting the 'unspeakability' of the homosexual, the passage employs a vocabulary of animality and entrapment. (The association of animality recurs in a letter to Gosse when James refers to some of the witnesses (rentboys) at Wilde's trials as 'little beasts of witnesses[.] What a nest of almost infant blackmailers!'.)[37] Figuring Wilde as luridly seductive, it posits two kinds of viewer: the compromised viewer who will walk into Wilde's 'trap', or the squirming viewer who will 'avert a discouraged gaze'. (Remember that James, in 1876, had described the reader of *Les Fleurs du Mal* as seeing 'a gentleman in a painful-looking posture, staring very hard at a mass of things from which, more intelligently, we avert our heads'.)[38]

Three years later, of course, Wilde is being tried; during the trials he is to figure largely in James's correspondence. James's prose hovers round the subject which it constitutes as 'hideous, sickening' but also 'interesting'. Here he is to Gosse on 8 April 1895:

it has been, it is, hideously, atrociously dramatic and really interesting – so far as one can say that of a thing of which the interest is qualified by a sickening horribility. It is the squalid gratuitousness of it all – of the mere exposure – that blurs the spectacle. But the *fall* – from nearly twenty years of a really unique kind of 'brilliant' conspicuity (wit, 'art', conversation – 'one of our two or three dramatists, etc.') to that sordid prison-cell and this gulf of obscenity over which the ghoulish public hangs and gloats – it is beyond any utterance of irony or any pang of compassion! He was never in the smallest degree interesting to me – but this hideous human history has made him so – in a manner.[39]

Richard Ellmann calls James's response to Wilde's fate 'repulsive'.[40] Certainly, James's lack of sympathy for Wilde, despite the severity and hardship of Wilde's punishment, makes for painful reading. James's earlier description of Wilde as creating a 'trap' suggests that, at some level, James himself feels implicated in the spectacle of Wilde's punishment. Given the nature of Wilde's crimes, one might feel that James's language – 'that sordid prison-cell and this gulf of obscenity' – appears to bring him close to the spectacle even as he wants to distance himself from it. Twice James figures himself as unwilling, passive participant in Wilde's drama, despite a violent disclaimer: 'it is *really interesting* although one's '*interest is qualified by a sickening horribility*'; 'He was *never in the smallest degree* interesting to me – but this hideous human history has made him so'. (James doesn't write here with his usual care: note the repetitions of 'hideous' and 'interesting'.)

Homosexual Self-Loathing: a book which needs to be written.[41] James's reaction to Wilde forms part of a somewhat sordid history of queers who hate other queers for the particular reason that they are queer. The particular form of James's loathing might be expressed by a law: *the discreet loathes the obvious*.[42] Namely, the circuitous, the genteel queer who refrains from underlining, who lets uncertainties ride, loathes the queer who makes everything unambiguous, beyond charitable doubt. If James's response to Wilde can be seen as an instance of what Sedgwick, in her reading of James's 'The Beast in the Closet', has termed 'homosexual panic', it needs to be emphasised that panic is by no means characteristic of James's feelings about (other) gay men. His comments about Wilde are unworthy of the man who is sympathetic to J. A. Symonds, is friends with the flamboyant Howard Sturgis, and has any number of young male friends, many of them to some degree gay-identified, whom he happens also to love. James was more likely to feel sympathy and affection for gay men than repugnance. Conflicted feelings were evident, however, in his friendship for the Russian Paul Zhukovski, whom he met through Turgenev in 1876. That year he wrote to Alice, '[Zhukovski] is much to my taste and we have sworn eternal friendship', yet meeting him again in Naples in 1880, James was less enthusiastic. Zhukovski's circle of Russian and German Wagnerians, he wrote to Grace Norton, had 'manners and customs' which 'were about as opposed to that of Cambridge as anything could well be – but to describe them would carry me too far'; to Alice he complained of their 'fantastic immorality and aesthetics'.[43] Edel's suggestion that James 'perhaps became aware [Zhukovski] was homosexual'[44] seems too mild; James seems fully aware of the homosexuality, and is shocked by its *boldness*, fearful of how it might implicate him. Interestingly, meeting Count Robert de Montesquiou in 1885, James is 'less terrified – and even amused'; James was a generous host to Montesquiou in London.[45] Montesquiou was, as Edel writes, already 'well-known in Paris as the homosexual eccentric and dandy who had furnished Huysmans his character of Des Esseintes in *A Rebours*'.[46]

The intensity of James's loathing for Wilde is striking, then. The queer language with which James writes about Wilde is audibly homophobic. In contexts other than that of a private letter, it might be used to incite hatred and loathing. Yet this does not mean that we should contrast a closeted, private James to an out, public Wilde, and view the two men as dramatically different. What touches a raw nerve in James is surely a recognition that the difference between them is not as palpable as might be desired. As Freedman writes, the antagonism between the two men is striking for 'the similarity of their personal situations: James and Wilde were two marginal immigrants – an Irishman and an American – each of whom was made doubly marginal as he grappled with a homoerotic sexuality'.[47] The writer of novels such as *Roderick Hudson*, *The Bostonians* and *The Tragic Muse* could himself be grouped with Wilde; if James's fiction involves an adventurous rethinking of the forms of human relationships, then Wilde, even before his 'fall', his 'squalid' and 'sordid' fate, provided too vivid a reminder of the danger attached to such explorations.

If one discerns panic in James's relation to Wilde, one needs to see this 'panic' as part of a much fuller, complex and profound response to Wilde and everything Wilde means – as a person, as a writer, as a public figure, as a 'homosexual'. James is extremely knowing and revealing about Wilde, even when his response is hostile, and this distaste masks a strong mutual influence between the two men. I have already suggested that the 'obscure' language of James's late style reflects the anxiety attaching to representations of same-sex desire in the wake of the Wilde trials and other Victorian sexual scandals.[48] Wilde's influence on James's writing is not merely to be seen in its evasions, however. Jonathan Freedman points to 'their mutual participation in an intricate intertextual chain of allusion, counterallusion, and outright theft – theft committed first by Wilde himself, but then recommitted, and with malice afterthought, by his victim'.[49]

When James looks at or averts his glance from Wilde, we see a specular encounter which locks the two men in a troubled relationship, in which the terms of similarity and difference between observer and spectacle threaten to collapse into one another. James's writing contains several such specular and spectral moments in which a troubled observer meets a seductive and destructive ghostly figure, often only to wonder who – observer or bespied figure – is more terrible. Such moments, almost invariably charged with homoerotic energies, can be found in 'Owen Wingrave', 'The Real Right Thing', 'The Turn of the Screw', 'The Beast in the Jungle', or 'The Jolly

Corner'.[50] Perhaps the most thrilling of such moments, however, is found in the first volume of James's autobiography, *A Small Boy and Others*, first published in 1913. James is recalling his childhood visits to the Galerie d'Apollon of the Louvre, setting of 'the most appalling yet most admirable nightmare of my life' which he remembered waking to 'in a summer dawn many years later' (James does not tell us when). The Galerie d'Apollon is, James writes, imbued with 'the ineffable, the inscrutable, . . . the incalculable'. The nightmare concerns an encounter not with a painting but with a 'dimly-descried figure'. Rather than looking at pictures, James finds himself desperately trying to avoid the scrutiny of a figure who fills him with an 'unutterable fear'. Yet the relationship between James and the spectre is ambivalent – James names it as one of 'the sources at which an intense young fancy . . . capriciously, absurdly drinks, . . . that of a love-philtre or fear-philtre which fixes for the senses their supreme symbol of the fair or the strange'. James's phrase 'love-philtre or fear-philtre' condenses the phobic and the erotic: a philtre is a drink exciting sexual love in the drinker. The apparition constitutes 'a splendid scene of things', 'the most appalling yet most admirable nightmare of my life', and the encounter is marked by an uncertain relation, the question of whether James will destroy or be destroyed by the spectre:

The climax of this extraordinary experience . . . was the sudden pursuit, through an open door, along a huge high saloon, of a just dimly-descried figure that retreated in terror before my rush and dash (a glare of inspired reaction from irresistible but shameful dread,) out of the room I had a moment before been desperately, and all the more abjectly, defending by the push of my shoulder against hard pressure on lock and bar from the other side. The lucidity, not to say the sublimity, of the crisis had consisted of the great thought that I, in my appalled state, was probably still more appalling than the awful agent, creature or presence, whatever he was, whom I had guessed, in the suddenest wild start from sleep, the sleep within my sleep, to be making for my place of rest . . . Routed, dismayed, the tables turned upon him by my so surpassing him for straight aggression and dire intention, my visitant was already but a diminished spot in the long perspective, the tremendous, glorious hall, as I say, over the far-gleaming floor of which . . . he sped for *his* life, while a great storm of thunder and lightning played through the deep embrasures of high windows at the right. The lightning that revealed the retreat revealed also the wondrous place and, by the same amazing play, my young imaginative life in it of long before, the sense of which, deep within me, had kept it whole, preserved it to this thrilling use; for what in the world were the deep embrasures and the so polished floor but those of the Galerie d'Apollon of my childhood?[51]

This extraordinary passage constitutes a superb example of what we might, following Terry Castle, call queer spectrality, or 'homospectrality',

in which 'homo' might suggest not only homoeroticism but the element of
sameness linking the haunted and the ghost.[52] James resembles his spectre
not only in that it is unclear who is the more appalling of the two, but
because his behaviour replicates that of the 'awful agent, creature or
presence': whereas he has been defending himself from the other's pursuit, he turns and gives chase, matching his visitant's 'straight aggression
and dire intention'. This encounter, both erotic and violent, plays out the
spatial dynamics of 'the closet' in hyperbolic terms: the passage shows
an obsession with doors, with enclosure and entrapment, hunting and
liberation, secrecy and visibility.

Leon Edel reads this dream as dramatizing James's 'fright perhaps at
the vaulting ambition of his own imagination', James's 'initiation to Style'
which was for James 'associated ... with power'.[53] Yet in so far as the
dream does undoubtedly dramatize the discovery of art, it merges art with
the erotic. If the dream is, for James, a recreation of a childhood scene, so
too the older James recreates the dream (even as he tells us that he calls it
'to this hour, with the last vividness'),[54] and in doing so gives it the form of
the fin de siècle queer horror story, the most distinguished examples of
which are written by Robert Louis Stevenson, James and Wilde, and
dramatize an anxious double life reminiscent of James's encounter in the
Galerie d'Apollon.

III 'A RAGE OF PERSONALITY': SHIFTING IDENTITY IN 'THE JOLLY CORNER'

In 1890, a year before the publication of Wilde's *The Picture of Dorian
Gray*, William James published 'The Hidden Self', his review of Pierre
Janet's *De l'Automatisme Psychologique*, in *Scribner's Magazine*. Just as Wilde's
novel described a decadent, beautiful young man with a 'hidden self' in
the old schoolroom at the top of his house, Janet, professor of philosophy
at the Lycée of Havre, describes how various feminine subjects, 'Léonie,
Lucie, Rose, Marie, etc.', hysterical patients at the Havre hospital, were
transformed into other selves, complete with separate life histories,
different physical attributes, moral standards and character traits.[55]
Janet's access to these women has been enabled by their doctors, 'who
were his friends, and who allowed him to make observations on them to
his heart's content' (93). Although William James begins his review by
lamenting science's failure to take account of '[p]henomena unclassifi-
able' within 'a closed and completed system of truth' (90), Janet's book
seems to stage the very meeting William James says does not take place,

that of '[t]he scientific-academic mind and the feminine mystical mind [which] shy from each other's facts, just as they fly from each other's temper and spirit' (91).

Janet's study is one of many late nineteenth-century studies dealing with 'multiple personality'. The condition was gendered female (most case studies were of women), seen 'as a typical if extreme example' of those almost definitively feminine conditions, neurasthenia and hysteria.[56] Frequently the other self (or selves) in cases of female multiple personality was more adventurous or transgressive than the patient. Janet's 'Léonie', when her normal self (Léonie 1), is 'serious and rather sad, calm and slow, very mild … and extremely timid', yet, as Léontine (Léonie 2) is 'gay, noisy, restless … has … a singular tendency to irony and sharp jesting', and remarks of Léonie 1 that 'she is too stupid' (98). (The various selves are often locked into an antagonistic relationship with one another.) Two of Morton Prince's cases, 'Miss Beauchamp' and 'B.C.A.', showed similar changes in the movement from first to second self.[57]

Many critics have connected turn of the century tales of gothic doubling with clinical writing on multiple personality and psychiatric writings on the 'divided self', such as William James's *The Varieties of Religious Experience* (1902).[58] In her reading of *Strange Case of Dr Jekyll and Mr Hyde* ('Dr. Jekyll's Closet'), Elaine Showalter gives an account of multiple personality disorders as a symptom of disaffection with culturally prescribed gender roles. She notes that Stevenson's novel, published in 1886, responds to 1880s accounts of male hysteria, and argues that the novel 'can most persuasively be read as a fable of fin-de-siècle homosexual panic, the discovery and resistance of the homosexual self'.[59] Such a reading is persuasive rather than conclusive, given that the story is notoriously vague as to the nature of the 'appetites' Jekyll regularly indulges. Yet the narrative abounds in innuendo which lends support to the claim advanced by critics such as Showalter and Sedgwick that 'secrets' in late nineteenth-century 'paranoid Gothic' texts are overwhelmingly 'homosexual' secrets,[60] or Karl Miller's assertion that '[t]he Nineties School of Duality framed a dialect, and a dialectic, for the love that dare not speak its name – for the vexed question of homosexuality and bisexuality'.[61] If Freud's analysis of Dr. Schreber explicitly relates paranoia in men to repressed homosexual desire, Stevenson's novella pushes at such a connection, particularly in 'Henry Jekyll's Full Statement of the Case', with which the narrative ends. Jekyll describes life as a choice between his respectable social self and the pariah Hyde: 'To cast in my lot with Jekyll, was to die to those appetites which I had long secretly indulged and had of late begun to pamper.

To cast it in with Hyde, was to die to a thousand interests and aspirations, and to become, at a blow and forever, despised and friendless.'⁶² The opposition is not so much between heterosexual and homosexual, but between a seemingly normal life in which forbidden appetites are secretly indulged, and the blatant assumption of an animal 'hide'. Jekyll talks of 'the animal within me licking the chops of memory'; when he metamorphoses into Hyde, he uses a figure suggesting the surfacing of evil, animal appetites: 'My devil had been long caged, he came out roaring.'⁶³ Hence in the classic gothic structure of queer doubling which Stevenson's exemplifies and inaugurates, one's self may appear 'straight' and one's other may appear 'queer', but they are united by the animality they respectively conceal or display.

James's 'The Jolly Corner' (1908) is a tale replete with intertextual echoes of *Dr Jekyll* and *Dorian Gray*. Its protagonist Spencer Brydon recalls Dr Jekyll in that he too is locked into a violent relationship with an abject double. In this tale, the 56–year-old Brydon returns after 33 years in Europe to New York, and renews his friendship with Alice Staverton, a woman with a 'slim mystifying grace of . . . appearance, which defied you to say if she were a fair young woman who looked older through trouble, or a fine smooth older one who looked young through successful indifference' (*CT* 12:197). Alice and Brydon are bonded through a shared eroticism of the closet, with its hushed secrets, its shame, its violence.

Brydon's life has been a Paterian 'surrender to sensations' (210), and he is haunted by 'the queerest and deepest of his own lately most disguised and muffled vibrations', the thought of 'opening a door behind which he would have made sure of finding nothing, a door into a room shuttered and void, and yet coming, with a great suppressed start, on some quite erect confronting presence, something planted in the middle of the place and facing him through the dusk' (198). Here the story's debt to Stevenson's *Dr Jekyll* is evident: as Stephen Heath has noted, *Dr Jekyll's* 'organizing image . . . is the breaking down of doors, learning the secret behind them'.⁶⁴ Indeed, James's comments on *Jekyll and Hyde* anticipate the way in which he rewrites Stevenson. 'There is something almost impertinent in the way . . . Mr Stevenson achieves his best efforts without the aid of the ladies', James writes, 'and *Doctor Jekyll* is a capital example of his heartless independence.'⁶⁵ 'The Jolly Corner' represents *Dr Jekyll with the aid of the ladies*: Alice Staverton and Mrs Muldoon are feminine presences who enter the very male space of Brydon's fantasy life. If Brydon has a 'homosexual secret' then Alice has 'staved' it in – 'to stave' meaning to burst or force a hole in something. Her easy ability to divine 'his strange sense' is experienced by Brydon as a liberation from the closet: 'her apparent understanding, with no protesting shock, no easy derision, touched him more deeply than anything yet, constituting for his stifled perversity, on the spot, an element that was like breathable air' (206). With Alice, Brydon's 'secret' is truly 'open': he talks of his past as his 'perverse young course', and notes

'I've not been edifying – I believe I'm thought in a hundred quarters to have been barely decent. I've followed strange paths and worshipped strange gods; it must have come to you again and again . . . that I was leading, at any time these thirty years, a selfish frivolous scandalous life.' (205)

Yet, in 'The Jolly Corner', Alice is not merely a sympathetic outside observer, but an active participant in Brydon's fantasy life. The fantasy of breaking into the closet, smashing down its door, is one that they create together.

Their shared fantasy involves an encounter with Brydon's 'fictional' double, the person he would have been if he had stayed in America.[66] Alice encounters this double in her dream life, whereas Brydon meets him in his childhood home, the 'house on the jolly corner, as he usually, and quite fondly, described it – the one in which he had first seen the light' (194). The description of this encounter, the core of 'The Jolly Corner', closely resembles James's description of his encounter with the appalling creature in the 'Galerie d'Apollon of [his] childhood'. Just as James does not know whether he or the creature is more appalling, for Brydon it is a matter of considerable anxiety which of his two selves would have been more depraved – the Brydon who has been 'blighted . . . for once and for ever' by being Europeanized, or the missing Brydon, the Brydon who might have escaped his 'father's curse' by following 'the rank money-passion', who would have become a businessman 'quite splendid, quite huge, and monstrous . . . quite hideous and offensive' (205).

Brydon's meeting with his spectral double is described in the middle section of the story, a section which appears to do 'without the aid of the ladies'. Brydon has begun to visit the house with compulsive regularity, 'sometimes . . . twice in the twenty-four hours' (207), and his life on the jolly corner achieves a greater definition than his social life:

He was a dim secondary social success . . . He projected himself all day, in thought, straight over the bristling line of hard unconscious heads and into the other, the real, the waiting life; the life that, as soon as he heard behind him the click of his great house-door, began for him, on the jolly corner, as beguilingly as the slow opening bars of some rich music follows the tap of the conductor's wand. (208)

Brydon is attempting to track down his '*alter ego*' (209), and James eroticizes this chase, figuring it as the 'stalking of a creature more subtle, yet at bay perhaps more formidable, than any beast of the forest' (210). If any sexual scenario carries within it the traces of other sexual scenarios, then the description of this chase combines several sexual narratives, to constitute an unstable semantic and erotic overload. Most obviously, the story charts a confluence of narcissism and homosexuality, a meeting of the two phases which, in Freud's sexual narrative, follow auto-eroticism and precede heterosexual object-choice.[67] In that the house is Brydon's childhood home, his return is also a return to his childhood past, to the ghosts of parental and ancestral authority.

Further, the house represents a typology of the human body, a spatial erotics, one of James's most 'bristling' architectural creations.[68] Brydon's progress up its 'ample back staircase' (212), during which he feels 'the sense of a need to hold on to something, even after the manner of a man slipping and slipping on some awful incline' (214), might suggest anal penetration: this suggestion is strengthened by a proliferation of double entendres. Brydon is shown to have a somewhat anxious 'phallic' relationship to a series of anal openings and passages. The house itself is compared to 'some great glass bowl, all precious concave crystal, set delicately humming by the play of a moist finger round its edge' (209). Just as the corridor of James's Galerie d'Apollon dream contains 'high deep embrasures', the house on the jolly corner allows Brydon to take shelter 'in an embrasure' (210) (defined in the *Collins English Dictionary* as an 'opening forming a door or a window, having splayed sides that increase the width of the opening in the interior'). It has 'nooks and corners, . . . closets and passages' (212); trying to leave, Brydon confronts the 'fan-tracery of the entrance' (223) and notices how 'the thin admitted dawn, glimmering archwise over the whole outer door, made a semicircular margin, a cold silvery nimbus that seemed to play a little as he looked – to shift and expand and contract' (224).

The phallic nature of Brydon's trial is made evident in the demand he feels to remain at the top of the stairs, which appears to become a test of sexual prowess and perseverance:

He had *stiffened* his will against going; without this he would have made for the stairs, and it seemed to him that, still with his eyes closed, he would have descended them, would have known how, straight and swiftly *to the bottom* . . . He took out his watch – there was light for that: it was scarcely a quarter past one, and *he had never withdrawn so soon* . . . It would prove his courage – unless indeed the latter might most be proved by his budging at last from his place. What he mainly felt now was that, since he hadn't originally scuttled, he had his dignities – which had never in his life seemed so many – all to preserve and *to carry aloft*. This was before him in truth as *a physical image* . . . (215; my emphasis)

The house's anality and masculinity are further intensified by contrasts of surface and texture. The proliferation of hard surfaces – the large black-and-white marble squares in the hall (on which 'the steel point of [Brydon's] stick' makes a 'dim reverberating tinkle' (209)), 'the points of [Brydon's] evening shoes' (209), even 'the hard silver of the autumn stars through the window-panes' (211) – contrast with the 'extraordinary softness and faintly refreshing fragrance' of Alice Staverton's lap, 'an ample and perfect cushion' (226), and the 'mantle of soft stuff lined with grey fur' (227) which caress Brydon in the third section of the story. It is difficult to miss the anality of the house's 'ample back staircase' (212), but this staircase is also figured as a water-closet, and as an underground community: Brydon thinks of it as a 'deep well . . . which might have been for queerness of colour, some watery underworld' (223–3). Descending the stairs (during which time '[h]e tried to think of something noble' (223)) Brydon reaches 'the glazed spaces of the vestibule . . . the bottom of the sea, which showed an illumination of its own and which he even saw paved . . . with the marble squares of his childhood' (223).

The story thus shows a fascination with waste products, and links anal eroticism to childhood. In Freud's theory of sexuality, the 'polymorphously perverse' child takes pleasure in bodily zones which are later stigmatized. In a footnote which he added to the *Three Essays on Sexuality* in 1920, Freud follows Lou Andreas-Salomé in stressing 'the significance of anal eroticism'. He writes that 'the history of the first prohibition which a child comes across – the prohibition against getting pleasure from anal activity and its products – has a decisive effect on his whole development . . . From that time on, what is "anal" remains the symbol of everything that is to be repudiated and excluded from life'.[69] Here Freud insists on the inherence of the social in the psychic; for Brydon anal fantasy represents both a psychic and a social threat.

'The Jolly Corner' symbolically merges psychic consequences of a sexuality generated by prohibition (is a prior anal eroticism prohibited? or does prohibition of the anus further eroticize it?) with the social regulation of sexuality. It emphasizes the surveillance of the 'fat Avenue "officer"' (208), whom Brydon 'had hitherto only sought to avoid' (220), but whose approach 'he would have welcomed positively' in order to dispel his fear. In pursuing his double Brydon is aware 'of the value of Discretion' (218), the need to remain concealed, yet also of the desire to see – he has an 'obsession of the presence encountered telescopically, . . . focussed and studied in diminished perspective' (217). His double demands that he show, reveal, confess: the door through which he hopes to see his double says to him, 'Show us how much you have!' (218).

The eventual meeting of Brydon and his double is an extraordinary fraught encounter in which desire merges with violence. The encounter posits sexuality as a shattering of self, or a phallicizing of the self in which sexual expression is a mode of power (the double is 'something all unnatural and dreadful, but to advance upon which was the condition for him either of liberation or of supreme defeat' (224)).[70] He begins the scene in the position of hunter, yet ends by being attacked; and the very uncertainty of his role is what excites him: 'he was already trying to measure by how much more he himself might now be in peril of fear; so rejoicing that he could, in another form, actively inspire that fear, and simultaneously quaking for the form in which he might passively know it' (214). Erotic tension is derived from the uncertainty of Brydon's relation to his double – a radical wavering between masochism and sadism. Is the other an 'animal brought at last to bay', the 'trodden worm', is the creature '[h]arder pressed' by Brydon, or will it in fact be Brydon who is 'harder pressed still' by the figure resembling a 'black-vizored sentinel guarding a treasure', by 'the stranger . . . advanced as for aggression' (213–4, 224, 226)?

Compulsive desire eradicates Brydon's subjectivity: he does not have the agency to say, 'I have this or that desire', but moves into a scenario the excitement of which depends on the possibility of his own agency or will being erased. Not only is Brydon's identification within the scene always changing; his involvement with the scene is contingent. The encounter is part of another narrative, an action not only intensely personal (it is called 'this completely personal act' (217)) but also deeply infused with the social and the historical. His fantasy life shows the traces of 'history' in his preoccupation with the closet, in the close linkage between narcissism and homosexuality, in the association of homoeroticism with the threat of violence and psychic transgression. These forces come together in the violent dénouement: '. . . the stranger, whoever he might be, evil, odious, blatant, vulgar, had advanced as for aggression, and he knew himself give ground. Then harder pressed still, sick with the force of his shock, and falling back as under the hot breath and the roused passion of a life larger than his own, a rage of personality before which his own collapsed, he felt the whole vision turn to darkness and his very feet give way. His head went round; he was going; he had gone' (226).

What is at stake in this violent encounter? The ghost of the jolly corner inspires both fascination and disgust in Spencer Brydon, who cannot isolate or stabilize the terms of difference and resemblance linking them. Brydon calls him a 'brute, with his awful face . . . a black stranger' (231), and the brute's repulsiveness stems from his 'vivid truth', his resemblance to a late nineteenth-century aesthete strongly marked with sexual alterity:

Rigid and conscious, spectral yet human, a man of his own substance and stature waited there to measure himself with his power to dismay . . . So Brydon, before him, took him in; with every fact of him now, in the higher light, hard and acute – his vivid truth, his grizzled bent head and white masking hands, his queer actuality of evening-dress, of dangling double eye-glass, of gleaming silk lappet and white linen, of pearl button and gold watch-guard and polished shoe. (224–5)

The palpable difference between Brydon and his double, his 'hidden self', is that the 'brute' seems more strongly defined or marked by his sexual alterity. Like the women who, under the directions of the hypnotist, produce more powerful and transgressive versions of themselves, Brydon creates and is repulsed by a version of himself whose 'queer actuality' is readily apparent. Note how the double's appearance suggests the very act of deceitful doubling, the 'white masking hands' and 'dangling double eye-glass' intensifying the story's unstable play with the terms of secrecy and visibility which are so potent in James's dream vision in the Galerie d'Apollon. The force of 'bent' and 'queer', and the way in which Brydon's double is 'thrust . . . out of his frame' (as if emerging from the closet), help explain Brydon's 'immense' 'revulsion', his '[h]orror', at the 'stranger . . . evil, odious, blatant, vulgar' (225–6).[71] (The discreet loathes the blatant: this description echoes many of James's remarks about the 'repulsive and fatuous' Wilde, who creates 'delicate trap[s] for the literalist'.) Brydon's relationship to his spectral double illustrates the ambivalence the late nineteenth-century homosexual subject feels towards a fantasy of masculinity as violent, sexually abusive and powerful, as this fantasy represents, all at once, an erotic object (the allure of 'rough trade'), a possible figure of identification, and also, in its possible homophobia (he resembles me, I am homophobic, therefore he is too), a threat.

Aspects of James's relation to Wilde feed into his representations of the spectral in 'The Jolly Corner' – a combination of fascination with disgust, a concern with hunting, with entrapment, with beastliness, with animality, a thrill at the very *fact* of the spectacle, of what is perceived as sordid becoming 'horribly' visible, an indecision over whether one should observe or look away from the spectacle, as to observe might implicate one, trap one, in some compromising pose. These qualities are present in 'The Jolly Corner', in James's relation to Wilde himself, and can be traced in an intertextual relation between James's writing and Wilde's writing; *Dorian Gray* in particular is a striking spectral intertext haunting 'The Jolly Corner'. Like *Dr Jekyll and Mr Hyde*, *The Picture of Dorian Gray* and 'The Jolly Corner' both describe troubled male protagonists with embarrassing doubles hidden in remote upper rooms. In Wilde's novel, Dorian's first compromising beast is not the picture but its painter, Basil Hallward. When Basil reproaches Dorian for having become 'bad, and corrupt, and shameful', Dorian shows Basil the portrait, which has become, like Spencer Brydon's *alter ego*, both 'hideous' and 'monstrous'.[72] Just as Brydon incurs the wrath of the 'hunted thing' who has been 'dodging, retreating, hiding', hunting him 'till he has "turned" ... the fanged or the antlered animal brought at last to bay' (213–14), Basil tracks down Dorian, who finds '[t]he mad passions of a hunted animal stirred within him' (158). (Later in the novel, when Dorian is pursued and threatened by James Vane, we are told that the 'consciousness of being hunted, snared, tracked down, had begun to dominate him' (199).) When Dorian stabs Basil repeatedly, Basil's actions suggest the three-fingered hand of Brydon's double: '[t]hree times [Basil's] outstretched arms shot up convulsively, waving grotesque stiff-fingered hands in the air' (158). If Brydon is encountering an *alter ego* whose vulgar material success is much greater than his own, so too, it appears, James is staging an intertextual encounter with Wilde, whose success in the market place so woundingly surpassed his own. Jonathan Freedman has shown that James wanted success in the market place without being tainted or compromised, as Wilde was, by the 'vulgarity' of popular tastes; the plays on which Wilde's success depends are, James claims, 'so helpless, so crude, so bad, so clumsy, feeble, and vulgar' – an accumulation of adjectives James might very well have applied to Wilde himself, and which suggests the description of the 'evil, odious, blatant, vulgar' spectre in 'The Jolly Corner'.[73] Even if it is difficult to say whether James is master or victim of queer spectrality, 'The Jolly Corner' contains strong auto-biographical resonances. Not only is the spectral encounter it describes similar to James's own Louvre nightmare, it dramatizes the fear of con-fusion with a spectral monster who, if not Wilde himself, frightens the spectator with qualities James perceives in Wilde. Moreover, the tale employs a privileged form of autobiographical narration: the dream which takes the dreamer back to the space of his childhood. As well as describing an encounter between Spencer Brydon and his 'spectral yet human' double, 'The Jolly Corner' *enacts* such an encounter, in its con-frontation with the queer spectre of Oscar Wilde's writing.

'The Jolly Corner' ends with Brydon, the male hysteric, in the role of invalid, receiving care and nurture from Alice Staverton. Alice seems not only nurse but also physician, or psychologist – counselling and reassuring the invalid Brydon as he lies 'on a deep window-bench of his high saloon, over which had been spread, couch-fashion, a mantle of soft stuff lined with grey fur' (227). That he should be tended by feminine hands emphasizes Brydon's passive, invalid status.

If there is a hint of a sexual attachment between them, then the story – in which a homoerotic narcissism gives way to a socialized heterosexuality – would echo Freud's theory of sexuality. Alice appears to have a teleological presence, as the endpoint of a process of hypnotherapy for the male homosexual in which a masculine image is faded out while a feminine image is faded in.[74]

Such a reading misunderstands, however, the bond between them. Alice's involvement with Brydon is not one of desire but one which moves between identification and desire. Her attraction to Brydon is not in doubt – she repeats, quite pointedly, the question, 'How should I not have liked you?' – yet this desire is not motivated by the thought of Brydon as object but by his fraught narcissism. Whereas many late nineteenth-century sexologists proposed that homosexuality was a result of sexual inversion – that it is the *female soul* of the male homosexual that loves the male object, and similarly the *male soul* of the female homosexual that loves the female object – and thereby maintained the primacy of heterosexual desire, Alice's fascination with Brydon appears to suggest that heterosexuality can also be based on involvement in a primarily *homosexual* scene. She dreams about Brydon only as doubled:

'You dream about me at that rate?'
'Ah about *him*!' she smiled. (206–7)

Alice kisses Brydon in 'cool charity and virtue' (228), and the closing embrace of the story is almost chaste in comparison with the erotic ardour of Brydon's adventures on the jolly corner. The erotic bond between them is not one of mutual desire but one of shared identification in Brydon's scene. This opens up the possibility that Alice's identity is just as fractured, as 'multiple', as Brydon's – if not more so.

Yet her manner of identification in the scene differs from Brydon's. Alice is attracted to the 'black stranger' for his battle scars, the way 'he's grim, he's worn – and things have happened to him' (232); she likes and accepts him 'for the interest of his difference' (231). Alice does not pity Brydon – or his double – out of the workings of a liberal conscience; and it is precisely this effortless empathy that nourishes Brydon, the fact that she doesn't 'disown' the spectral double, that, as she tells Brydon, she is reconciled to him more than Brydon is himself:

as *I* knew him – which you at last, confronted with him in his difference, so cruelly didn't, my dear – well, he must have been, you see, less dreadful to me. (232)

The story then responds imaginatively to the demands of identity. Whereas therapeutic responses to multiple personality, both at the turn of the century and today, 'assume a notion of the already-constituted . . . subject, understood as comprising a functional plurality of component parts to which violence comes entirely from the outside to shatter its functional unity into dysfunctional multiplicity',[75] Alice strives to preserve the multiplicity of Brydon's identity/ies, without seeking integration. (She ends the story by murmuring 'he isn't – no, he isn't – *you!*' (232)) The tale contrasts Brydon's repulsion towards and rejection of the stranger with Alice's warm acceptance of him.[76] As often in James's tales, the violent reactions felt by men towards a perceived homosexuality (in other men *or* in themselves) is not shared by his female characters, possibly because the female subject is not threatened by a loss of masculine entitlement, has no investment in a construction of masculinity which could be threatened by her failure to acknowledge the taboo on homosexuality. Yet there is more at stake. I have shown that the stern Jane Traffle, in 'Mora Montravers', softens markedly and takes up a maternal interest in Walter Puddick after she learns so much about his 'interesting' state. If the paternal law is responsible for instituting the taboo on homosexuality,[77] then the masculine subject of James's late fiction, in transgressing this taboo, makes a turn towards the maternal. This turn is thematized in 'The Altar of the Dead'.

CHAPTER SEVEN

Suicide and blackmail: James's 'poor sensitive gentlemen'

I SUICIDE AND COMIC SPECTACLE

According to two homosexual polemicists from the turn of the century, young homosexual men frequently killed themselves, whether from low self-esteem or because of concrete social pressures, such as blackmail or the fear of prosecution. The Criminal Law Amendment Act of 1885 was known as the 'blackmailer's charter', yet more than the fear of specific legal punishment feeds into the dread inspired by the approach of the man who knows too much. For the late nineteenth-century gentleman who does not constitute himself as queer, the bearer of shady secrets threatens much, including marriage or other heterosexual relationships, social standing and professional status. J. A. Symonds wrote in 'A Problem in Modern Ethics' (1891) that 'many unexplained cases of suicide in young men' can be accounted for by homosexuality, and 'Xavier Mayne' (Edward Irenaeus Prime Stevenson), in his study *The Intersexes* (1908, but written over the previous two decades), describes a virtual epidemic of homosexual suicides: 'uranianism', he writes, 'has a long yearly chronicle of murders that are – self-murders'.[1]

As Xavier Mayne's melodramatic tone suggests, queer suicides could be luridly sensationalized, and provided fertile ground for fictional treatment. Consider a number of fictional representations of young men who have taken their own lives, usually at the close of the novel, anticipating the popular films which reserved a nasty fate for their queer characters in the last reel.[2] In the last pages of *The Princess Casamassima*, Hyacinth Robinson's corpse is discovered by the princess and Schinkel, who tells Hyacinth's landlady that 'Mr Robinson has shot himself through the heart'.[3] In Stevenson's *Strange Case of Dr Jekyll and Mr Hyde*, first published, like *The Princess Casamassima*, in 1886, Utterson breaks down the door into Jekyll's laboratory to behold 'the face of Edward Hyde ... [B]y the crushed phial in the hand and the strong smell of kernels that hung upon the air, Utterson knew that he was looking on the body of a self-destroyer.'[4]

At the close of *The Picture of Dorian Gray*, first published five years later, Dorian's servants break into his room to find their master, 'a dead man, in evening dress, with a knife in his heart'.[5]

The Picture of Dorian Gray is without doubt the classic queer suicide text of the 1890s. Wilde's novel might be thought of as a hyperbolically and mythically queer text, containing (and establishing) standard queer motifs such as narcissism and the double, but also working in what are to become characteristic queer plots of subsequent film and fiction: the blackmail plot, the corruption plot (found, for instance, in Hitchcock's *Rope*, of 1948), the murder (*Rope* again, Hitchcock's 1951 movie *Strangers on a Train*, or Tennessee Williams's *Suddenly Last Summer*), the suicide plot (Lilian Hellman's play *Children's Hour*, or the 1968 movie *The Detective*, directed by Gordon Douglas), the fall from social respect (Basil Dearden's *Victim*, 1961, or Otto Preminger's *Advise and Consent*, 1962).[6] The only major queer plot missing from this list is the mourning plot, inaugurated by Tennyson and Whitman in such poems as *In Memoriam* and 'When Lilacs Last in the Dooryard Bloom'd', and developed by James in 'The Altar of the Dead'.

Whereas the queer plot of *Strange Case of Dr Jekyll and Mr Hyde* is perpetually hinted at but never quite confirmed, at several points in *Dorian Gray* a queer reading is inescapable. When faced with the problem of how to dispose of Basil Hallward's corpse, Dorian Gray calls on the help of the morally scrupulous doctor Alan Campbell, with whom he had been 'great friends once, five years before – almost inseparable, indeed', although 'the intimacy had come suddenly to an end.' Dorian persuades Alan Campbell to dispose of the corpse by writing something on a piece of paper, which he folds and hands to Campbell. On reading it, Campbell's 'face became ghastly pale ... A horrible sense of sickness came over him.'[7] The novel keeps Dorian's text from the reader, yet still makes it clear that we are witnessing an act of homosexual blackmail.

In the final chapter of *Dorian Gray* we are told that 'Alan Campbell had shot himself one night in his laboratory, but had not revealed the secret that he had been forced to know' (165). His fate echoes that of a number of noblemen who have associated with Dorian, as Basil Hallward makes clear in the interrogation of Dorian which leads Dorian to murder him:

Why is your friendship so fatal to young men? There was that wretched boy in the Guards who committed suicide. You were his great friend. There was Sir Henry Ashton, who had to leave England, with a tarnished name. You and he were inseparable. What about Adrian Singleton, and his dreadful end? What about

Lord Kent's only son, and his career? I met his father yesterday in St. James's Street. He seemed broken with shame and sorrow. What about the young Duke of Perth? What sort of life has he got now? What gentleman would associate with him? (117)

Just as Dorian is ostracized by decent London society ('so many gentlemen in London will neither go to your house nor invite you to theirs' (117)), friendship with him leads to social ostracization, professional disgrace, or to suicide.

At least some of the novel's readers could discern the queer implications of Dorian's sins, in particular because these sins clearly recalled details of the recent Cleveland Street Scandal of 1889–90, involving liaisons between members of the aristocracy and a number of telegraph boys in a brothel run by Charles Hammond, in the West End of London. The reviewer who famously claimed that Wilde 'can write for none but outlawed noblemen and perverted telegraph boys' was making connections between such fictional characters as 'Sir Henry Ashton, who had to leave England, with a tarnished name', and the historical Lord Arthur Somerset, who left England to escape arrest at the time of the scandals. Like Ashton, Somerset had 'a tarnished name': Earnest Parke, in reporting the case in detail in the *North London Press*, stoked the affair's scandalous flames with the suggestion that justice was being delayed in order to allow the escapes.[8] Discussing the novel's reception, Regenia Gagnier argues that the novel 'conceded to two distinct audiences': '[m]embers of the homosexual community could read *Dorian Gray* sympathetically,' whereas 'the story's obliqueness regarding Dorian's sins and . . . its entirely moralistic conclusions' could free Wilde from any public airing of hostile suspicions.[9]

The Cleveland Street Scandals, and Wilde's use of them in *The Picture of Dorian Gray* to consolidate the association of queerness, shameful secrets and a corrupt aristocracy, meant that in the 1890s queer secrets had a greater specificity than in the 1880s. If the Labouchère amendment had made possible the paranoid linkage of homosexuality, blackmail and suicide, the Cleveland Street Scandals gave these associations a wide cultural currency. By the time James writes 'The Altar of the Dead' in 1894, oblique references to undivulged misdemeanours – which might be traced in 'old newspapers' and which have attracted a 'horrible publicity' (*CT* 9:259, 237) – have a peculiarly queer colouring. On the one hand, homosexuality has a greater importance in the 1890s, in that it has the status of a particular identity. On the other hand, the formation and greater visibility of gay identities means that public displays of affection between men now risked identification *as* homosexual. This new 'queer régime' of silence and speech is difficult to characterize, as it involves both an excess of speech and a proliferation of silence.

My reading of 'The Jolly Corner' and of James's reactions to Wilde suggests that panic is one of James's responses to late Victorian homosexual culture and to modern notions of homosexuality. However, James is more often a shrewd, ironic and humorous commentator. If Oscar Wilde was to provide the public face of homosexuality, his fate – of imprisonment and public shame – was certainly not the universal, or even usual, experience of late Victorian bourgeois homosexuals. The lives of men such as Howard Sturgis, in which homoerotic experiences and relationships were enjoyed openly within a private sphere, were no doubt more typical. These men acknowledged queer experiences as an important part of their lives, without making public declarations. If James and Sturgis do, however, explore same-sex affection and the consequences of homophobia in their writing,[10] it is with a degree of caution: what might appear obvious to some readers of their fiction could be ignored by others.

If James is cautious, however, he is not timid. In a number of tales published in the 1890s and 1900s, he explores issues of secrecy and publicity, blackmail, scandal, fear of exposure and suicide, and these explorations may be related to the simultaneous repression and promotion of sexuality engendered by the trials.[11] Like *The Picture of the Dorian Gray*, these tales both invite queer readings, yet avoid concrete specification, thereby making it possible for the reader to ignore their queer context.

Often this cat and mouse game is played with considerable humour. James consciously evokes Wilde in his comic satire 'The Papers', first published in 1903. James's satire portrays the inroads of the mass-market press into British life at the turn of the century, with the founding of the *Daily Mail* in 1896, which made new breakthroughs in reaching a large readership, and the growth of gossip columns in journals such as *The Lady's World* (precursor to Wilde's *The Woman's World*).[12] 'The Papers' describes the efforts of the rather masculine, beer-drinking, cigarette-smoking Maud Blandy, a 'mannish Rosalind' who exhibits a 'superiority to sex', and her 'comparatively feminine' friend Howard Bight, to get themselves mentioned in 'the Papers', the 'Daily Press', which they think of as 'the oracle', 'the glory of the age' (*CT* 12:14–18, 48). Yet the Papers are only interested in 'the comings and goings, the doings and undoings, the intentions and retractions of Sir A. B. C. Beadel-Muffet K.C.B., M.P.' (18), a widower with a Wildean instinct for publicity, who may be able to marry the wealthy Mrs Chorner if he can satisfy her demand that he should keep out of the Papers. According to Maud's imaginative analysis,

Beadel-Muffet is unable to settle for a genteel (and comfortable) bourgeois existence because of the Wildean monster he has created: 'I see him having for some reason, very imperative, to seek retirement, lie low, to hide, in fact, like a man "wanted," but pursued all the while by the lurid glare that he has himself so started and kept up, and at last literally devoured ("like Frankenstein," of course!) by the monster he has created' (24). (It will be recognized how Maud's scenario comically reworks the tragic dénouements of *Dr Jekyll* and *Dorian Gray*.) Howard agrees with Maud: Beadel-Muffet 'must die as he has lived – the Principal Public Person of his time' (33). (While Beadel-Muffet unmistakably recalls Wilde, he is a politician; James appears to exact a comic revenge on Wilde by creating another minor character, 'Mortimer Marshal', a playwright who attracts no publicity at all.)

Lurid puns and innuendo attach to Beadel-Muffet's public appearances with seeming inevitability. His attempts to lie low are frustrated by the obsessive detail with which the press records his movements:

Sir A. B. C. Beadel-Muffet K.C.B., M.P. had returned on Monday from Undertone, where Lord and Lady Wispers had, from the previous Friday, enter-tained a very select party; . . . Sir A. B. C. Beadel-Muffet K.C.B., M.P. had kindly consented to preside on Wednesday, at Samaritan House, at the opening of the sale of work of the Middlesex Incurables. (52)

Here James hints that we should pay attention to the 'undertones' and 'whispers' we might associate with the name of 'Middlesex Incurables', but tells us no more about them; he is inviting a sophisticated readership to enjoy the pleasures of queer reading.

Just as 'Sir Henry Ashton' in *The Picture of Dorian Gray* leaves England with a tarnished name, and Lord Arthur Somerset flees to the continent to escape prosecution, Sir A. B. C. Beadel-Muffet K.C.B., M.P. disappears, but the invisibility of his physical body is matched only by the ubiquity of his name in the Papers, which 'fairly raged' with the 'question of his whereabouts, of his antecedents, of his habits, of his possible motives, of his probable, or improbable, embarrassments', with 'very wonderful' 'rumours and remarks' and 'wild surmises' (67–8). The Papers rage more loudly still when they finally produce Beadel-Muffet's body, and can describe 'the rich grim fact . . . lighting into blood-colour the locked room, finally, with the police present, forced open, of the first hotel at Frankfort-on-the-Oder' (91). Maud Blandy is shaken by this

fact . . . that she had in her eyes . . . the vision of the scene in the little German city: the smashed door, the exposed horror, the wondering, insensible group, the English gentleman, in the disordered room, driven to bay among the scattered personal objects that only too floridly announced and emblazoned him, and several of which the Papers were already naming – the poor English gentleman, hunted and hiding, done to death by the thing he yet, for so long, always *would* have, and stretched on the floor with his beautiful little revolver still in his hand and the effusion of his blood, from a wound taken, with rare resolution, full in the face, extraordinary and dreadful. (94)

This chillingly humourous passage writes queer suicide as a homoerotic act, floridly announcing and emblazoning instead of diverting attention from its compromised victim. Its melodramatic tone perfectly anticipates queer blackmail films of the 1960s such as *Victim* (1961) or *The Children's Hour* (1962). The shocking death becomes newspaper fodder; the moral issues of Beadel-Muffet's suicide become, in James's analysis of the press, secondary to the potential for sensationalism in his violent mode of death.[13] The papers are figured as devouring animals, 'roar[ing] and resound[ing] more than ever with the new meat flung to them' (103); this metaphor recalls the beastly language James used to describe witnesses in the Wilde trials, and is typical of his resentment of the growing intrusiveness of modern life.

James's critique of the turn of the century culture of celebrity and publicity is pointed, then, and would be even more specific to his most knowing readers. After Beadel-Muffet's suicide, the hawkers are roaring new headlines: 'The Beadel-Muffet Mystery, Startling Disclosures, Action of the Treasury' (106). Here James refers quite specifically to allegations made by Alfred Douglas in 1896 in articles in the *Mercure de France* and *La Revue Blanche*. Regenia Gagnier discusses Douglas's claims in her book *Idylls of the Marketplace*. Douglas wrote that Wilde's enemies and Queensberry threatened the Liberal government with compromising disclosures unless Wilde were found guilty: 'The mock moralists threatened a series of actions against members of the government which would have produced a scandal without precedent. If Oscar Wilde were found guilty and punished, there would be an end of the matter.'[14] Gagnier adds that More Adey, a close friend of Robert Ross (Wilde's first lover, and a friend of James), 'wrote but did not send a letter that supports Douglas's allegations':

I am certain that the Treasury were forced by a body of private persons ... headed by the infamous Lord Queensberry, to obtain a conviction by some means or other against Mr. Wilde. These individuals, I believe, *blackmailed* the Treasury, holding over the Treasury the threat that, if Wilde were not convicted, damning evidence would be produced against important and exalted persons.[15]

It seems we have here the source for the Papers' 'Startling Disclosures, Action of the Treasury', yet the full content of the Papers' claims do not find their way into the tale, which swerves back into a comic register. (This kind of swerve supports Regenia Gagnier's view of James as one of the 'subtlest authors' of the fin de siècle, who 'could employ the decadent themes of the time and remain above suspicion.')[16] 'The Papers' ends with the 'Tremenjous Sensation!' – the 'Return of Beadel-Muffet' to 'splendidly explain' questions such as '*Who was the dead man in the locked hotel room?*' – and with Maud Blandy's conviction that Mrs Chorner will '[n]ow, at any rate . . . marry him', just as Maud decides to marry the comparatively feminine Howard Blight. The tale's 'undertones' and 'whispers', however, show James ironically mocking the terms of 'decency' and sexual prurience of fin de siècle England, and the manipulation of secrets and scandals for political ends. If the tale ends with a marriage – and Maud and Howard are in many ways ideal companions – marriage itself has become, in the tale, a mere item of publicity, in the service of professional, social and financial status.

Wilde plays a comic, spectral role in another tale near the turn of the century. James's 'In the Cage', of 1898, a tale of potential blackmail in which a female telegraph clerk working in Mayfair obtains compromising information about her aristocratic customers, again comments ironically on an England which is both sexually censorious and addicted to sexual sensationalism. As Eric Savoy has recently argued, the Cleveland Street Scandals and the Wilde trials make up the tale's 'historical register': the tale interrogates the 'sexual panic and class panic' generated by these scandals.[17] Having established that one of her clients, 'Captain Everard', is involved in an affair with the married 'Lady Bradeen', the (nameless) telegraph clerk comes to fear that she will be 'pounced upon for some lurid connection with a scandal' (*CT* 10:224). The telegraphist's knowledge is threatening to the two aristocrats, and Everard offers her sovereigns in an effort to try and keep her quiet – although he has misunderstood her, as she has had no intention to betray them. Betrayal is for her not a concrete intention but a fantasy. She dreams of saying to Everard, 'I know too much about a certain person now not to put it to you – excuse my being so lurid – that it's quite worth your while to buy me off. Come, therefore, buy me!' (176). When she shows her mastery of the situation by pointing out to Lady Bradeen errors in a coded telegram she had wanted to send, she is figured in terms recalling those James uses to describe the 'little beasts of witnesses . . . a nest of almost infant blackmailers' of the Wilde trials:[18] 'It was as if she had bodily leaped – cleared the top of the cage and alighted on her interlocutress' (182). As he does in 'The Papers', James preserves the comic register in 'In the Cage', averting the impact of scandal with the convenient death of Lord Bradeen. Yet the tale's exploration of the ethical questions and the potential abuses of power arising from sexual curiosity and black-mail is profound; it diagnoses anxieties at the centre of Britain's newly emerging queer culture.[19]

II MELANCHOLIA AND SUICIDE: 'A ROUND OF VISITS' AND 'THE ALTAR OF THE DEAD'

Suicide involves the body at war with itself, just as fin de siècle tales of queer doubling show egos at war with alter egos, selves attempting to repudiate and destroy 'others' who bear shameful, stigmatized identity traits. If the paranoid homosexual wages war with a spectral double, the melancholic homosexual loathes himself. Freud, in his 1917 essay 'Mourning and Melancholia', speculated that melancholia arose when the subject's ambivalent feelings towards a lost loved object (which could be an object which the subject forbids himself) frustrated the 'normal', healthy process of mourning in which

the existence of the lost object is psychically prolonged. Each single one of the memories and expectations in which the libido is bound to the object is brought up and hypercathected, and detachment of the libido is accomplished . . . the ego becomes free and uninhibited again.[20]

Melancholia, according to Freud, is a 'pathological disposition' (*MM* 252), in which the ability of the self to function breaks down. He writes that

The distinguishing mental features of melancholia are a profoundly painful dejection, cessation of interest in the outside world, loss of the capacity to love, inhibition of all activity, and a lowering of the self-regarding feelings to a degree that finds utterance in self-reproaches and self-revilings, and culminates in a delusional expectation of punishment. (*MM* 252)

Although 'inhibition and loss of interest are fully accounted for by the work of mourning . . . [t]he melancholic displays something else besides, which is lacking in mourning – an extraordinary diminution in his self-regard, an impoverishment of his ego on a grand scale' (*MM* 254).

Freud's theory suggests that homosexuals, at least in a homophobic social order, will be predisposed towards melancholia. Judith Butler has clearly described the different implications of Freud's theory for frustrated heterosexual and homosexual bonds:

In the case of a prohibited heterosexual union, it is the object which is denied, but not the modality of desire . . . But in the case of a prohibited homosexual union, . . . both the desire and the object require renunciation and so become subject to the internalizing strategies of melancholia.[21]

This consequence of Freud's theory was recognized by Freud himself, when he speculated that his 'theory would require . . . that the disposition to fall ill of melancholia (or some part of that disposition) lies in the predominance of the narcisstic type of object choice' (*MM* 259). (As Laplanche and Pontalis have noted, Freud first used the term narcissism 'to account for object-choice in homosexuals'.)[22] Noting that 'the melancholic's erotic cathexis in regard to his object has . . . undergone a double vicissitude: part of it has regressed to identification, but the other part, under the influence of the conflict due to ambivalence, has been carried back to the stage of sadism which is nearer to that conflict', Freud argues that '[i]t is this sadism alone that solves the riddle of the tendency to suicide which makes melancholia so interesting – and so dangerous' (*MM* 261). If his analysis of melancholia seems to invite a linkage of homosexuality and suicide, this linkage may be read both as historical commentary and as an account of the psychic difficulty in occupying a homosexual position.

One might expect then that queer melancholia would not be found where same-sex affection is affirmed, but where it is denied, or where its status is uncertain. In James's late tales, bonds between men are so often sites of tangled ambiguity, fraught mixtures of identification, love, hatred, reproach, cameraderie and denial: can one find in these tales an exploration of the dynamics of 'queer melancholia'? Consider the illness which lays up Mark Monteith, the protagonist of 'A Round of Visits', James's last tale, first published in 1910. Monteith has returned to New York from London to look into 'the dismal subject of his anxiety', and manages to gather information which 'measured his loss, measured, above all, his pain' (*CT* 12:427). As Mark absorbs the 'two things' he has heard, 'though both bad, one much worse than the other', he comes to know 'himself for so badly wounded', and gains a 'sense, together, of a blinding New York blizzard and of a deep sore inward ache' (427). Monteith is suffering because his friend Phil Bloodgood has betrayed him financially, yet, in Monteith's account of the situation, what is so hurtful about this betrayal is not 'the beastly values themselves', but 'the horror of *his* having done it, and done it to *me*' (430).

Like Freud's melancholic, Monteith suffers not only from self-reproach, but from a disgust in what Freud calls 'the outside world', which anthropomorphically takes on gruesome symptoms of his own disorder. Monteith finds nothing that might encourage him to participate in or take a libidinal interest in his environment. Instead he withdraws into an engagement with a highly ambivalent incorporated form of the lost erotic object, feels himself in charge of some horrid alien thing, some violent, scared, unhappy creature whom there was small joy, of a truth, in remaining with, but whose behaviour wouldn't perhaps bring him under notice, nor otherwise compromise him, so long as he should stay to watch it. A young jibbering ape of one of the more formidable sorts, or an ominous infant panther smuggled into the great gaudy hotel and whom it might yet be important he shouldn't advertise, couldn't have affected him as needing more domestic attention. (427–8)

The kind of 'ominous infant panther' which one might smuggle into a hotel and which should not be advertised is suggested by Wilde's *De Profundis*: in a famous passage, Wilde notes that 'to have entertained at dinner the evil things of life, and to have found pleasure in their company . . . was like feasting with panthers'.[23]

Monteith's illness takes the form of a bad 'throat and a probable temperature', and the location of the symptom in the mouth helps account for the orality of Monteith's name, as well as the filling good bloodiness of the name of his friend. These associations are brought together as Monteith looks at the photograph of Bloodgood he has displayed in his hotel room:

It was *because* [Phil Bloodgood] was so beautifully good-looking, because he was so charming and clever and frank – besides being one's third cousin, or whatever it was, one's early school-fellow and one's later college classmate – that one had abjectly trusted him. To live thus with his unremoved, undestroyed, engaging, treacherous face, had been, as our traveller desired, to live with all of the felt pang; had been to consume it in such a single hot, sore mouthful as would so far as possible dispose of it and leave but cold dregs. (429)

Monteith goes to visit an old acquaintance, Newton Winch, who is also laid up in bed. He remembers Winch 'as constitutionally common, as consistently and thereby doubtless even rather powerfully coarse, clever only for uncouth and questionable things' (41). Together in Winch's apartment, the two men try to find out as much as possible about each other while revealing as little as they can about themselves; yet this anxious probing is flirtatious:

'Well,' Mark kept on, 'to try and make out with him how, after such things – !' But he stopped; he couldn't name them.

It was as if his companion knew. 'Such things as you've done for him, of course – such services as you've rendered him.'

'Ah, from far back. If I could tell you,' our friend vainly wailed – 'if I could tell you!'

Newton Winch patted his shoulder. 'Tell me – tell me!'

'The sort of relation, I mean; ever so many things of a kind – !' Again, however, he pulled up; he felt the tremor of his voice.

'Tell me, tell me,' Winch repeated with the same movement.

The tone in it now made their eyes meet again, and with this presentation of the altered face Mark measured as not before, for some reason, the extent of the recent ravage. 'You must have been ill indeed.' (452)

This meeting is further complicated by the news Newton Winch has to tell Monteith: that he is 'worse' than Bloodgood, but unlike Bloodgood, who has deserted New York, he has 'stayed to take it' (457). The story ends with two police officers demanding entry into Winch's apartment, to discover what can now be recognized as an archetypal scene of queer suicide: 'their rush availed little; Newton was stretched on his back before the fire; he had held the weapon horribly to his temple, and his upturned face was disfigured' (459).

James, like Freud, is as interested in the psychic states accompanying such suicides as in the suicide itself. Recent cultural analysis of the work of mourning, in queer theory and in writing on AIDS, has tended to affirm the importance of Freud's identification of melancholia as a state in which a sadistic attitude directed towards an incorporated object doubles as masochistic self-destruction. Leo Bersani, Douglas Crimp and Tim Dean are only three scholars who have recently looked to Freud in order to ask questions about responses to AIDS.[24] Dean characterizes 'the American response to AIDS as psychotic', and writes:

Ambivalence toward the object of love may indeed be endemic to any love relation, yet Freud emphasizes ambivalence as one of the prerequisites for the transformation of mourning into melancholia. How much more ambivalent must homosexual love be in a homophobic culture, and therefore how much more prone to melancholic identification – and the subsequent unleashing of murderous aggression – must gay men be in the age of AIDS?[25]

A whole series of further questions emerges from this. How, for instance, is it possible to mourn a lost loved object when the bond between subject and object is proscribed? The question might be differently posed in relation to James's fiction: how is it possible to mourn a lost loved object when the bond between subject and object lacks an adequate signifier? Is it possible to mourn a bond which cannot be named, which is subject to psychic censorship? Another question compounds the problem. Is the homosexual subject free from or isolated from the homophobia which characterizes her culture? And, if not, will ambivalence, a commingling of love and hatred, characterize every homosexual bond and remain after loss to frustrate mourning? Remarkably, all of these questions are addressed in James's 'The Altar of the Dead'.

James conceived of and wrote 'The Altar of the Dead' in 1894. The tale was first published in 1895 in the volume poignantly entitled *Terminations*.

At this time, the circle of male literary figures in London which included James and which made a major contribution to the shaping of modern conceptions of the 'homosexual'[26] – men like Howard Sturgis, Robert Ross and Edmund Gosse – was watching with fascination the train of events which was to lead up to the Wilde trials of 1895. 'The Altar of the Dead' is one of James's first tales which takes homosexuality as its (more or less unambiguous) subject matter – an earlier example is of course 'The Pupil' of 1891, which describes a passionate bond between a tutor and his boy charge. This is not to say that homoerotic tension is not present throughout much of his earlier short fiction: rather, that in 'The Altar of the Dead' a notion of homosexual identity is at stake as opposed to the sporadic expression of homoerotic desire, and that relations between men in this tale are more easily recognizable as 'homosexual'. A further refinement is necessary: the tale interrogates the *possibility* of expression of homosexual identity; it does not merely 'represent' such an identity, but questions the psychic consequences of the difficulties of such a representation. This interrogation needs to be viewed as part of a dynamic cultural process rather than as an isolated incident.

Just over a year before James wrote 'The Altar of the Dead' Edmund Gosse had lent him J. A. Symonds' *A Problem in Modern Ethics*; in returning Symonds' study, James referred to it as 'those marvellous outpourings' and an 'infinitely remarkable' 'exhibition'.[27] 'The Altar of the Dead' addresses the specifically modern 'problem' of homosexual identity which Symonds takes as the subject of his writing. The tale returns to territory James had established in novels like *Roderick Hudson*, *The Princess Casamassima* and *The Bostonians*, all of which deal with difficult same-sex friendships or 'passions'. However, a crucial shift registers the new awareness of homosexual identities in 1890s Britain. Whereas the three novels present same-sex affection boldly, and foreground the absence of a space in which such affection might be acknowledged as constituting an important, lasting bond, 'The Altar of the Dead' describes a context in which same-sex affection cannot be acknowledged. Same-sex affection itself is subject to prohibition, and James analyses the force of this prohibition in what is his most forceful and perceptive presentation of melancholia. The story anticipates Freud's analysis of the role played by the affect of mourning in identity-construction, and his identification of melancholia as a failed mourning, and joins Freud in exploring a queer context for melancholia.

James's preface to 'The Altar of the Dead' contains one of the rare occasions in the New York prefaces when his focus shifts from aesthetic and critical concerns to an issue which is overtly political. James complains that London society shows too great an indifference to the dead. Remembering the dead, he insists, is not a 'morbid' or sentimental ritual but a vital social task – yet 'to be caught in any rueful glance at [the dead] was to be branded at once as "morbid"'. James writes that '[t]he sense of the state of the dead is but part of the sense of the state of the living; and, congruously with that, life is cheated to almost the same degree of the finest homage (precisely this our possible friendships and intimacies) that we fain would render it' (*AN* 244–5).

Although James's preface inveighs against what he calls 'the awful doom of general dishumanisation' (*AN* 245), his tale implies that, even among this pervasive malaise, different situations pose different challenges to mourning. Freud's 'Mourning and Melancholia' makes the now classic remark that 'people never willingly abandon a libidinal position' (*MM* 253). In the state of melancholia, the subject can neither relinquish a hopeless libidinal position, nor transfer the highly cathected libido bound up in that position to another position. Compare with this the question James asks in the preface: 'it was impossible for any critic or "creator" at all worth his wage not, as a matter of course, again and again to ask himself what may not become of individual sensibility, of the faculty and the fibre itself, when everything makes against the indulgence of it save as a conscious, and indeed highly emphasised, dead loss' (*AN* 242).

George Stransom, the tale's protagonist, is a subject who can only indulge his sensibility as 'a conscious, and indeed highly emphasised, dead loss'. Stransom is shocked to see that others do, in fact, mourn and form other relations. Early in the tale he meets Paul Creston, who has re-married, and is disgusted at what he perceives as disloyalty to the first Mrs Creston, as a discrepancy between the cheerful man he meets and 'the different face, the wholly other face the poor man had shown him last, the blurred, ravaged mask bent over the open grave by which they had stood together' (*CT* 9:234). 'Creston was not in mourning now', the tale continues, and Stransom's disposition to melancholia is hinted at by his refusal to accept what he perceives as the 'frivolity, the indecency' of mourning completed (237).

Stransom's dismay is soon compounded by his discovering, from a newspaper article, the death of his former friend, Sir Acton Hague, K.C.B. Hague has died from 'the bite of a poisonous snake': the sexual innuendo attached to his mode of death is strengthened by a number of hints that punctuate the tale. Reading the article Stransom feels 'relief at the absence of any mention of their quarrel, an incident accidentally tainted at the time, thanks to their joint immersion in large affairs, with a horrible publicity' (237). As is common in James, business activity and financial connection have erotic overtones. The 'publicity' given their quarrel is a violation to intimate rather than professional bonds: Stransom feels he has suffered a 'wrong', an 'insult ... blankly taken from the only man with whom he had ever been intimate; the friend, almost adored, of his University years, the subject, later, of his passionate loyalty' (237). We have here some typical delicately nuanced Jamesian innuendos. Following a description of Kate Creston as 'the only *woman* for whom [Stransom] might perhaps have been unfaithful', Hague is referred to as 'the only *man* with whom he had ever been intimate' (236–7; my emphasis). Further, the quarrel has mixed privacy and publicity: '[t]he shock of interests had been private, intensely so; but the action taken by Hague had been in the face of men' (237). Already the question needs to be asked: was this scandal a (homo)sexual scandal?

Stransom transforms a small chapel of a suburban Roman Catholic church into his own mourning-altar, an altar devoted in particular to his dead fiancée, Mary Antrim, but also dedicated to the many friends of his who are inevitably dying, seeing that he 'had entered that dark defile of our earthly descent in which some one dies every day' (242). He is figured as a Christ-like 'shepherd of a huddled flock, with all a shepherd's vision of differences imperceptible' (242). However, 'there were gaps in the constellation', gaps which are, moreover, not arbitrary, but pointed: the altar is remarkable for its one exclusion: '[t]he greatest blank in the shining page was the memory of Acton Hague, of which he inveterately tried to rid himself. For Acton Hague no flame could ever rise on any altar of his' (243).

Stransom's involvement with his altar is strongly eroticized. His first entry into the church is figured as a penetration, a lifting of veils (a 'leathern curtain' beyond which there is 'a glimpse of an avenue of gloom with a glow of tapers at the end' (238)) the passing of which enables him to quit 'the great grey suburb and come nearer to the warm centre' (239). He is at once struck by 'the sombre presence of a woman, in mourning unrelieved', and expresses a desire to occupy *her* position: 'He wished he could sink, like her, to the very bottom, be as motionless, as rapt in prostration' (239).[28] Stransom and the woman (who remains nameless) form a bond in which 'they grew quite intimate' over 'the idea that they didn't care for each other'. Rather they are drawn to each other because they 'feel deeply together about certain things wholly distinct from themselves' (248).

Ironically, they do not know how similar the 'certain things' they both care about are. Only when Stransom visits his friend's home after her aunt's death, and sees Hague's picture on the wall, does he realize that all of her candles have been lit for Hague, just as Hague is the one person for whom he has refused to light a candle. The story develops into a contest for the right to mourn the dead man. The woman insists that Stransom 'give [Hague] his candle' (258), thereby forgiving Hague and giving him the same status as Stransom's other mourned friends. Stransom, meanwhile, realizing the depths of the woman's intimacy with Hague, experiences 'a chill . . . like an ague in which he had to make an effort not to shake' (258). He learns that the woman had not wanted him to learn from her aunt what Hague had done to her (259). The unspeakability shrouding Hague's injuries to them both – 'from Acton Hague any injury was credible', the woman 'convey[s] with exquisite mildness' to Stransom (255) – hints at a reciprocating symmetry in their stories. Hague had ended their friendship 'in the face of men': it seems Hague may have publicly made indecent suggestions about Stransom. This helps explain Stransom's relief that 'no mention of their quarrel' was made in the reports of Hague's death (237). Similarly, the woman's fear that her aunt may betray something ignominious about Hague's treatment of her makes it seem possible that Hague had in fact left her for a man. This possibility is supported by Stransom's consideration that 'of [Acton's] previous life she should have ascertained only what [Hague] had judged good to communicate. There were passages it was quite conceivable that even in moments of the tenderest expansion he should have withheld . . . A man, in her place, would have "looked up" the past – would even have consulted old newspapers' (259).[29] (The woman, we are told, had 'lived apart from public affairs' (259).) Asking himself what form the rupture between Hague and the woman might have taken, Stransom 'made . . . out that this relation of Hague's, whatever it was, could only have been a deception finely practised . . . Stransom knew enough of his other ties, of his obligations and appearances, not to say enough of his general character, to be sure there had been some infamy. In one way or another the poor woman had been coldly sacrificed' (264).

That is to say, the condition of shared widowhood Stransom and his female friend have been enjoying so long as their mourned objects remained anonymous collapses when they find that they are both 'widow' to the same man. Each reminds each other of what they had found most disagreeable in Hague: his lack of commitment not only to their person, but to their gender. James's freedom is not curtailed but enhanced by this schema. James can convey both characters' attachment to Hague indirectly: the story can convey that both attachments are erotic by showing how jealous the characters are of each other. 'Acton Hague was between them, that was the essence of the matter; and he was never so much between

them as when they were face to face' (263). Stransom wants to know everything about her relationship with Hague, even if this knowledge should
make him miserable: 'He had never for a moment admitted that he was in
love with her; therefore nothing could have surprised him more than to
discover that he was jealous. What but jealousy could give a man that sore,
contentious wish to have the detail of what would make him suffer?' (263)

Yet, as James's description of the woman makes clear, and as subsequent
accounts of mimetic desire would confirm, in any triangular rivalry the
rival can always become the object of desire. If one's partner desires
another, then mimesis, or identification, makes that other an object of
hatred and of desire. The story notes that 'the woman with whom
[Stransom] had had for years so fine a point of contact was a woman
whom Acton Hague, of all men in the world, had more or less fashioned'.
Freud's account of mourning and identity-formation is implicit in the
story's claim that 'Such as she sat there to-day, she was ineffaceably
stamped with [Hague]' (260). Just when the demands of exclusive constructions of sexuality intervene in Stransom's and the woman's friendship,
challenging both of their claims on the dead Acton Hague, the instability
of identity and desire propels them together. The self-sufficiency of
Stransom's sexuality is undermined as it is unclear who has the strongest
claim on his affections: his dead fiancée, Acton Hague, or the woman he
has met in the chapel. To the extent that her identity is shaped by Hague,
Stransom's desire for Hague tips over into desire for the woman; and as a
love-object of Hague's, she becomes an object of Stransom's desire through
the workings of mimesis. Moreover, the woman's whole-hearted mourning for Hague is de-stabilized by Stransom's obviously peculiar relationship to him. What Judith Butler calls a 'heterosexual matrix' assumes the
separability of identification and desire: for the boy, identification with the
father initiates desire for the woman.[30] In this messy triangle, however,
desire and identification are hopelessly confused. How 'identity' might be
shaped out of these knotty entanglements is the very problem set up by
the tale, the problem needing to be solved so that some kind of narrative
resolution might be reached.

Stransom responds to the crisis by making what Freud calls, in discussions of hysteria, a 'flight into sickness'. 'His irritation took the form of
melancholy', James writes, 'and his melancholy that of the conviction that
his health had quite failed' (266). Like the malady of Mark Monteith of
'A Round of Visits', Stransom's illness arises from the ambivalence obtain-
ing between him and the loved object in a context where both affection
and object are subject to shame. The difficulty of mourning Acton Hague,

the tale implies, is a difficulty arising from a particular social arrangement, a kinship structure privileging certain bonds at the expense of other repudiated bonds.

Hence it is interesting that the story foregrounds a process of legitimization, centred on the Church. The Catholic chapel gives Stransom the opportunity to establish 'rites more public', rites legitimized by the approval of the Church's 'bland ecclesiastics' and the 'delightfully human' Bishop (240). The Roman Catholic Church is of course one of the most powerful Western institutions involved in the supervision of kinship and the administration of mourning rituals. This constitutes the Church's attraction to Stransom: it bestows on him a space 'consecrated to an ostensible and customary worship' (241).

Stransom's project is similar then to the American Names Project and the AIDS quilt, which aim to supplement a lack in American institutional life, to assert the importance of and provide a prominent cultural face for mourning deaths from AIDS. Peter S. Hawkins claims that 'the NAMES Project may well have invented a hybrid form that owes as much to war memorials as to traditional quilting – a "folk art" made for the mass audience of the late twentieth century . . . [T]he AIDS Quilt has in effect made intimacy its object; it has enabled quite private reality (sometimes sentimental and homey, sometimes kinky and erotic) to "come out" in public'.[31] Now in refusing to allot Acton Hague any space on his altar, Stransom is also refusing such a 'coming out' gesture, a gesture which is at once historical impossibility and psychic necessity.

James's use of fantasy and camp enables him to address apparently contradictory demands – the demands of a social structure that Stransom's bond to Hague be refused legitimization, and the psychic demands that the bond be acknowledged in order that Hague may be mourned, may take his place on the altar. The altar bridges private and public, but does so in according public respect to private sentiments rather than subjecting these sentiments to the scandalizing gaze of the press. Stransom tells his friend that his 'chapel will never be full till a candle is set up before which all the others will pale' (250). By this he means '[his] own' candle (250), but the absence which comes to be painfully felt by Stransom is the absence of a candle for Hague.

Stransom wants his altar to have the same aesthetic qualities which James, according to the account he gives of his fiction in the New York prefaces, wants to give to the novel: symmetry, harmony, a resolution of whole and component parts. He is striving for what Leo Bersani calls a 'redemptive aesthetic', that is, a cultural symbolization seen as 'essentially ·

reparative'.[32] 'Symmetry was harmony', Stransom notes, and 'harmony was of course everything. He took, in fancy, his composition to pieces, redistributing it into other lines, making other juxtapositions and contrasts. He shifted this and that candle, he made the spaces different, he effaced the disfigurement of a possible gap'. Yet he cannot avoid 'moments in which he . . . catch[es] a glimpse of the void so sensible to the woman who wandered in exile or sat where he had seen her with the portrait of Acton Hague'. To arrive at his 'conception of the total, the ideal' he is faced with the need of adding 'just another figure': ' "Just one more – to round it off; just one more, just one," continued to hum itself in his head.' This murmur, 'just one more', echoes repeatedly in the closing paragraphs of the tale. In other words, Stransom's structure can only be complete if it can incorporate the shameful, ugly, unspeakable attachment he wishes to exclude (268).

Ghost tale, fairy tale, 'The Altar of the Dead' moves from the non-performativity of Stransom's melancholia to close in that most performative and utopian of modes, camp. Stransom's last visit to his altar reads like a Sirkian melodrama, complete with all the trimmings, such as 'a passion of light' and 'a choir of angels' (271). Anticipating later camp and homoerotic appropriations of Catholic iconography (most notorious in Ronald Firbank's fiction), James brings Stransom to the angel who can prepare him to accommodate Hague. His dead fiancée Mary Antrim, in the guise of Virginal (and libidinal) Mother, 'smiled at him from the glory of heaven – she brought the glory down with her to take him . . . In the midst of his joy . . . he felt his buried face grow hot as with some communicated knowledge that had the force of a reproach. It suddenly made him contrast that very rapture with the bliss he had refused to another. This breath of the passion immortal was all that other had asked; the descent of Mary Antrim opened his spirit with a great compunctious throb for the descent of Acton Hague' (270). Mary's divine intervention and sanction enable him to accomplish the identification he had always been wanting to make, to attain the masochistic ecstasy of the 'prostrate figure, . . . a woman in deep mourning, bowed in grief or in prayer' (270). He is able to fulfil the desire he felt when he first saw the mourning woman, the desire to 'sink, like her, to the very bottom, be as motionless, as rapt in prostration' (239).

James's use of camp assigns the fulfilment of Stransom's desire to an unrealized space, a 'historical moment' yet to arrive. In his portrayal of Stransom James comments on the difficulties arising from the foreclosure of homoerotic possibilities, and examines the ills attending any construction of sexuality depending on repudiation and exclusion. If J. A. Symonds's writings anticipate the rhetoric of gay liberation, a rhetoric which demands legal and civil rights for a homosexual subject assumed to be self-sufficient, James's fiction seems to imply that the very construction of a 'homosexual subject' is fraught with difficulty, that the assertion of a 'homosexual identity' is a project doomed to failure within our present social arrangement.

A sexual identity cannot admit proscribed bonds without a sense of panic or shame: to acknowledge such bonds without anxiety would only be possible with what Judith Butler, in *Gender Trouble*, calls 'an alternative logic of kinship'.[33] James's fiction sets itself the task of imagining such an alternative logic. 'The Altar of the Dead' uses any tools it can find to tackle this task – parodic subversion, fictional fantasy – and in doing so makes a break with its own narrative procedure, as it swings out of a realist mode into comic melodrama. This switch in mode enables the story to escape the law of prohibition which governs its own production. George Stransom's 'great compunctious throb for the descent of Acton Hague' constitutes the performative enactment of a marriage ceremony joining two men in the arms of that omnipotent body which offers or denies recognition to human relationships: the Roman Catholic church. If the tale implies that the very construction of a 'homosexual subject' is fraught with difficulty, it does not ascribe this difficulty to an inherent pathology of homoerotic desire, but to the fact that same-sex desire has no adequate symbolization. James is asking whether the stringent conditions of masculine entitlement in late Victorian culture can be reconciled with an acknowledgement of emotional and erotic affiliations such entitlement appears to foreclose.

'That queer monster the artist'

'It's, I suppose, because I am that queer monster the artist, an obstinate finality, an inexhaustible sensibility.'

James to Henry Adams, 29 March 1914[1]

In the preceding pages we have seen how James's fiction negotiates the thrills and ravages and difficulties of sexual identity and of the failure of identity, working through masochistic fantasy, the melancholia of systemic prohibition, and the shame and *frisson* of transgressive sexual desires. We have noted how the fiction names that which should not be named and creates a poetics of the obscene at odds with its perfectly genteel surface. These poetic figurations of the queer body and of transgressive desires are surprising in a corpus of writing frequently regarded as sexually timid, and lie like violent surprises, fractures, land mines in a deceptively serene landscape.

These faultlines might open up a biographical question: could James have been aware of the extreme eroticism contained on the figurative surface of his prose? Such a question might be asked of James's earliest fiction. Leon Edel writes that *Watch and Ward*, his first novel, written in 1870, contains 'persistent erotic imagery and innocent erotic statement which seems to have been set down with bland unconsciousness on the author's part'.[2] Here the 'seems' acknowledges, however, that the 'unconsciousness' is hypothesized by the critic. Perhaps James, at twenty-seven, was not so naive. The extreme self-consciousness of James's late writing – the way in which the fiction humourously alludes to the unsaid or that which is nearly said – suggests an authorial irony, one aspect of which is the author's own absence and consequent inability to verify whether or not the fiction means what it appears to be meaning.[3]

Yet a consideration of the vexed question of James's biography can only take us so far. For a notion of James's personal capabilities should not predetermine our reading of his fiction, or we risk missing its daring negotiations with the forbidden. If we consider rather that 'identity' might be worked out (rather than expressed) within a text, then the transgressive eroticism cutting across the genteel surface of the Jamesian text might measure the failure of identity, in so far as identity acknowledges constraints, injunctions and the social ordering of sexual relations according to gender and kinship. Yet such a 'failure' might lead to a reworking of identity along other lines. The performativity of James's text might include a dismantling and rebuilding of identity – of a queer identity, an identity which will include the repudiated, the transgressive, the taboo. Hence the swing, at the close of 'The Altar of the Dead', from the melancholia and shame of unacknowledged, forbidden, scandalous desire, to the camp incorporation of the pariah in Stransom's altar. Hence the breaking and remaking of the bowl, the remaking of Maggie Verver's marriage based on a changed perception of the relation between herself and her husband, and an acknowledgement of the flaws inherent in the structure of marriage itself.

The movement from a régime of prohibition and shame to a reworked symbolic order finds its fullest exploration in *The Ambassadors*. In the first chapter of this book I discussed how the London theatre reworks the laws of sexual difference for Lewis Lambert Strether. In the theatre, the Woollett, Massachusetts law of two, of 'two exactly', 'the male and the female', breaks down, is supplanted by 'a series of strong stamps'; Strether discovers that 'the personal and the sexual range ... might be greater or less'.[4] *The Ambassadors* is a comedy which notoriously doesn't end in marriage (just as John Little Bilham is ' "notoriously", as he put it himself, not from Boston' (70)); its comic movement leads Strether away not only from the heterosexual imperative and the birds and the bees of Woollett, but also from the stark oppositions of puritanism, into an exotic, accomodating, forgiving and permissive landscape. Paris, 'the great ironic city' (65), is a 'vast bright Babylon, like some huge iridescent object, a jewel brilliant and hard, in which parts were not to be discriminated nor differences comfortably marked. It twinkled and trembled and melted together, and what seemed all surface one moment seemed all depth the next' (59). In Paris duty and obligation don't need to be resisted, for they fall away: Little Bilham, for instance, 'had an occupation, but it was only an occupation declined; and it was by his general exemption from alarm, anxiety or remorse on this score that the impression of his serenity was made' (82). Just as Henry James appreciates the 'tragic or ironic (or even comic) felicity' of 'dear, queer, deeply individual + homogeneous W. H. P. [Pater]', Strether takes pleasure in 'the delicate daubs and free discriminations' of Little Bilhams's 'quaint and queer and dear and droll' friends, who 'twanged with a vengeance the esthetic lyre' (83). Miss Barrace of Paris calls Waymarsh of Milrose, Connecticut 'a type, the grand old American – what shall one call it? The Hebrew prophet, Ezekiel, Jeremiah' (75). She might be Salome appraising John the Baptist, but Miss Barrace does not want Waymarsh's fine pate upon a platter. Her appreciation of Waymarsh is benign – 'the sight of him warms my poor old chilled heart' – and she admires his 'sombre glow', not knowing 'that what was behind it was his grave estimate of her laxity' (75).

It is of course possible to discern an embodied homoerotic thematics in *The Ambassadors*, but here I'd like simply to note the novel's spirit of camp affirmation in the face of prohibition and restraint. While Strether learns so much from Little Bilham and his circle, he also has much to teach, and his instruction, in the novel's most famous speech, is to 'Live as you can; it's a mistake not to ... The right time is *any* time that one is still so lucky as to have' (140). Henry James makes a similar speech, to Hugh Walpole, 'Belovedest little Hugh', 'my irrepressible Hugh', 'dearest, dearest Hugh', 'darling, darling little Hugh', 'D. D. L. H.', 'my damnedest little Hugh', 'Darlingest and delightfullest old Hugh'.[5] 'Cultivate with me, darlingest Hugh, the natural affections, so far as you are lucky enough to have matter for them.' James develops this at length:

Don't say to me, by the way, apropos of jinks – the 'high' kind that you speak of having so wallowed in previous to leaving town – that I ever challenge you as to *why* you wallow, or splash or plunge, or dizzily and sublimely soar (into the jinks element), or whatever you may call it: as if I ever remarked on anything but the absolute inevitability of it for you at your age and with your natural curiosities, as it were, and passions ... We must know, as much as possible, in our beautiful art, yours and mine, what we are talking about – and the only way to know is to have lived and loved and cursed and floundered and enjoyed and suffered. I think I don't regret a single 'excess' of my responsive youth – I only regret, in my chilled age, certain occasions and possibilities I *didn't* embrace. (21 August 1913, *Letters* 4:679–80)

This humourous and passionate *carpe diem* expresses beautifully the spirit of James's late letters, in which James pioneers and cultivates and develops an exquisitely refined camp prose and sensibility.

Why is camp peculiarly appropriate to the tribulations of *la vie gaie*? Because camp is ironic about prohibition. It knows that what we do is wrong, but shrugs its shoulders, raises its eyebrows (consider Eartha Kitt: she knows she's sinful, but this doesn't seem to bother her). Because camp, knowing that love will fail – how could it succeed? – is unperturbed, and remains faithful to the ideal of perfect love. (These are the lessons of *The*

Ambassadors, as learned and taught by Lewis Lambert Strether.) Hence camp allows one to be a tart without compromising one's romantic integrity.

Psychoanalysis shares much of camp's knowledge: love will fail, identification with the fantasmatic ideal will fail, the object of desire is impossible. Yet psychoanalysis and camp propose different solutions. Psychoanalysis recommends therapy and a reworking of trauma and pain, a long arduous battle. Camp offers compensatory fantasies – tomorrow, somewhere over the rainbow – and immediate, reliable gratifications – a martini, a cigarette, music. Psychoanalysis insists we cannot have what we most desire; camp knows we can't have it right now, but in the meantime suggests we try what's available. The psychoanalytic and puritan superego insists on the futility of our investments in glamour (Marlon Brando, Jimmy Dean . . .). Camp tells us we all can vogue, and realize glamour in our own lives. Camp is a disco lyric, and refuses to recognize imperfection.

Hence psychoanalytic readings of James's life emphasize renunciation, repression, fear, chastity – and unworldliness.[6] In his correspondence, however, James fashions himself in the spirit of camp affirmation. Sweeping aside the materiality and physicality of detail and fact, the letters – whether to A. C. Benson, Morton Fullerton, Howard Sturgis, Jonathan Sturges, Jocelyn Persse, Hugh Walpole, or Gaillard Lapsley – lavishly construct a fantasy of absolute devotion to the beautiful object. Whether the object reciprocates affection is of no importance, for James is the adorer, he emphasizes the beloved's charms, not his own. Physical expressions of affection are unchecked in these camp epistolary outpourings, untroubled by mundane circumstances such as the beloved's reluctance, embarrassment, nervousness, shyness, by the various ways desire can falter in the pressure of the moment.

Biography has shown itself preoccupied with the question of whether Henry James obtained physical gratification – genital sharing – in his relations with other men.[7] This question seems to be regarded as the litmus test of whether or not we can call Henry James 'homosexual'. Yet this preoccupation with James's sexual behaviour leads us away from a much more important and remarkable fact about James: within his own circle, James was increasingly daring in the way he constituted himself as a sexual and desiring subject, and acknowledged freely – indeed, with pleasure – that his desires were for (young and attractive) men. In homophobic turn-of-the-century Britain, verbal expressions of affection and erotic endearment between men required more courage than acts of physical gratification.

James's self-fashioning has an importance that goes beyond the question of his own biography, as it plays a role in the history of queer subjectivities: he should be regarded as a key figure in the development of modern camp. Here once more his relation with Oscar Wilde is important, for Wilde is camp's most prominent progenitor. As Gregory W. Bredbeck remarks, 'Wilde's almost mythical status as the origin of modern gay Camp has been constantly reinscribed'.[8] Wilde's influence on subsequent queer writers – from Ronald Firbank to Harvey Fierstein – is palpable. But James's influence on camp and queer writers is far from negligible – whether on writers of his immediate circle, such as E. F. Benson, Percy Lubbock, Sturgis, Wharton, or more distant admirers, such as Forster, Compton Mackenzie, Marcel Proust (who liked to tell a probably apocryphal tale of a fan letter received from James).[9]

James inaugurated his own mode of camp writing, which differs from Wilde's, even as the two are intimately related. It is easy to identify Wildean qualities in Jamesian camp, such as the witty, indulgent dialogue, or the admiration of powerful, desiring women (whether Mrs Brookenham of *The Awkward Age*, or friends like Edith Wharton and Jessie Allen, or historical figures like George Sand), whose example serves to make the lapses of men modest and timid. Always, however, James makes these qualities his own. Wildean camp is loud, flashy and aggressively clever; Jamesian camp is quiet, self-effacing and subtle. Wildean camp says: 'I said this, you didn't'; Jamesian camp says: 'I said this because of you and the inspiration you give me.' Wildean camp is 'in your face', the public act of queer defiance; Jamesian camp is of the nudging, hinting variety, and assumes its audience is complicit in naughtiness.

James developed and refined his camp style in letters to various beloveds, to fellow worshippers at the masculine shrine, such as Howard Sturgis (although the beloveds can also play the role of devotees), and to close women friends, like Edith Wharton and Elizabeth Jessie Jane Allen. The art of Jamesian camp is always to say the beautiful and witty thing, and in so doing draw attention to the utterance rather than the speaker, to the medium rather than to the message, as if the language is creating itself and we merely behold its playful and extravagant diversions. Writing to Wharton in 1909, James tells her, 'You are indeed my ideal of the dashing woman, and you never dashed more felicitously or fruitfully, for my imagination, than when you dashed, at that particular psychologic moment, off to dear old rococo Munich' (*Letters* 4:537). Here 'dash' seems to take over the sentence, the dashing rococo form of which seems to derive from Wharton's own flamboyant extravagance rather than from the writer's.

Such camp decorativeness – the creation of a narcissistic prose which draws attention to its own beauty rather than to the skills of its creator – is recognizable in James's late fiction, beginning in particular with *The Spoils of Poynton* and *What Maisie Knew* (both 1897). One notes for instance the extravagant length of James's extended metaphors, resulting in a prose which is densely cross-referenced. In *What Maisie Knew* we have the continual references to Ida Farange's billiard cue and balls, and a prose which is as illustrative of the workings of the mind as it is playful, as when Maisie uses a visit to the dentist's as 'a term of comparison for the screwed-up intensity' of her movements from one guardian to the other: 'the "arrangement", as her periodical uprootings were called, played the part of the horrible forceps'.[10]

This prose is camp because it is hedonistic: it is not in a hurry to get somewhere, but content to follow the various delights leading from its path. It is reverential in that it implies its subject requires grandeur. No situation is unfit for this luxuriant excess. Muir Mackenzie, appointed 'Hereditary Grand Governess' of the Lamb House garden, is apostrophized and apotheosized: 'You are grand indeed . . . We cling to you; we will walk but by your wisdom and live in your light; we cherish and inscribe on our precious records every word that drops from you' (15 June 1901, *Letters* IV, 190). The life and death of a dog should be suitably memorialized. Virginia Woolf knew that Flush, Elizabeth Barrett Browning's spaniel, deserved a whole book; J. R. Ackerley's German shepherd, Queenie, deserved two.[11] James similarly rose to the occasion on the death of Mitou, Edith Wharton's Pekingese (mourned by Nicette),[12] or of Clare Benedict's companion, Othello:

I send you both . . . my tenderest condolences on the death of poor little gallant, romantic Tello . . . [E]ven while I write, the companion of my so much tamer adventures (than yours and Tello's), *my* little terrier, Nicholas by name, . . . slumbers gently at my elbow, and making me doubly feel for you, reminds me of the frailty of these attachments. He has climbed into my best drawingroom armchair, pillowed his charming black-and-tan little impudent head on my most Pompadour cushion; and so, though he is old enough to know better, he asserts his youth and his impunity. But – on the other hand – while you were making Tello the cosmopolite of his race, I committed to earth the three valued friends whose names are inscribed on the small tomb-stones in my garden – so I know the particular pang of loss. (2 May 1902, *Letters* 4:228–9)

It goes beautifully on; it is difficult to stop quoting.

If a more comprehensive edition of James's letters should be published – of the nearly 12,000 letters in existence, a mere 2,000 are in print – James's camp style would emerge in fuller splendour. Lyall Powers' *Henry James and Edith Wharton: Letters: 1900–1915* showed the full extent of James's camp banter with Wharton – in James's mythology, the 'Angel of Devastation', or 'Alexandria the Great'. Their camp extravagance came into play not only in their discussions of George Sand's love life, but also in their figuration of Wharton's automobile as a motorcar named desire – the 'Chariot of Fire', the 'Vehicle of Passion'.[13] Wharton is a great American bird, and James is a humble, superannuated chook: 'so does a poor old croaking barnyard fowl advise a golden eagle!', I 'am as ungarnished in every way as an aged plucked fowl before the cook has dealt with him' (*Letters* 4:519, 573). Fripperies and frivolities abound in James's letters to Howard Sturgis and Jessie Allen. James's letters show his participation in a camp milieu, of shared gossip, in which friends' behaviour is subject to amused scrutiny. Here is James to Sturgis, in 1909: 'I daresay it is written in the book of fate that I shall even motor with [Wharton] to Folkestone and wait upon her departure there. The iridescent track of her Devastation – the phosphorescent lights of her wake – suffer, I suppose, at Qu'acre, gradual extinction' (*Letters* 4:525).

This flamboyance might be seen as the flipside of melancholia. If James shows himself afflicted by the melancholia of loneliness, then his camp writing persona abandons introspective consideration of his wounds to place the self in relation to the delights of the world, observing which the self is lost. Such delights might be the immoralities and desires of others, about which James shows himself endlessly curious, as when he hears from Hugh Walpole in 1914 that Walpole's father, Anglican Bishop at Edinburgh, had spoken disparagingly of Father John Gray – for whom Wilde named *The Picture of Dorian Gray* – and André Raffalovich. Walpole is reproached for not having said more: 'When you refer to their "immorality on stone floors," and with prayerbooks in their hands so long as the exigencies of the situation permit of the manual retention of the sacred volumes, I do so want the picture developed and the proceedings authenticated' (*Letters* 4:695). Here as so often the Jamesian euphemism – 'the exigencies of the situation' – highlights the indecency of the subject matter.

James's passionate addresses to young men are not always camp, of course. Should the young man suffer, James is there with peculiar balms. Learning of Morton Fullerton's being troubled with threats of blackmail by a former mistress, who had stolen letters documenting his involvement with various society men and women, James 'aches':

there was always a muffled unenlightened ache for my affection in my not knowing ... I think of the whole long mistaken perversity of your averted *reality* so to speak, as a miserable *personal* waste, that of something – ah, so tender! – in *me* that was only quite yearningly ready for you, and something all possible, and all deeply and admirably appealing in yourself, of which I never got the benefit.

The sense of missed erotic opportunity – rather than of resigned chaste devotion – is explicit. James aches 'intelligently now, where I only ached darkly . . . before', and in his pain gives himself the role of erotic healer: 'I can't believe I can't somehow, bit by bit, help you and ease you by dividing with you . . the heavy burden of your consciousness. *Can* one man be as mortally, as tenderly attached to another as I am to you . . . without its counting effectively at some right and preappointed moment for the brother over whom he yearns' (14 November 1907, *Letters* 4:473).

When James ails, the thought of the young man can heal – 'Haply I think on thee'. 'Dearest, dearest Boy, more tenderly embraced than I can say!' he writes Hendrik Andersen on 28 February 1902, not long after the death of Hendrik's brother Andreas. '*But*, dearest Boy, I've been dismally *ill* . . . with a malignant sudden attack, through a chill, of inflammation of the bowels: which threw me into bed, for a week, howling'. Yet 'nursed, tended, cared for, with all zest and needfulness', James announces that

I've pulled though – and am out . . . of a very deep dark hole. *In* my deep hole, how I thought yearningly, helplessly, dearest Boy, of *you* as your last letter gives you to me and as I take you, to my heart.' (*Letters* 4:227)

Here the erotic nuances of James's prose, at a time when physical affliction makes his metaphor more concrete, are so loud that one might think James unaware of what he is saying – if he were, it might be argued, he would be more defensive. James goes on to urge Andersen to 'hold fast, sit tight, *stick hard*' (James's emphasis, as always); again one might think the double entendre uncomfortable (to add another double entendre), particularly as James is advising Hendrik how he might preserve Andreas, who 'is *all* yours now: he lives in you and out of all pain'. Yet intentions seem irrelevant, as the letter is a passionate, breathless outpouring. James is transported, ecstatic, he is on fire. Here, as in the letter to Fullerton, we see an unrestrained queer James, writing a prose which conjoins homoerotic and brotherly love. What is perhaps surprising is the way James's prose combines the sacred and the profane, is so sexy in condolence, in the presence of death: 'Beautiful and unspeakable your account of relation to Andreas. Sacred and beyond tears', James writes in this same letter (*Letters* 4:228). Yet when else might James's prose be so erotic? The pangs of grief and of love may be similarly intense, and intensify each other. When feelings thus vibrate, why should the body not tremble? The death of Andreas has itself left a 'deep dark hole' for James to fill. Hence in a letter of 9 February – the first from James to Hendrik after Andreas' death – we see James explicitly make a claim to fill Andreas' place, 'sooner or later to *have* you there and do for you, to put my arm round you and *make* you lean on me as on a brother and a lover, and keep you on and on, slowly comforted or at least relieved of the first bitterness of pain' (*Letters* 4:226). These letters proudly take their place among James's finest queer writing.

It is not only in the throes of illness and grief or when writing to passionately loved friends that James figures himself so intimately connected to his addressee, however. His language of physical adoration is ironically reworked in letters to writers, which contain an amusing teasing; in them the very act of *reading* is construed as a passive and receptive erotic act. The licence James shows is that of the elder statesman of fiction, who might be allowed his eccentricities, but it also derives from the difficulty of giving an authoriative answer to the question: could he really have meant that? One hopes that Joseph Conrad found pleasure in James's appreciation of *The Sea and the Mirror*:

I read you as I listen to rare music – with deepest depths of surrender, and out of those depths I emerge slowly and reluctantly again, to acknowledge that I return to life. To taste you as I do taste you is *really* thus to wander far away . . . (1 November 1906, *Letters* 4:418)

Kipling's *Kim* also moved James powerfully; in fact, it made him overflow:

I overflow, I beg you to believe, with *Kim*, and I rejoice in such a saturation, such a splendid dose of you. That has been the great thing, I find; that one could sink deep and deep, could sit in you up to one's neck . . . I've surrendered luxuriously to your genius. Don't scoff at me . . . when I tell you that I take you as you are. It might be that I wished you were quite different – though I don't. I should still, after this, just fatalistically take you. You are too sublime – you are too big and there is too much of you. (30 October 1901, *Letters* 4:210)

Some might feel James's appreciation is vulgar, yet what better description of the *jouissance* of writing? What greater compliment could the creative artist receive, than such a physical, sensual appreciation of his gifts? Certainly such appreciations were solicited, as writers sent their wares to James. Thanking H. G. Wells for sending him *Marriage*, James exceeded even his own standards of bodily enjoyment:

I live with you and (almost cannibal-like) *on* you H. G. W. . . . I simply decline – that's the way the thing works – to pass you again through my cerebral oven for critical consumption: I consume you crude and whole and to the last morsel, cannibalistically, quite, as I say; licking the platter clean of the last possibility of a savour and remaining thus yours abjectly

Henry James (18 October 1912, *Letters* 4: 636–7)

Is James figuring himself as queer? His letters never make such a direct profession (what might this claim mean, if he did?).[14] Nor does his autobiography. There James does talk of his erotic awareness, however, describing his fascination with 'the beautiful young manly form of our cousin Gus Barker, then on a vivid little dash of a visit to us and who, perched on a pedestal and divested of every garment, was the gayest as well as the neatest of models . . . [O]ur genial kinsman's perfect gymnastic figure meant living truth'.[15] Yet this camp performativity has a seductive queer power. Campness asserts queerness without needing to say 'queer'. It does not fear or repudiate this designation, but wants to get past the bathos, the melodrama, the flatness of identity assertions. Camp concentrates on the stylistic performance of a queerness it takes for granted. This camp performance is conducted for an appreciative audience, which is itself fit for appreciation.

In his late life James was not exactly fighting away the admiring hordes, but more than enough tokens of admiration came his way from the youthful. In 1909 James was invited for the second time to Cambridge by the 'dear Triumvurate', two Cambridge undergraduates, Geoffrey Keynes and Theodore Bartholomew, and Charles Sayle, Under-Librarian at the University Library.[16] This time he accepted, writing to Gaillard Lapsley, 'I feel rather like an unnatural intellectual Pasha visiting his Circassian Hareem!'[17] The greatest good yielded by the visit for James came in the picturesque form of the youthful Rupert Brooke: Keynes describes 'an unforgettable image of [James] . . . lying comfortably on the cushions and gazing up through prominent half-closed eyes at Brooke's handsome figure clad in white shirt and white flannel trousers'.[18] Thanking Sayle for his hospitality, James was unsure how to spell Rupert's surname, but this failing was a pretext for the serene Jamesian liberty – exempt from alarm, anxiety and remorse – which must end this book:

I have come back to sterner things; you did nothing but beguile and waylay – making me loll, not only figuratively, but literally (so unforgettably – all that wondrous Monday morning), on perfect surfaces exactly adapted to my figure. For their share in these generous yet so subtle arts please convey again my thanks to all concerned – and in particular to the gentle Geoffrey and the admirable Theodore, with a definite stretch toward the insidious Rupert – with whose name I take this liberty because I don't know whether one loves one's love with a (surname terminal) *e* or not. (*Letters* 4:524)

Notes

1 HENRY JAMES AND THE LANGUAGES OF SEX

1 Butler, *Gender Trouble*, p. 136.
2 This point is made at some length in Fuss, *Essentially Speaking: Feminism, Nature and Difference*. Another valuable discussion of constructionist and essentialist approaches to sexuality is found in David Halperin's *One Hundred Years of Homosexuality and Other Essays on Greek Love*, pp. 15–53.
3 See Frank Sulloway, *Freud, Biologist of the Mind*, pp. 259–63, 290–6 and *passim* for the importance of ontogeny/phylogeny debates in nineteenth-century psychiatry and psychoanalysis; pp. 91–4 and *passim* for the importance of 'nature versus nurture' debates. Gillian Beer's *Darwin's Plots* discusses the opposition between ontogeny and phylogeny in Darwin's work and in nineteenth-century fiction.
4 James, *The Portrait of a Lady*, pp. 205, 206, 216.
5 Symonds, 'A Problem in Greek Ethics', p. 9.
6 See pp. 17–19 for a discussion of the word 'sex' in *The Ambassadors*, and chapter seven, pp. 148–9, for reference to the pun on 'Middlesex' in 'The Papers', and p. 193 n. 68 for a discussion of the word 'sex' in *A Little Tour in France*. See also Stephen Heath, *The Sexual Fix*, pp. 7–18, for an account of the entry of 'sexuality' (both word and concept) into late Victorian culture, and the changes 'sex' undergoes in this period.
7 To Stevenson, 17 February 1893, *Letters*, vol. 3, pp. 406–7.
8 James, *Literary Criticism: French Writers*, pp. 696–798.
9 James, 'Charles Baudelaire', ibid., p. 158.
10 James, 'Gabriele D'Annunzio', ibid., p. 942.
11 Heath, *The Sexual Fix*, p. 123. *The Sexual Fix* is also interesting for its account of James's revisions: see pp. 99–100.
12 Hardy, *Tess of the d'Urbervilles*, p. 172.
13 Ludmilla Jordanova discusses how medical theory and practice, in the eighteenth and nineteenth centuries, formalized 'the idea of the body as signs', and 'sanctioned a particular form of inferential thinking, that moved from visible indicators on a surface (either the body itself or clothes) to invisible traits inside the body' (*Sexual Visions*, pp. 26–7). For useful accounts of the medicalization of femininity in the Victorian period see Mary Poovey, 'Scenes of an Indelicate

Character: The Medical Treatment of Victorian women', in *Uneven Developments*, pp. 51–88; Elaine Showalter, *The Female Malady;* and Carroll Smith-Rosenberg, *Disorderly Conduct.*

14 Hardy, *Tess of the d'Urbervilles*, p. 176. For readings of sexuality and gender in Hardy see Rosemarie Morgan's *Women and Sexuality in the Novels of Thomas Hardy* and Marjorie Garson's *Hardy's Fables of Integrity.*

15 See especially my reading of *The Wings of the Dove* in chapter two.

16 Heath, *The Sexual Fix*, p. 11.

17 Foucault, *The History of Sexuality*, pp. 57–8. An unreflective Orientalism accompanies Foucault's use of these terms: the *scientia sexualis* is found in Western societies whereas 'China, Japan, India, Rome, the Arabo-Muslim societies' have the *ars erotica.* In 1983 he expressed reservations about his use of these terms: 'One of the numerous points where I was wrong in *[La Volonté de Savoir]* was what I said about this *ars erotica*' (*The Foucault Reader,* p. 347).

18 White, *The Uses of Obscurity*, p. 136.

19 See chapter two.

20 James frequently discusses the necessary moves he must make in conforming to the market and publishing standards in his notebooks. See Michael Anesko, *"Friction with the Market"*, for an account of James's dealings with fiction markets.

21 See in particular Christopher Craft's 'Alias Bunbury: Desire and Termination in *The Importance of Being Earnest*' in *Another Kind of Love.*

22 Dollimore, *Sexual Dissidence*, p. 103.

23 Freedman, *Professions of Taste*, p. 76.

24 For Brooks, 'forepleasure' is characteristic of what he calls 'perversity, and ultimately the possibility of the polymorphous perverse, the possibility of a text that would delay, displace, and deviate terminal discharge to an extent that it became nonexistent'. Although Brooks says such a 'textual practice is evident in writers like Barthes and Beckett, 'we find as good an illustration of effective perversity in the text of Henry James'. ('The Idea of a Psychoanalytic Literary Criticism', p. 151.)

25 Dowling, *Language and Decadence in the Victorian Fin de Siècle*, p. 130.

26 See Freedman, *Professions of Taste*, for a detailed account of the influence of British aestheticism in James's late fiction.

27 James, *The Ambassadors*, p. 2. Subsequent references are given in the text.

28 Ellis, 'A Note on Paul Bourget', pp. 51–2.

29 See my reading of *The Golden Bowl*, chapter three, in which I describe James's presentation of perversion as a force threatening disruption of familial cohesion.

30 Lyotard, *The Postmodern Condition*, p. xxiv.

31 Hoggart, 'All Present and Incorrect', p. 38.

32 Bayley, 'The Master at War', p. 9.

33 Stephen Marcus, in *The Other Victorians*, discusses the importance of the Victorians' production of pornography, and argues that Victorian sexual life was much more varied than traditional historical accounts allow for. However, insofar as he regards the sexual material he discusses as emerging from a *subculture*, he reinforces an idea of a high Victorian culture which veils sexual life

in obscurity. Yet, through the veil, the Victorians' sanitized self-representations and the activities of the 'other Victorians' are intimately related.

34 Wendy Graham's 'Henry James's Subterranean Blues: A Rereading of *The Princess Casamassima'* notes common strands between the male eroticism in that novel and the figuration of the male body in texts as diverse as Richard Burton's 'Terminal Essay' from his translation of 'One Thousand and One Nights', the case studies of Krafft-Ebing's *Psychopathia Sexualis* and J. A. Symonds' 'A Problem in Modern Ethics'.

35 Warner, *Mr. Fortune's Maggot*, p. 93.

36 Waugh, *Brideshead Revisited*, p. 208.

37 Stevenson, *Strange Case of Dr Jekyll and Mr Hyde*, pp. 10–11.

38 Stevenson, *The Strange Case of Dr Jekyll and Mr Hyde and Other Stories*, p. 302.

39 This is Elaine Showalter's contention; she cites other scholars, such as William Veeder and Karl Miller in support. See *Sexual Anarchy*, pp. 111–12.

40 Cited in Shand-Tucci, *Boston Bohemia 1881–1900*, p. 147.

41 To Edmund Gosse, 7 January 1893, *Letters*, vol. 3, p. 398.

42 Bristow, *Effeminate England*, pp. 128–9.

43 Cited in Brake, *Subjugated Knowledges*, p. 211. This letter is not in any of the published collections of James's letters.

44 There is much scholarship on the Wilde trials, of which the best recent account is Ed Cohen's *Talk on the Wilde Side*.

45 Quoted ibid., p. 128.

46 Quoted ibid., p. 164.

47 Bartlett writes, 'by wearing [the green carnation] Wilde ceased to be an individual homosexual with a flair for creating his own public image, and subscribed to a homosexual fashion. He declared himself to be one of an anonymous group of men for whom the wearing of the green carnation *meant* homosexuality' (*Who Was That Man?*, p. 50). See also Richard Dellamora's *Masculine Desire: The Sexual Politics of Victorian Aestheticism*, which traces the tacit linkage between aestheticism and sexuality implicit in Wilde's image back to Tennyson's *In Memoriam*. Freedman, in *Professions of Taste*, argues that James's work (especially 'The Author of "Beltraffio"') ironizes the relationship between aestheticism and homosexuality (pp. 171–2).

48 Kucich, *Repression in Victorian Fiction*, p. 3.

49 Sedgwick, *Epistemology of the Closet*, p. 167.

50 Ibid., pp. 164–70 and *passim*.

51 Ibid., p. 73.

52 The first usages recorded in the *OED* of 'perverse' and 'perversion' in a sexual sense date from the 1890s.

53 This is clear in my readings of *Roderick Hudson* and *The Golden Bowl*. In 1912 Otto Rank wrote (in reference to literature in German): 'modern literature tends most strongly to the undisguised depiction of sexual, especially incestuous themes' (*The Incest Theme in Literature and Legend*, p. 549).

54 Sedgwick, *Epistemology of the Closet*, p. 10.

55 Quoted ibid. The passage is from *Roland Barthes by Roland Barthes*.

56 Heath, *The Sexual Fix*, p. 156.

57 For a discussion of the problematic conflation of *différance* and sexual difference, see Heather Findlay, 'Is There a Lesbian in this Text?', in Weed, (ed.), *Coming to Terms*, pp. 59–69.

58 Cohen, *Talk on the Wilde Side*, p. 92.

59 For a more detailed account of the importance of these scandals to 'In the Cage' and 'The Papers', see chapter seven.

60 Cohen, *Talk on the Wilde Side*, p. 144.

61 Harold Beaver, in 'Homosexual Signs', points out that 'the qualities predicated of "homosexuality" (as a dependent term) are in fact a condition of "heterosexuality"; . . . "heterosexuality", far from possessing a privileged status, must itself be treated as a dependent term' (p. 115).

62 The importance of money in sexual fantasy is considered by Marcus in *The Other Victorians*, and Freud's 'Character and Anal Eroticism' (1908) makes a famous linkage between money and sex. See also pp. 58–9 for the shared importance of money and sex in James's late fiction.

2 GENDER AND REPRESENTATION IN *THE WINGS OF THE DOVE*

1 James, *Literary Criticism: Essays on Literature*, pp. 68–9.

2 Ibid., pp. 66–7.

3 Eagleton, 'Text, Ideology, Realism', in Edward Said (ed.), *Literature and Society*, p. 162.

4 Brooks, *The Well Wrought Urn*, p. 164.

5 James, *The Art of the Novel*, p. 115; *The Golden Bowl*, p. 119.

6 Barthes, *The Pleasure of the Text*, pp. 7, 13–14.

7 Bradbury, '"Nothing that is not there and the nothing that is": The Celebration of Absence in *The Wings of the Dove*', in Ian F. A. Bell (ed.), *Henry James: Fiction as History*, pp. 82–97.

8 Seltzer, *Henry James and the Art of Power*, pp. 15–16.

9 Holland, *The Expense of Vision: Essays on the Craft of Henry James*, p. 287.

10 Nietzsche, *The Will to Power*, pp. 317–18, 272.

11 Seltzer, *Henry James and the Art of Power*, pp. 88–9.

12 James, *The Portrait of a Lady*, p. 408.

13 See Smith-Rosenberg, *Disorderly Conduct*, pp. 245–96.

14 Ibid., p. 176.

15 Dowling, 'The Decadent and the New Woman in the 1890's', pp. 440–1. See also Carol A. Senf's '*Dracula*: Stoker's Response to the New Woman', and A. R. Cunningham, 'The "New Woman Fiction" of the 1890's' for discussions of the 'New Woman' and fiction.

16 Sedgwick, *Between Men*, p. 8.

17 Seltzer, *Henry James and the Art of Power*, p. 66.

18 James, *The Golden Bowl*, pp. 526, 528.

19 The portrayal in Densher's consciousness of 'something repressed which *recurs*,' something 'that ought to have remained secret and hidden but has come

to light' suggests Freud's class of the 'uncanny', and shows an affinity between *The Wings of the Dove* and James's many shorter fictions in which characters are threatened by (frequently violent) apparitions, the precise nature of which (the realm of the supernatural? products of a deluded mind?) remain unclear. An unhappy relationship between past and present is of course a major element in literature of the supernatural, and appropriately plays an important part in Freud's essay. See Freud, 'The "Uncanny"', *PFL* 14:335–76.

20 Lacan, *Écrits*, pp. 3, 5.

21 The governess of *The Turn of the Screw*, who, as an adult, sees herself 'for the first time . . . from head to foot' (p. 7), is the most striking instance in James of a retarded mirror stage, aligned with an obsession with father figures and recurrent (metaphorical?) violence towards children.

22 Sadoff, *Monsters of Affection*, p. 146.

23 Holland, *The Expense of Vision*, p. 315.

24 James, *The Princess Casamassima*, p. 582.

25 Lacan, *Écrits*, p. 67.

26 The imitative structure of desire in *The Golden Bowl* is pointed out by Seltzer in *Henry James and the Art of Power*, pp. 78–9.

27 Sedgwick, *Between Men*, pp. 25–6.

28 de Lauretis, 'The Violence of Rhetoric: Considerations on Representation and Gender', in Armstrong and Tennenhouse (eds.), *The Violence of Representation*, p. 253.

29 Nietzsche, *Beyond Good and Evil*, p. 13.

30 George Bernard Shaw, quoted by Hynes, *The Edwardian Turn of Mind*, p. 132.

31 Freud, 'Femininity', *The Standard Edition*, vol. 22, p. 116.

32 Haller and Haller, *The Physician and Sexuality in Victorian America*, pp. 41, 48.

33 See in particular Gallagher and Laqueur (eds.), *The Making of the Modern Body*, pp. 42–82.

34 Ibid., p. viii. See, in the same volume, Mary Poovey, '"Scenes of an Indelicate Character": The Medical "Treatment" of Victorian Women', pp. 137–68 for an excellent account of the relationship between the biologization of femininity and debates over the use of chloroform in childbirth.

35 AIDS provides a contemporary illustration of such an ideological battle centering on a disease: see Sontag, *AIDS and Its Metaphors*.

36 Sontag, *Illness as Metaphor*, pp. 21, 32, 25.

37 Ibid., p. 25.

38 Strouse, *Alice James: A Biography*, p. 236. Quoted by Seltzer, *Henry James and the Art of Power*, p. 82. I am indebted here to Seltzer's discussion of what he calls 'the steady expansion of the medico-tutelary complex' (p. 83).

39 James, *The Complete Notebooks*, p. 103.

40 Ibid.

41 Sontag, *Illness as Metaphor*, pp. 21–2.

42 Strouse, *Alice James: A Biography*, p. 236.

43 Edel (ed.), *The Diary of Alice James*, pp. 206–7.

44 Fowler, 'Milly Theale's Malady of Self', *Novel* 14 (1980): 57–74, pp. 58–9.

45 See Habegger, 'Henry James's Rewriting of Minny Temple's Letters', and *Henry James and the 'Woman Business'*, pp. 126–49.
46 Dumas *fils*, *La Dame aux Camélias*, p. 60. In *A Small Boy and Others* James describes a memory of 'the *régime* of Honorine's young train, who were fresh for the early sparrow and the chiffonier even after shedding buckets of tears the night before, and not so much as for the first or the second time, over the beautiful story of La Dame aux Camélias' (*Autobiography*, p. 217).
47 Henry Mürger, *Scènes de la vie de la Bohème*; Edmond About, *Germaine*. In the notebooks James notes the resemblance of his plot to About's *Germaine*.
48 Groos, 'Amore e Morte: Dying of Consumption', p. 40.
49 Eagleton, *The Ideology of the Aesthetic*, p. 106.
50 Freedman, *Professions of Taste*, p. 100.
51 For feminist studies of Dora see Charles Bernheimer and Claire Kahane (eds.), *In Dora's Case: Freud, Hysteria, Feminism*, and Jane Gallop, 'Keys to Dora', in *Feminism and Psychoanalysis: The Daughter's Seduction*; also, for a dramatic treatment of Dora, see Hélène Cixous, *Portrait de Dora*, in *Théâtre: Portrait de Dora et La Prise de l'École de Madhubaï*.

3 SEXUALITY AND THE AESTHETIC IN *THE GOLDEN BOWL*

1 Bersani, *The Freudian Body*, p. 42.
2 Barthes, *The Pleasure of the Text*, p. 30.
3 Psychoanalytic literature frequently uses the term 'perversion' as if it is unproblematic: see for example Jean Clavreul, 'The Perverse Couple', in Stuart Schneiderman, (ed.), *Returning to Freud*, or several references to perversion in the work of Julia Kristeva. In Freud's writing however use of the term is troubled, and efforts made to separate 'normal' and 'perverse' are often undermined. In *Three Essays* Freud writes that the 'normal sexual aim is regarded as being the union of the genitals in the act known as copulation, which leads to a release of the sexual tension and a temporary extinction of the sexual instinct ... But even in the most normal sexual process we may detect rudiments which, if they had developed, would have led to the deviations described as "perversions" ... Perversions are sexual activities which either (a) *extend*, in an anatomical sense, beyond the regions of the body that are designed for sexual union, or (b) *linger* over the intermediate relations to the sexual object which should normally be traversed rapidly on the path towards the final sexual aim.' *Three Essays on the Theory of Sexuality*, *PFL* 7:61–2.
4 As Seltzer points out, the Assinghams are part of a structure of (disciplinary) surveillance – in a Foucauldian sense (*Henry James and the Art of Power*, pp. 63–4). More attention needs to be paid, however, to how James eroticizes such disciplinary mechanisms.
5 Barthes, *The Pleasure of the Text*, pp. 9–12. In his coinage 'the perverse text', Barthes is alluding directly to Freud's unstable notion of the perverse – denoting all non-reproductive sexual acts but connoting, in particular, sadomasochism and homosexuality.

6 Mulvey, 'Visual Pleasure and Narrative Cinema', in *Visual and Other Pleasures*, p. 20.

7 Ibid., p. 25.

8 Freud, 'Femininity' (1933), *PFL* 2:167.

9 Barthes, *S/Z*, p.36.

10 See Stephen Heath, 'Difference', for a critique of the scopic drive as phallo-centric, and Sadoff, *Monsters of Affection*, especially the chapter on Brontë, for an application of contemporary theories of the gaze to the Victorian novel.

11 Mitchell and Rose, (eds.), *Feminine Sexuality. Jacques Lacan and the* École Freudienne, p. 64.

12 See Victoria Glendinning, *Vita: The Life of V. Sackville-West*.

13 Mitchell and Rose, (eds.), *Feminine Sexuality. Jacques Lacan and the* École Freudienne, p. 51.

14 Krafft-Ebing, *Psychopathia Sexualis*, p. 130.

15 James, 'The Jolly Corner', *Complete Tales* 12, p. 226.

16 See chapter seven for a fuller analysis of 'The Jolly Corner'.

17 See Gayle Rubin, 'The Traffic in Women: Notes Toward a Political Economy of Sex' for an analysis, which draws from Lévi-Strauss, of patriarchal hetero-sexuality as male traffic in women.

18 Freud, 'Instincts and their Vicissitudes', *PFL* 11:138. The translation of *Trieb* as 'instinct' is one of the most famous errors of the English version of Freud. Freud also uses the term *Instinkt*, and in quite different contexts from those in which he uses *Trieb*. In order to distinguish when Freud is using *Trieb* from when he is using *Instinkt*, *Trieb* should be translated as 'drive'.

19 Krafft-Ebing, *Psychopathia Sexualis*, p. 130.

20 The idea that masochism in a woman is less 'pathological' than in a man still has some currency: Silverman writes in her recent *Male Subjectivity at the Margins* that 'it does seem to me that it is only in the case of men that feminine masochism can be seen to achieve pathological proportions. Although that psychic phenomenon often provides a centrally structuring element of both male and female subjectivity, it is only in the latter that it can be safely acknow-ledged' (p. 189).

21 Ibid., pp. 8–9.

22 Hall, *Adolescence*, pp. 112–13.

23 Ellis, *Analysis of the Sexual Impulse*, vol. 3, pp. 66, 67, 69, 72, 82.

24 Freud, 'The Economic Problem of Masochism', *PFL* 11:418.

25 Ibid., p. 424. Bersani, in *The Freudian Body*, writes that 'the pleasurable unplea-surable tension of sexual excitement occurs when the body's "normal" range of sensation is exceeded, and when the organization of the self is momentarily disturbed by sensations or affective processes somehow "beyond" those com-patible with psychic organization' (p. 38). The human subject is shattered into sexuality; sexual excitement is conceptualized as a desire to be shattered out of coherence. This means that 'sexuality . . . could be thought of as a tautology for masochism' (p. 39). Bersani goes on to write that *'masochism serves life,'* 'allows us to survive our infancy and early childhood,' and that, 'far from being

an individual aberration, [masochism] is an inherited disposition resulting from an *evolutionary conquest*' (p. 39). Although Bersani does not discuss the way in which modes of masochism may vary historically and culturally, his insight that masochism is a means of survival is helpful in considering the way in which, for Maggie, masochism is a means of wrestling with the psychic cost of femininity.

26 Freud, 'The Economic Problem of Masochism', p. 419.

27 Laplanche, *Life and Death in Psychoanalysis*, p. 100 (Laplanche's emphasis).

28 In *The Standard Edition of Sigmund Freud*, vol. 23.

29 Compare Melanie Klein on sublimation and reparation: Klein writes of 'the specific importance for sublimation of the bits to which the loved object has been reduced and the effort to put them together. It is a "perfect" object which is in pieces; thus the effort to undo the state of disintegration to which it has been reduced presupposes the necessity to make it beautiful and "perfect"' (*Selected Melanie Klein*, pp. 124–5).

30 See Gallop, 'The Other Woman', in *Thinking Through the Body*, pp. 160–78, and Moore, 'Sexual Agency in Manet's *Olympia*', for just two readings of criticism's failure to see the 'other woman'.

31 See in particular Habegger, *Henry James and the 'Woman Business'*, which describes Henry James, Jr., as a male chauvinist writing in the wake of his father.

32 As Borch-Jacobsen shows, the separation of spectator from scene is difficult to maintain: see *The Freudian Subject*, pp. 26–48. To maintain a distinction between 'I am being beaten by my father' and 'My father is beating the child whom I hate' requires a separation of self and other. However, as Borch-Jacobsen writes, there is a 'close connivance between this "sadism" [of the first phase] and the "masochism" of the second phase, for if the "other" is beaten to the extent that I identify with him or her, it goes without saying that I "myself" will also be the beaten one' (p. 37).

33 The images of rings, cords, cages imprisoning Charlotte resemble Sylvia Plath's description in 'The Rabbit Catcher' of 'a mind like a ring / Sliding shut on some quick thing, / The constriction killing me also', discussed by Rose in *The Haunting of Sylvia Plath* (especially pp. 135–43), to which I am indebted for its incisive use of psychoanalytic conceptions of fantasy.

34 Lévi-Strauss, *The Elementary Structures of Kinship*, p. 12.

35 Gilbert and Gubar, in *Sexchanges*, show how a number of late nineteenth-century texts, including Rider Haggard's *She* and *King Solomon's Mines*, George MacDonald's *Lilith*, and Bram Stoker's *The Lair of the White Worm*, juxtapose colonialist scenarios of invasion, penetration and conquest with male anxieties concerned with the perception of a threatening growth in female power ('Femme Fatale', pp. 3–46).

36 James, 'Covering End', in *Complete Tales* 10, p. 350.

37 Kristeva, *Powers of Horror*, p. 186.

38 Freedman, 'Henry James and the Discourses of Antisemitism'.

39 It is certainly tempting to compare the breaking of the bowl with the breaking

of the vessels – but the similarity of the two gestures will have to remain 'uncanny' in the absence of more solid historical evidence of James's awareness of Judaism. The question of James and Judaism is so complex and in the absence of any intelligent, thorough study it would seem rash to try to arrive at any inevitably premature answers.

40 As Bersani writes in *The Freudian Body*, 'Maggie does nothing but adhere, without the slightest defection into truth, to the decorous lie, fed to her by the others, that nothing is wrong with her marriage' (p. 84).

4 MASOCHISM AND THE LAW IN *RODERICK HUDSON*

1 Butler, *Bodies That Matter*, p. 94.

2 See Sedgwick, 'The Beast in the Closet: Henry James and the Writing of Homosexual Panic', *Epistemology of the Closet*, pp. 182–212, 'Queer Performativity: Henry James's *The Art of the Novel*', and 'Is the Rectum Straight? Identification and Identity in *The Wings of the Dove*', *Tendencies*, pp. 73–103; Graham, 'Henry James's Subterranean Blues'; Eric Savoy, '"In the Cage" and the Queer Effects of Gay History'; Terry Castle, 'Haunted by Olive Chancellor', *The Apparitional Lesbian*, pp. 150–85; Michael Moon, 'A Small Boy and Others: Sexual Disorientation in Henry James, Kenneth Anger, and David Lynch'. Other important readings include Robert K. Martin, 'The "High Felicity" of Comradeship: A New Reading of *Roderick Hudson*', and Richard Hall, 'Henry James: Interpreting an Obsessive Memory'.

3 See in particular Judith Fetterley's discussion of criticism of *The Bostonians*, in *The Resisting Reader*.

4 Sedgwick, *Epistemology of the Closet*, p. 197.

5 Freedman, *Professions of Taste*, pp. xv–xvi.

6 Crucial to such a construction is the role played by two absences in James's life: the potential of romance with both Minnie Temple and Constance Fenimore Woolson is foreclosed by James's refusals, and the deaths of these two women. Although Kaplan's recent biography does look at the structure of masculine friendships which was so important in James's life, James is still seen as cautious, avoiding erotic involvement. Both constructions seem hugely problematic, and ignore the extent to which James, in his letters to male friends, freely cast himself as an erotic subject. Although such letters cannot be taken to imply any actual sexual activity, the assumption that an absence of evidence means that James was a virginal creature should not remain unchallenged. It is very difficult to prove virginity! But beyond the issue of what sexual activity James may or may not have indulged in, the erotic adventurousness of his letters – and, of course, of his fiction – in itself constitutes an adventurousness and boldness in matters 'sexual'. Interrogations of sexuality in James's fiction must assume that a biographical construction of James will only be helpful to the extent that the problematic nature of such a construction is always accounted for.

7 Geismar, *Henry James and his Cult*, pp. 359–60. (This book was called *Henry James and the Jacobites* when published in the States.)

8 Notably Esch, in 'A Jamesian About-Face: Notes on "The Jolly Corner"', reads the tale as an allegory of reading (Esch is to this tale as Paul de Man is to Proust), dramatizing the incompatability of literal and figurative readings, and the consequent impossibility of reading oneself in one's *alter ego*, of identifying oneself in 'a notation – the narrative's system of written signs' (p. 603).

9 Habegger, *Gender, Fantasy, and Realism in American Literature*, pp. 255, 294–5.

10 Sedgwick, *Epistemology of the Closet*, p. 167.

11 Wilde, 'The Decay of Lying', *Complete Works*, p. 981. See Beer, *Darwin's Plots*, for an account of the far-reaching influences of Darwin on nineteenth-century fiction; see also Freedman, *Professions of Taste*, and Dowling, *Language and Decadence in the Victorian Fin de Siècle*, for an account of the growth of decadence out of nineteenth-century philology and evolutionary theory.

12 See Nordau, *Degeneration*, pp. 317–21. Nordau's attack on Wilde and decadence sounds curiously like Habegger's attack on James! For an account of Nordau's response to decadence see Cohen, *Talk on the Wilde Side*, pp. 15–19. As Cohen shows, the press specifically represented Wilde as a degenerate at the time of his trials.

13 Pater, *The Renaissance*, pp. 152–3.

14 The full extent to which James's work responds to nineteenth-century discourses on reproductive sexuality is only beginning to be realized. See Susan Mizruchi, 'Reproducing Women in *The Awkward Age*', for an account of that novel's incorporation of upper-class anxieties surrounding reproduction and changing perceptions of maternity. In 1927 Forster, in *Aspects of the Novel*, writes that '[m]aimed creatures can alone breathe in [James's] pages – maimed yet specialized. They remind one of the exquisite deformities who haunted Egyptian art in the reign of Akhnaton – huge heads and tiny legs, but nevertheless charming. In the following reign they disappear' (p. 143). James is being attacked for his degeneracy (which is opposed to the full fertile art of Tolstoy), but it seems that Forster takes pleasure in what he attacks.

15 Shakespeare, *Othello* III.3.354 (p. 118). See Adrian Poole, 'Henry James, War and Witchcraft', for an essay which describes James's fascination with *Othello* and the many textual echoes of the play to be found in James's work.

16 James, *Roderick Hudson* (Harmondsworth: Penguin, 1986), p. 386–7 (my emphasis). All further quotations from the novel are given parenthetically in the text, and are to this edition, a reprint of the first English edition of the novel (1878); however, when referring to the New York edition I cite from the Oxford University Press reprint of 1986, edited by Tony Tanner.

17 This linkage of familial and erotic affection anticipates by many years James's letter comforting Hendrik Andersen after the death of his brother Andreas: 'I return to Rye April 1st, and sooner or later to *have* you there and do for you, to put my arm round you and *make* you lean on me as on a brother and a lover . . .' (9 February 1902, *Selected Letters*, p. 541; James's emphasis).

18 Martin, 'The "High Felicity" of Comradeship'.

19 Katz, 'The Invention of the Homosexual, 1880–1950', *Gay/Lesbian Almanac*, pp. 141–52.

20 Seidman, *Romantic Longings*, p. 7. See Smith-Rosenberg's 'The Female World of Love and Ritual', *Disorderly Conduct*, pp. 53–76, for an analysis of female intimacy in Victorian America.

21 An article by Martin Duberman, '"Writhing Bedfellows" in Antebellum South Carolina: Historical Interpretation and the Politics of Evidence', discusses letters written between two men in the 1820s and shows that for these two men male-male sexual contact was not stigmatized, and was not regarded as in any way inconsistent with married life (in *About Time*, pp. 3–23). Duberman's analysis would support Foucault's general claim that before the medicalization of the homosexual homoerotic activity was not a particular marker of identity. However, as my reading of Bayard Taylor's *Joseph and His Friend* shows (below, pp. 70–3), the American novel was beginning to conceptualize a relation between homoerotic desire and 'identity' before such a relation became a topic of medical discussion.

22 John D'Emilio and Estelle B. Freedman note that the *reading* of 'romantic' friendships as 'devoid of sexual contact' in fact enabled an expression of eroticism within friendship – which may or may not have accompanied genital intimacy. Before the 1880s, 'romantic friendships could be erotic in part because they were assumed to be sexually innocent' (*Intimate Matters*, pp. 121, 129. Smith-Rosenberg's 'Davy Crockett as Trickster: Pornography, Liminality, and Symbolic Inversion in Victorian America' is an interesting reading of homoerotic expression in mid-century (*Disorderly Conduct*, pp. 90–108).

23 See Roger Gard, ed., *Henry James: The Critical Heritage*, and Kevin J. Hayes, ed., *Henry James: The Contemporary Reviews*, for selections of the book's first reviews. The reception of *The Bostonians* (1886) and Wilde's *The Picture of Dorian Gray* (1891) show a growing explicitness in condemnations of homoeroticism: see pp. 95–6 and 147 below.

24 In *Gay American History* Jonathan Katz describes Walt Whitman's correspondence with J. A. Symonds and Edward Carpenter, which began in the 1870s – Symonds in particular tried to get Whitman to tell him more about the 'love of man for man' and the 'Love of Friends', but Whitman always remained evasive.

25 James, *French Writers*, pp. 153, 156–7.

26 James, *Essays on Literature*, pp. 629, 632–4.

27 James, *Selected Letters*, p. 348–9.

28 James, *Essays on Literature*, pp. 1,278–83.

29 Famously in *Hawthorne* James laments the lack of the 'items of high civilization' in 'American life'. To his long list of American absences, he might have added . . . no princes, no princesses! See *Hawthorne, Essays on Literature*, pp. 351–2. Of course eroticism in James's America is never democratic. Rowland's relation to Roderick prefigures Olive Chancellor's relation to Verena Tarrant, and in both financial differences – and the ability of money to buy off or take over familial influences – are important.

30 Sedgwick, 'Shame and Performativity', p. 29. A classic instance of such a stance is found in the introduction to the Penguin edition: Geoffrey Moore writes that Rowland 'is also (in the Victorian sense) a lover, not – as *James's con-*

scious mind would have us believe – of Mary alone. Rowland's real love, from the beginning, has been Roderick' (p. 16).

31 The review, submitted to the *North American Review*, was unpublished, and first appeared in the *Harvard Literary Bulletin* of 1957. It is now available in the Library of America volume, *Essays on Literature; American Writers; English Writers*. The similarities between *Joseph and His Friend* and *Roderick Hudson* would suggest James was familiar with Austen's novel. See also p. 97.

32 Austen, *Playing the Game*. This study has received little attention, but contains much interesting material.

33 Taylor, *Joseph and His Friend*, p. 112. Subsequent references are given parenthetically in the text.

34 This work is already proceeding in a British and an American context, but such a history remains patchy. See e.g. Michael Moon, *Disseminating Whitman*, Dellamora, *Masculine Desire*, Craft, 'Tennyson's Strange Manner of Address' in *Another Kind of Love*, Jeff Nunokawa, '*In Memoriam* and the Extinction of the Homosexual'.

35 See Sedgwick, *Epistemology of the Closet*, pp. 182–200. Sedgwick's readings in this book of *Billy Budd*, *Dorian Gray*, 'The Beast in the Jungle' and Proust are all relevant here. See also Showalter, 'Dr Jekyll's Closet', in *Sexual Anarchy*, pp. 105–26.

36 See e.g. pp. 123–5 for my discussion of 'Mora Montravers'.

37 See Martin, 'The "High Felicity" of Comradeship', pp. 102–3, for an analysis of the significance of these figures.

38 Keats, *Endymion*, *Poetical Works*, pp. 89–90.

39 Whitman, 'States!', *Complete Poems*, p. 620.

40 When revising this passage for the New York edition, the older James accentuates the anthropomorphic homoeroticism of the scene; this last sentence becomes: 'He sat up beside his companion and looked away at the far-spreading view, which affected him as melting for them both into such vast continuities and possibilities of possession' (New York edition, p. 25).

41 In the revised version the potential of the scene to invade Rowland's body is heightened, making him a passive vehicle subject to 'haunting': 'It touched him to the heart; suddenly a strange feeling of prospective regret took possession of him. Something seemed to tell him that later, in a foreign land, he should be haunted by it, should remember it all with longing and regret' (New York edition, pp. 25–6). In the revised edition 'possession' is used twice in close succession.

42 Sedgwick, *Between Men*, p. 35.

43 James writes in the preface to *The Golden Bowl* that '[w]e are condemned, ... whether we will or no, to abandon and outlive, to forget and disown and hand over to desolation, many vital or social performances' (*AN* 348).

44 Notes to *Roderick Hudson* (Penguin edition), p. 392.

45 In the revised edition Gloriani compares her with Salomé, not Herodias. See below.

46 Freud, *PFL* 11:369.

47 Miller, *Bringing Out Roland Barthes*, p. 29.

48 As Martin remarks, Roderick's dress associates him 'with the florid Romanticism of the American South.' 'The "High Felicity" of Comradeship', p. 103.

49 In *Masochism in Modern Man* Reik writes, 'I maintain that the birthplace of masochism is phantasy' (p. 186).

50 Christina's attraction to Rowland remains opaque – it is an example of a bond in James in which the distinctness of love, obligation and respect is not legible.

51 Having invoked the latter metaphor for the artist's work, James writes that 'the comforts of the artist [are] just the raw essence of fantasy' (*AN* 69). These two descriptions of the novelistic canvas are from the prefaces to *Roderick Hudson* and *The Princess Casamassima*. A comment from Laplanche and Pontalis, *The Language of Psycho-Analysis*, is relevant here: speaking of the workings of defence in their entry on phantasy, they note that 'defences are themselves inseparably bound up with the function of phantasy, namely the *mise-en-scène* of desire – a *mise-en-scène* in which what is *prohibited* (*l'interdit*) is always present in the actual formation of the wish' (p. 318).

52 See René Girard's *Deceit, Desire, and the Novel*, and Sedgwick's *Between Men*, for the best analyses of erotic triangles within literature.

53 Deleuze points to the 'preoccupation with arrested movement' in Masoch's novels, one example being Wanda 'with her furs and her whip, adopting a suspended posture, like a *tableau vivant*' (*Coldness and Cruelty*, p. 70).

54 Donald notes how stanza 8 of 'Ode to a Nightingale' 'luxuriates unashamedly in morbid, masochistic pleasures', and that, through figuring death as the speaker's male lover, Keats 'literalizes and socializes imaginative passivity and celebratory self-annihilation as homoerotic.' 'Coming out of the Canon: Sadomasochism, Male Homoeroticism, Romanticism', p. 248. The description also recalls Baudelaire – think of his 'Une Martyre', with its corpse 'In a room like a greenhouse, both stuffy and warm, / An atmosphere heavy with death, / Where arrangements of flowers encoffined in glass, / Exhale their ultimate breath' (*Flowers of Evil*, p. 229).

55 Deleuze, *Coldness and Cruelty*, p. 71. Deleuze's emphasis on the importance of suspense in masochism and a masochistic aesthetic is echoed by Gaylyn Studlar in her study *In the Realm of Pleasure*.

56 Sedgwick, 'Shame and Performativity', pp. 214, 218–19.

57 Sedgwick, *Epistemology of the Closet*, pp. 49, 72.

58 *ridden*: 'afflicted, affected, or dominated by something specified' (*Collins English Dictionary*).

59 Wilde, 'The Ballad of Reading Gaol', *Complete Works*, p. 860.

60 Tintner, *The Museum World of Henry James*, pp. 133–4. As Tintner points out, Wilde admired James, so a complex network of influence goes from the early English edition of *Roderick Hudson*, through Wilde's *Salomé*, to James's New York edition of the novel.

61 In the revised text Roderick's genitals are discreetly referred to in that campy rhetoric of negation the novel employs so easily: Rowland tells Roderick that '"[Gloriani] only thinks ... that Herodias must much have resembled Miss

Light – unless indeed he also sees our young woman with *your* head on her charger." "Ah," Gloriani laughed, "it isn't a question of Hudson's 'head'!"' (New York edition, p. 141). See also Showalter's reading of Wilde's *Salomé* in *Sexual Anarchy*, pp. 143–56.

62 Barthes, *Roland Barthes by Roland Barthes*, pp. 1–5.

5 QUEER PLOTTING

1 In Hayes, (ed.), *Henry James: The Contemporary Reviews*, p. 169.

2 Girard's *Deceit, Desire, and the Novel* is the seminal discussion of the triangular rivalry plot in European fiction. Sedgwick's *Between Men* discusses the homo-erotic elements of male-male rivalry plots.

3 More research is needed on the role of class identities and class images in lesbian and gay culture: in a literary context, Hopkins, Forster and Lawrence are only three writers for whom cross-class attraction seems to hold a potent and compelling allure. See Joseph Bristow, '"Churlsgrace": Gerald Manley Hopkins and the Working-Class Male Body', for an account of cross-class eroticism in Hopkins.

4 'The Author of "Beltraffio"' was published in the *English Illustrated Magazine* of spring 1884.

5 Leon Edel claims that James 'did not know at the time that Symonds's homo-sexuality was the real issue' (*The Life of Henry James*, vol. 1, p. 743; Edel does not mention Symonds's homosexuality in the earlier version of the biography: see *The Middle Years*, p. 80). According to Frank Kermode, Symonds's 'taste (though not his homosexuality) is reflected in the narrator's praise of Mark Ambient's' (Kermode, (ed.), *The Figure in the Carpet and Other Stories*, p. 447).

6 Freedman, *Professions of Taste*, p. 172.

7 Symonds, 'A Problem in Greek Ethics', pp. 9, 95–6. In his notebook James does not mention Symonds's sexuality as the cause of difference between him and his wife – in James's '*drame intime*' which was to become 'The Author of "Beltraffio"', the wife was to find the husband's books 'immoral, pagan, hyper-aesthetic, etc.', and the husband was to be 'impregnated – even to morbidness – with the spirit of Italy, the love of beauty, of art, the aesthetic view of life, and aggravated, made extravagant and perverse, by the sense of the wife's disapproval'. Yet the coupling of Greek, pagan and immoral in the story suggest a more knowing re-creation of Symonds's own aestheticist appropriation of the ancient world.

8 See Dellamora, *Masculine Desire*, pp. 167–92, and Linda Dowling, *Hellenism and Homosexuality in Victorian Oxford*, pp. 89–92, for accounts of 1870s debates around Symonds's Hellenism.

9 Edel, *The Life of Henry James*, vol. 1, p. 743.

10 Castle, *The Apparitional Lesbian*, p. 151.

11 For example, Leon Edel argues (but only in the later version of the biography) that it is more accurate to see the relationship between Olive and Verena in its 'overt nature' than as 'latent homosexuality' (*The Life of Henry James*, vol. 1, p. 740).

12 See Fetterley, *The Resisting Reader*, pp. 103–12, for a detailed analysis of criticism of the novel.
13 Introduction to *The Bostonians*, pp. xxviii, xxxiii.
14 Quoted in Fetterley, *The Resisting Reader*, p. 104.
15 Faderman, *Surpassing the Love of Men*, p. 190.
16 Faderman writes: 'In 1884, before the popularization of the sexologists, [James] would have had no reason for viewing love between women as a "mental malady" and an abnormality' (ibid., p. 195).
17 James, *The Bostonians*, p. 142. Further references are given parenthetically in the text.
18 Fetterley, *The Resisting Reader*, p. 132.
19 Quoted ibid., p. 118.
20 Castle, *The Apparitional Lesbian*, pp. 171, 177.
21 Quoted in Faderman, *Surpassing the Love of Men*, p. 190.
22 As Edel points out, '[t]he drama of *The Bostonians* resides in a struggle for possession not unlike the drama of Katharine Loring, her sister, and Alice James' (*The Life of Henry James*, vol. 1, p. 739).
23 See below, p. 108.
24 In Hayes, (ed.), *Henry James: The Contemporary Reviews*, p. 169.
25 Ibid., p. 166.
26 Ibid., p. 164.
27 Gard, (ed.), *Henry James: The Critical Heritage*, p. 162.
28 Hayes, (ed.), *Henry James: The Contemporary Reviews*, p. 170.
29 Gard, (ed.), *Henry James: The Critical Heritage*, p. 154.
30 *The Nation* 40 (12 March 1885): p. 226. Although it is possible that this reviewer's distaste for British aestheticism motivates his virulent disapproval of Mark Ambient, it seems more likely that his sympathy for Mrs Ambient's fears is more knowledgeable, and does not arise merely from an unthinking wish to censor *risqué* literature.
31 Castle, *The Apparitional Lesbian*, pp. 150–85.
32 Olive's opinion of Bayard Taylor's *Faust* translation was shared by James, who despite a disparaging review of *John Godfrey's Fortunes* could be enthusiastic about Taylor. On 16 January 1871 (one year after *Joseph and His Friend* was published) he wrote to Charles Eliot Norton, 'When I say that Bayard Taylor has published a very good (I believe) translation of Faust and that Lowell is to republish more of his delectable essays ... I shall have mentioned the only serious literary facts of our hemisphere.' (*Letters*, vol. 1, pp. 252–3)
33 Warner, *Joan of Arc: The Image of Female Heroism*, p. 241.
34 Ibid., p. 19.
35 Schiller, *Joan of Arc*, in *Mary Stuart; Joan of Arc*, p. 157.
36 Ibid., pp. 192, 193. Castle writes that 'Joan of Arc travels through time as a peculiarly sapphic heroine' (*The Apparitional Lesbian* p. 185).
37 Warner, *Joan of Arc*, p. 149.
38 Ibid., pp. 15–23.

39 In *The Apparitional Lesbian*, Castle discusses the intertextual relations between *The Well of Loneliness* and *The Bostonians*.

40 Smith-Rosenberg, 'The Female World of Love and Ritual: Relations Between Women in Nineteenth-Century America', *Disorderly Conduct*, pp. 53–76.

41 Jeffreys, *The Spinster and Her Enemies*, p. 126.

42 Raitt, *Vita and Virginia*, p. 7.

43 Castle, *The Apparitional Lesbian*, p. 178.

44 Litvak, *Caught in the Act*, pp. 235–40.

45 Graham, 'Henry James's Subterranean Blues', p. 57.

46 See his letter to Edmund Gosse, 7 January 1893, *Letters*, vol. 3, p. 398.

47 James, *The Princess Casamassima*, pp. 127, 135, 217. Further references are given parenthetically in the text.

48 If James did read *Venus in Furs*, he would not have done so before 1902, when it was first translated into French and English (Gilles Deleuze, 'Coldness and Cruelty', p. 12). However, he certainly knew Swinburne's poetry, and the 'cruel woman' was a common late nineteenth-century icon (see Bram Djikstra, *Idols of Perversity*, for the fullest exploration of cruel late nineteenth-century *femmes fatales*). *The Princess Casamassima* joins *Venus in Furs* in adding a queer supplement to the dyad of passive man and cruel woman: the 'cruel man', whether Paul Muniment or, in Masoch's novel, the Prince.

49 Such a reading is given by Silverman in *Male Subjectivity at the Margins*, pp. 168–9. By relentlessly placing such moments in James's fiction within the dynamics of the Oedipus complex, Silverman ignores the way in which the anxious eroticism of James's writing might be responding to and critiquing a specific social context – the legal and cultural critique of his work is ignored. Instead James becomes a case study of tortured, ambivalent and marginal masculinity.

50 *The Well of Loneliness* gives two such situations for good measure: the first occurs when Angela Crossby forms a liaison with Roger Antrim, the second when Mary Llewellyn leaves Stephen for Marin Hallam.

51 See Graham, 'Henry James's Subterranean Blues', pp. 59–69, for discussion of other *double entendres* in the text.

52 Ibid., pp. 64–65.

53 Patricia Highsmith's *Carol*, published pseudonymously in 1952, is a rare example of a novel written before the 1970s which enables the lesbian couple it portrays to stay together.

54 'The Fox', in Lawrence, *The Complete Short Novels*, pp. 135–205.

55 Lawrence, *Women in Love*, p. 9. Further references to the novel are given parenthetically in the text.

56 Lawrence, *The Rainbow*, p. 326.

57 Lawrence, 'Prologue' to *Women in Love*, *Women in Love*, p. 505.

58 Lawrence, *The Rainbow*, p. 325.

59 Bristow, *Effeminate England*, p. 68. Bristow's chapter on Forster, 'Against "Effeminacy": the Sexual Predicament of E. M. Forster's Fiction' (pp. 55–99),

gives a detailed account of the tensions between same-sex bonds and hetero-sexuality in Forster's fiction.

60 Forster, *The Longest Journey*, p. 82. Further references are given parenthetically in the text.

61 Hall, *The Well of Loneliness*, p. 447.

62 In her introduction to the 1988 Penguin edition of the novel, Elizabeth Heine documents these connections; she argues that Forster would have become aware of sexological theories though the Cambridge Apostles (p. xxi).

63 The best discussion of this debate is Fuss's *Essentially Speaking*; see also Halperin, *One Hundred Years of Homosexuality and Other Essays on Greek Love*.

64 Sinfield, *The Wilde Century*, p. 17.

65 Posnock, *The Trial of Curiosity*, p. 82.

6 THE SPECTACLE OF MODERN HOMOSEXUALITY

1 See Sedgwick, *Epistemology of the Closet*, pp. 182–212, for her reading of 'The Beast in the Jungle', and Moon, 'A Small Boy and Others', for his reading of James's 'The Pupil'. I am certainly not discussing all of James's tales with queer themes here: the reader might also like to consider 'A Light Man', 'Collaboration', 'The Real Right Thing', 'The Great Good Place'.

2 James, 'Fordham Castle', *Complete Tales* 12, p. 142. All further references to James's tale are to this edition and are given parenthetically in the text (to *CT*) by volume and page number.

3 My thanks to an anonymous reader of an earlier version of this chapter for pointing this out.

4 An 1891 usage is cited in the *OED* supplement.

5 James, *Complete Notebooks*, pp. 183, 187, 194. All the names in the following analysis are in the *Complete Notebooks*, in lists between pages 13 and 202.

6 Ibid., pp. 257–8, 268.

7 Freud, *Jokes and Their Relation to the Unconscious*, *PFL* 6:222.

8 Ibid., pp. 227–30.

9 Kristeva, *Revolution in Poetic Language*, pp. 16, 78.

10 Kristeva, *Desire in Language*, p. 65.

11 Stallybrass and White, *The Politics and Poetics of Transgression*, pp. 10–11.

12 Beckett, *Waiting for Godot*, *The Complete Dramatic Works*, p. 42.

13 Sedgwick, *Epistemology of the Closet*, pp. 196–7.

14 Neil Bartlett's *Who Was That Man?*, describes the simultaneous publicity and caution of (homo)erotic languages in late Victorian London. This book, Sedgwick's *Epistemology of the Closet*, and Craft's 'Alias Bunbury: Desire and Termination in *The Importance of Being Earnest*' (*Another Kind of Love*, pp. 106–39) are the best analyses of the discursive terrain of the 'closet' and the 'open secret'. For good descriptions of the historical conditions which engendered such linguistic circuitousness, see Weeks, *Coming Out: Homosexual Politics in Britain from the Nineteenth Century to the Present* and *Sex, Politics and Society: The Regulation of Sexuality Since 1800*.

15 To Gardner, *Letters*, vol. 2, p. 372; to Godkin, quoted in Edel, *Henry James: The Conquest of London*, p. 462.
16 See Katz, *Gay American History*, and *Gay/Lesbian Almanac*, and George S. Chauncey, *Gay New York*, for accounts of late nineteenth-century American gay subcultures; and Jeffrey Weeks, *Coming Out: Homosexual Politics in Britain from the Nineteenth Century to the Present*, and *Sex, Politics and Society: The Regulation of Sexuality Since 1800* for accounts of gay communities in fin-de-siècle Britain.
17 Dowling's *Hellenism and Homosexuality in Victorian Oxford* describes the pioneering construction of homosexual subjectivities among Oxford intellectual and artistic circles.
18 Foucault, *The History of Sexuality*, p. 43.
19 Cohen, *Talk on the Wilde Side*, p. 131. This study provides the most detailed account of how Wilde's trials made him the public face of homosexuality.
20 Sinfield, *The Wilde Century*, p. vii.
21 Forster, *Maurice*, p. 136.
22 Sinfield, *The Wilde Century*, pp. 118, vii.
23 Ellmann, *Oscar Wilde*, p. 129.
24 Gilbert, *Patience; or, Bunthorne's Bride*, in *The Savoy Operas*, p. 165.
25 Ellmann, *Oscar Wilde*, p. 130.
26 Edel, *Henry James: The Conquest of London*, p. 462.
27 Shand-Tucci, *Boston Bohemia*, p. 15.
28 Edel, *Henry James: The Conquest of London*, p. 462.
29 See Shand-Tucci, *Boston Bohemia*, pp. 222–37 and *passim*.
30 James, *Letters*, vol. 2, p. 372.
31 'Hyacinth' is a name with an extensive homoerotic genealogy. As Wendy Graham points out, 'Hyacinthus was dear to Apollo', and sexually available youths in Georgian England were called 'Hyacinths' ('Henry James's Subterranean Blues', p. 63). See Bartlett's *Who Was That Man?* for a wonderful account of Wilde's association with hyacinths and other flowers, and the erotic meanings that attach to them.
32 One of the book's first reviewers wrote in the San Francisco *Chronicle* that '[T]he portrait of Gabriel Nash ... has the air of being taken from life, so clearly outlined it is, and were it a few years back it might have been surmised to be a clever sketch of Oscar Wilde' (In Hayes, (ed.), *Henry James: The Contemporary Reviews*, p. 221). See Richard Ellmann, 'Henry James Among the Aesthetes', in *a long the riverrun*, pp. 132–49, and Freedman, *Professions of Taste*, pp. 182–92, for accounts of the relation between Wilde, British Aestheticism and *The Tragic Muse*.
33 Gagnier, *Idylls of the Marketplace*, p. 163. Gagnier's source is W. Graham Robertson, *Time Was*, p. 135.
34 Ibid., pp. 163–4.
35 James, *Letters*, vol. 3, p. 373.
36 Freedman gives a very fine analysis of this speech in *Professions of Taste*, pp. 173–5.
37 James, *Letters*, vol. 4, p. 12.
38 James, 'Charles Baudelaire', *Literary Criticism: French Writers*, p. 158.

39 James, *Letters*, vol. 4, pp. 9–10.

40 James 'wrote to Paul Bourget that Wilde's sentence was too severe, that isolation would have been more just . . . What made James's finely shaded discrimination particularly repulsive was that Wilde had experienced both hard labor and isolation.' Ellmann, *Oscar Wilde*, p. 474.

41 I am thinking of Sander L. Gilman's *Jewish Self-Hatred: Anti-Semitism and the Hidden Language of the Jews*.

42 For Freedman, Wilde and James 'perfectly exemplify two distinct styles of late Victorian homoeroticism: the latent and the blatant' (*Professions of Taste*, p. 171). I am viewing James as cautious and secretive rather than 'latent'.

43 Quoted in Edel, *The Conquest of London*, pp. 234, 409.

44 Edel, *The Life of Henry James*, vol. 1, p. 409. Edel does not make this claim in the earlier version of the biography.

45 Ibid., volume 1, pp. 750–2.

46 Ibid., volume 1, p. 751. In the earlier version of the biography, Edel leaves out the word 'homosexual' from this sentence (*The Middle Years*, p. 88).

47 Freedman, *Professions of Taste*, p. 169.

48 See chapter one, p. 17.

49 Freedman, *Professions of Taste*, p. 168.

50 John Fletcher, in 'The Haunted Closet: Henry James's Queer Spectrality', analyses the homoerotic ghostly encounter which takes place in 'The Real Right Thing'.

51 James, *A Small Boy and Others*, in *Autobiography*, pp. 196–7.

52 Castle's *The Apparitional Lesbianism* inspiringly demonstrated the importance of ghosts to lesbian and gay studies. A conference of May 1996 at Warwick University entitled 'Homospectrality' was helpful to me in developing this analysis of James and the ghostly.

53 Edel, *The Life of Henry James*, vol. 1, pp. 60–1.

54 James, *A Small Boy and Others*, p. 196.

55 William James, 'The Hidden Self', p. 93. Janet's study was first published in 1889.

56 Leys, 'The Real Miss Beauchamp: Gender and the Subject of Imitation', p. 169. In this article Leys shows how the period's fascination with 'multiple personality' frustrates the quest for a '"real" or "original" identity' (p. 169). One of the first essays on multiple personality is Frederick Myers's 'Multiplex Personality', published in *Nineteenth Century* in 1886.

57 See Morton Prince, *The Dissociation of a Personality* and *Psychotherapy and Multiple Personality*.

58 See especially Karl Miller, 'Queer Fellows', in *Doubles*, pp. 209–44.

59 Showalter, *Sexual Anarchy*, p. 107.

60 Sedgwick uses the term 'paranoid Gothic' to indicate 'Romantic novels in which a male hero is in a close, usually murderous relation to another male figure, in some respects his "double," to whom he seems to be mentally transparent' (*Epistemology of the Closet*, p. 186).

61 Miller, *Doubles*, p. 216. However, Miller goes on to read 'The Jolly Corner' as

negotiating an Oedipal family romance and the tensions of James's 'double nationality' and his ambivalent relationship with America (*Doubles*, pp. 229–34).

62 Stevenson, *Strange Case of Dr Jekyll and Mr Hyde*, p. 121.

63 Ibid., p. 126.

64 Heath, 'Psychopathia Sexualis', p. 95.

65 James, 'Robert Louis Stevenson', *Essays on Literature*, p. 1,252.

66 The American context of the story is illuminated by recent studies by Chauncey (*Gay New York*) and Shand-Tucci (*Boston Bohemia*) which describe the development of urban gay subcultures in America at the turn of the century. James Gifford, in *Dayneford's Library: American Homosexual Writing, 1900–1913*, places 'The Jolly Corner' in a tradition of American queer writing associated with the emergence of a gay tradition in the early twentieth century, and reads Brydon's ghost as a 'homosexual apparition' Brydon sees as *other* than himself (p. 86).

67 See e.g. Freud, 'Notes on a Case of Paranoia' ('Schreber'), *PFL* 9:198.

68 Describing his visit to the church of Saint Julian at Tours in *A Little Tour in France* James writes: 'I have always thought there is a sex in fine buildings; and Saint Julian, with its noble nave, is of the gender of its patron' (p. 17). He frequently uses buildings to create an erotic discourse.

69 Freud, *Three Essays*, *PFL* 7:104.

70 See Bersani's 'Is the Rectum a Grave?' for an examination of the fantasies surrounding active and passive sexuality, and the relationship between sexuality and politics. In what reads almost uncannily like a description of the eroticism of 'The Jolly Corner', Bersani writes that '[i]t is possible to think of the sexual as, precisely, moving between a hyperbolic sense of self and a loss of all consciousness of self' (p. 218).

71 See pp. 11–12 for a discussion of the meaning of the word 'queer'.

72 Wilde, *The Picture of Dorian Gray*, pp. 155–6. Further references are given parenthetically in the text.

73 In Freedman, 'James, Wilde, and the Incorporation of Aestheticism', *Professsions of Taste*, pp. 167–201.

74 Donna Przybylowicz argues that 'in [his] acceptance of Alice's love [Brydon] acknowledges sexual difference and desire' and 'returns to the intersubjective realm of the superego and social authority' (*Desire and Repression*, p. 124).

75 Leys, 'The Real Miss Beauchamp', p. 197.

76 Krishna Baldev Vaid, in a study published in 1964, comes tantalizing close to the interpretation offered here. He writes that at the end of the first section of the tale 'we have all that we need to know about the nature of Brydon's obsession and his determination to see the "wretch," an appellation that beautifully indicates the interlocked knot of his desire and his dread'. However, Vaid does not tell us *what it is* that we know so fully, or *what exactly* the wretch indicates. He also writes, noting the tale's 'clarity': 'The "moral" of the tale is clear: given the type of alternative self that Brydon, or any man like him, might have had, his wholeness and health follow an exorcization of that other self. In other words, it does not celebrate the repudiation of all the unfulfilled possibilities of the

past, but only of certain kinds of unfulfilled possibilities.' (*Technique in the Tales of Henry James* p. 237.) Vaid does not specify what these 'certain kinds of unfulfilled possibilities' are, but his analysis of the repudiation mechanism taking place is acute. However, the tale does not seem to 'celebrate' such repudiation.

77 For a superb analysis of the taboo on homosexuality, see Butler, *Gender Trouble*, pp. 59–72.

7 JAMES'S 'POOR SENSITIVE GENTLEMEN'

1 Symonds, 'A Problem in Modern Ethics', p. 150; Mayne, *Intersexes*, p. 505.

2 See Vito Russo's *The Celluloid Closet* for an account of the many macabre deaths reserved for lesbian and gay male characters in Hollywood cinema, many of which are listed in his 'necrology' (pp. 347–9).

3 James, *The Princess Casamassima*, p. 590.

4 Stevenson, *Strange Case of Dr Jekyll and Mr Hyde*, pp. 83–4.

5 Wilde, *The Picture of Dorian Gray*, p. 167. Subsequent references are given parenthetically within the text.

6 Russo's *The Celluloid Closet* discusses the recurrence of such plots in twentieth-century cinema.

7 Wilde, *The Picture of Dorian Gray*, pp. 127, 129.

8 For detailed discussions of the Cleveland Street Scandal see H. Montgomery Hyde, *The Cleveland Street Scandal*, and Colin Simpson et al, *The Cleveland Street Affair*.

9 Gagnier, *Idylls of the Marketplace*, p. 61.

10 Sturgis's *Tim* and *Belchamber* both show the tragic fate of same-sex friendships, particularly friendships formed in school or at university.

11 The notion that a "repression" of alterior sexual experiences and identities might in fact constitute a promotion of subversive sexuality is central to Anna Marie Smith's *New Right Discourse on Race and Sexuality*. Her insights, although derived from a study of Thatcherite Britain, can productively be brought to consideration of the 1890s. The staged suicide of Sir A. B. C. Beadel-Muffet in 'The Papers' (1903), and the actual suicide of Newton Winch in 'A Round of Visits' (1910) both can be related to a queer context, but there is not space to discuss the issue of suicide here.

12 For an account of turn of the century mass-circulation newspapers, see Stephen Koss, *The Rise and Fall of the Political Press in Britain*, pp. 356–408.

13 See Cohen, *Talk on the Wilde Side*, and Brake, *Subjugated Knowledges* for accounts of late nineteenth-century journalistic representations of homosexuality.

14 Gagnier's translation, in *Idylls of the Marketplace*, p. 206.

15 Ibid., pp. 205–6.

16 Ibid., p. 155.

17 Savoy, '"In the Cage" and the Queer Effects of Gay History', p. 287.

18 Letter to Edmund Gosse, *Letters*, vol. 4, p. 12.

19 For full discussions of the queer context of *In the Cage*, see Savoy, '"In the Cage" and the Queer Effects of Gay History', and my 'Queer Henry *In the Cage*'.

20 Freud, 'Mourning and Melancholia', *PFL* 11:252–3. Subsequent references (to *MM*) are given parenthetically in the text.
21 Butler, *Gender Trouble*, p. 59. Butler's extensive work on mourning, melancholia and queer identity in this study and in *Bodies that Matter* has been invaluable in helping me formulate this reading of James.
22 Laplanche and Pontalis, *The Language of Psycho-Analysis*, p. 255.
23 Wilde, *De Profundis, Complete Works*, p. 938. This phrase was left out of the 1905 edition published by Robert Ross; however, it is quite possible that James, who was friendly with Ross, saw the typescript of *De Profundis*. In any case, as Richard Ellmann points out, Wilde often talked of his youthful male acquaintances as panthers – panthers who were of course eventually to compromise Wilde. (*Oscar Wilde*, pp. 423, 427.)
24 See Bersani, 'Is the Rectum a Grave?', Douglas Crimp, 'Mourning and Militancy', and Tim Dean, 'The Psychoanalysis of AIDS'.
25 Dean, 'The Psychoanalysis of AIDS', pp. 95, 104.
26 See Weeks, *Coming Out* and *Sex, Politics and Society*.
27 To Gosse, 7 January 1893, *Letters*, vol. 3, p. 398.
28 This passage recalls the way in which Rowland Mallet envies the position occupied by Mary Garland in *Roderick Hudson*.
29 A similar situation arises in 'Crapy Cornelia' (1909). In this story White-Mason, the protagonist, who plans to propose to the widow Mrs Worthingham, is forestalled by his learning of her acquaintance with Cornelia Rasch, a 'little clever queer creature' (*CT* 12:351) who possesses compromising information about his past. The tale does not divulge this information, which White-Mason thinks of as 'a massive little bundle of data' (p. 352), but connects it with White-Mason's former association with Mary Cardew, a 'girl long since dead' with whom he used to flirt, and who thought, for some reason, that White-Mason wasn't 'fair' (pp. 359, 366). At the end of the tale White-Mason says that both he and Cornelia are 'high', that is, like 'high game' (p. 366), and decides that he doesn't after all want to marry Mrs Worthingham.
30 Butler, *Gender Trouble*, p. 60.
31 Hawkins, 'Naming Names', p. 770.
32 Bersani, *The Culture of Redemption*, p. 7.
33 Butler, *Gender Trouble*, p. 39.

CONCLUSION: 'THAT QUEER MONSTER THE ARTIST'

1 James, *Letters*, vol. 4, p. 706.
2 Introduction to *Watch and Ward*, p. 6.
3 My article 'Queer Henry *In the Cage*' analyses in depth the way in which this tale foregrounds the erotic discourse encoded on its surface, and ironizes the circulation of sexual secrets in fin de siècle Britain.
4 James, *The Ambassadors*, p. 36. Further references are given in the text.
5 From letters to Walpole, *Letters*, vol. 4, pp. 574, 577, 585, 694. Subsequent references to *Letters*, by volume and page number, are given in the text.

6 For example: 'Allowance must be made for James's long puritan years, the confirmed habits of denial, the bachelor existence, in which erotic feeling had been channelled into hours of strenuous work … One must also remember that James had a fear of loss of masculinity.' Edel, *The Treacherous Years*, p. 299.

7 The question has been what to do in the absence of concrete evidence. To conclude from this absence that Henry James must have remained virginal is regarded as proper scholarly caution, but it is of course to make a claim without any evidence. Briefly, Leon Edel hypothesizes that James did not 'act out' his 'verbal passion', while acknowledging that '[w]e simply do not know' (*The Treacherous Years*, p. 298), while Fred Kaplan stresses the importance of James's friendships with young men, but claims, without evidence, that these friendships remained chaste: 'James had with these young men the tacit understanding that anything beyond warm embraces would be distasteful to him' (*Henry James: The Imagination of Genius*, p. 453). Sheldon Novick's recent *Henry James: The Young Master* claims James was sexually active with other men from the age of twenty-two, but this claim is as hypothetical as those put forward by Edel and Kaplan.

8 Bredbeck, 'Narcissus in the Wilde: Textual Cathexis and the Historical Origins of Queer Camp', in Moe Meyer, (ed.), *The Politics and Poetics of Camp*, p. 51.

9 See a footnote by Edel in *Letters*, vol. 4, p. 702.

10 James, *What Maisie Knew*, pp. 33–4.

11 Woolf, *Flush: A Biography*; Ackerley, *My Dog Tulip* (1956), *We Think the World of You* (1960).

12 James to Wharton, 2 December 1911, in Powers, (ed.), *Henry James and Edith Wharton: Letters, 1900–1915*, p. 211.

13 See Powers, (ed.), *Henry James and Edith Wharton: Letters, 1900–1915*, p. 14.

14 See Judith Butler, 'Imitation and Gender Insubordination', for a provocative discussion of the strengths and pitfalls of identity statements.

15 James, *Notes of a Son and Brother*, in *Autobiography*, p. 293.

16 The visit is descibed in Geoffrey Keynes, *Henry James in Cambridge*.

17 Quoted in Edel, *Henry James: The Master*, p. 403.

18 Keynes, *Henry James in Cambridge*, pp. 18–19.

Bibliography

1 WORKS BY HENRY JAMES

I give the first date of publication of each text and the specific edition I quote from. (For some novels more than one version is referred to; as far as possible, works are listed in order of first publication.)

Watch and Ward. 1878. Ed. Leon Edel. London: Rupert Hart-Davis, 1960.

Roderick Hudson. London: Macmillan, 1878. Ed. Geoffrey Moore. Harmondsworth: Penguin, 1986.

Roderick Hudson. New York: Scribner's, 1907. Ed. Tony Tanner. Oxford: Oxford University Press, 1980.

The American. London: Macmillan, 1879. Ed. William Spengemann. Harmondsworth: Penguin, 1981.

Confidence. 1879. London: Chatto and Windus, 1880.

The Portrait of a Lady. 1881. New York: Scribner's, 1908. Ed. Geoffrey Moore. Harmondsworth: Penguin, 1986.

A Little Tour in France. 1884. Intr. Leon Edel. Harmondsworth: Penguin, 1985.

The Bostonians. 1886. Harmondsworth: Penguin, 1966.

The Princess Casamassima. 1886. Ed. Derek Brewer. Harmondsworth: Penguin, 1987.

The Tragic Muse. 1890. Harmondsworth: Penguin, 1978.

The Spoils of Poynton. 1897. Harmondsworth: Penguin, 1963.

What Maisie Knew. 1897. New York: Scribner's, 1909. Harmondsworth: Penguin, 1966.

The Turn of the Screw. 1898. Norton Critical Edition. Ed. Robert Kimbrough. New York: Norton, 1966.

The Awkward Age. 1899. Ed. Vivien Jones. Oxford: Oxford University Press, 1984.

The Sacred Fount. 1901. New York: Grove Press, 1979.

The Wings of the Dove. 1902. New York: Scribner's, 1909. Ed. Peter Brooks. Oxford: Oxford University Press, 1984.

The Ambassadors. 1903. New York: Scribner's, 1909. Ed. Christopher Butler. Oxford: Oxford University Press, 1985.

English Hours. 1905. Ed. Leon Edel. Oxford and New York: Oxford University Press, 1905.

The Golden Bowl. 1905. New York: Scribner's, 1909. Ed. Gore Vidal. Harmondsworth: Penguin, 1985.

The Question of Our Speech and The Lesson of Balzac: Two Lectures. Boston: Houghton, Mifflin & Co. 1905.

'The Speech of American Women'. *Harper's Bazar*, 40 (1906): 979–82, 1,103–6; 41 (1907): 17–21, 113–17.

'The Manners of American Women'. *Harper's Bazar*, 41 (1907): 355–9, 453–8, 537–41, 646–51.

The American Scene. 1907. London: Granville, 1987.

A Small Boy and Others. London: Macmillan, 1913.

Notes of a Son and Brother. London: Macmillan, 1914.

The Ivory Tower. 1917. Fairfield, NJ: Augustus M. Kelley, 1976.

Letters to A. C. Benson and Auguste Monod. Ed. E. F. Benson. London: Elkins Mathews & Marrot, 1930.

The Art of the Novel: Critical Prefaces. Ed. Richard P. Blackmur. New York: Scribner's, 1934.

The Complete Plays of Henry James. Ed. Leon Edel. London: Rupert Hart-Davis, 1949.

Autobiography. Ed. Frederick W. Dupee. London: W. H. Allen, 1956.

The House of Fiction: Essays on the Novel by Henry James. Ed. Leon Edel. London: Rupert Hart-Davis, 1957.

The Complete Tales of Henry James. Ed. Leon Edel. 12 vols. London: Rupert Hart-Davis, 1962–4.

Letters. Ed. Leon Edel. 4 volumes. London: Macmillan, 1974–84.

Literary Criticism: Essays on Literature; American Writers; English Writers. Ed. Leon Edel and Mark Wilson. New York: Library of America, 1984.

Literary Criticism: French Writers; Other European Writers; The Prefaces to the New York Edition. Ed. Leon Edel and Mark Wilson. New York: Library of America, 1984.

The Figure in the Carpet and Other Stories. Ed. Frank Kermode. Harmondsworth: Penguin, 1986.

The Complete Notebooks of Henry James. Ed. Leon Edel and Lyall H. Powers. New York and Oxford: Oxford University Press, 1987.

Henry James: Selected Letters. Ed. Leon Edel. Cambridge, MA and London: Harvard University Press, 1987.

Henry James and Edith Wharton: Letters, 1900–1915. Ed. Lyall H. Powers. London: Weidenfeld and Nicolson, 1990.

2 OTHER PRIMARY SOURCES

About, Edmond. *Germaine*. Paris, 1858.

Baudelaire, Charles. *The Flowers of Evil*. Trans. James McGowan. Oxford: Oxford University Press, 1993.

Beckett, Samuel. *The Complete Dramatic Works*. London: Faber and Faber, 1986.

Benson, E. F. *The Challoners*. London: William Heinemann, 1904.

Brontë, Emily. *Wuthering Heights*. Ed. Ian Jack. Oxford and New York: Oxford University Press, 1981.

Browning, Robert. *Selected Poetry*. Ed. Daniel Karlin. Harmondsworth: Penguin, 1989.

Coleridge, Samuel Taylor. *Biographia Literaria*. Ed. George Watson. London: J. M. Dent, 1960.

Selected Letters. Ed. H. J. Jackson. Oxford, 1987.

Douglas, Lord Alfred. *Lyrics*. London: Rich and Cowan, 1935.

Dumas *fils*, Alexandre. *La Dame aux Camélias*. 1848. Trans. David Coward. Oxford: Oxford University Press, 1986.

Eliot, George. *The Mill on the Floss*. 1860. Ed. Gordon S. Haight. Oxford and New York: Oxford University Press, 1980.

Daniel Deronda. 1876. Ed. Barbara Hardy. Harmondsworth: Penguin, 1967.

Forster, E. M. *The Longest Journey*. 1907. Ed. Elizabeth Heine. Harmondsworth: Penguin, 1984.

Maurice. 1971. Harmondsworth: Penguin, 1972.

Gilbert, W. S. *The Savoy Operas*. London: Macmillan, 1926.

Haggard, Rider. *She*. 1887. Ed. Daniel Karlin. Oxford: Oxford University Press, 1991.

Hall, Radclyffe. *The Well of Loneliness*. 1928. London: Jonathan Cape, 1956.

Hardy, Thomas. *Tess of the d'Urbervilles*. Ed. Juliet Grindle and Simon Gatrell. Oxford and New York: Oxford University Press, 1988.

Harrison, Fraser, ed. *The Yellow Book: An Anthology*. Woodbridge: The Boydell Press, 1982.

Highsmith, Patricia. *Carol*. London: Bloomsbury, 1990. (First published pseudonymously as *The Price of Salt*, by Claire Morgan, 1952.)

Huysman, J.-K. *Against Nature*. Trans. Robert Baldick. Harmondsworth: Penguin, 1959.

James, Alice. *The Diary of Alice James*. Ed. Leon Edel. Harmondsworth: Penguin, 1982.

The Death and Letters of Alice James: Selected Correspondence. Ed. Ruth B. Yeazell. Berkeley: University of California Press, 1981.

James, William. 'The Hidden Self', *A William James Reader*. Ed. Gay Wilson Allen. Boston: Houghton Mifflin, 1971, pp. 90–108.

Kafka, Franz. *Collected Stories*. Ed. Gabriel Josipovici. London: Everyman's, 1993.

Keats, John. *Poetical Works*. Oxford: Oxford University Press, 1901.

Lawrence, D. H. *The Rainbow*. Ed. Mark Kinkead-Weekes. Cambridge: Cambridge University Press, 1989.

Women in Love. 1920. Ed. David Farmer, Lindeth Vasey and John Worthen. Cambridge: Cambridge University Press, 1987.

The Complete Short Novels. Ed. Keith Sagar and Melissa Partridge. Harmondsworth: Penguin, 1987.

MacDonald, George. *Lilith*. 1895. London and New York: Allison & Busby, n.d.

Mayne, Xavier [Edward Irenaeus Prime Stevenson]. *Imre: A Memorandum*. 1906. New York: Arno, 1975.

Melville, Herman. *Redburn: His First Voyage; White-Jacket; or The World in a Man-of-War; Moby-Dick; or, The Whale.* New York: Library or America, 1983.

Mürger, Henry. *Scènes de la vie de Bohème.* Paris, 1851.

Sackville-West, Vita. *Family History.* London: The Hogarth Press, 1932.

Schiller, Johann Christoph Friedrich von. *Mary Stuart; Joan of Arc.* Trans. Robert David MacDonald. Birmingham: Oberon Books, 1987.

Shakespeare, William. *Othello.* Ed. Kenneth Muir. Harmondsworth: Penguin, 1968.

The Sins of the Cities of the Plain, or The Recollections of a Mary-Ann. With Short Essays on Sodomy and Tribadism. 2 vols. London: privately printed, 1881.

Stevenson, Robert Louis. *Strange Case of Dr Jekyll and Mr Hyde.* London: Longmans, Green, and Co., 1886.

The Strange Case of Dr Jekyll and Mr Hyde and Other Stories. Ed. Jenni Calder. Harmondsworth: Penguin, 1979.

Stoker, Bram. *Dracula.* 1897. Ed. A. N. Wilson. Oxford and New York: Oxford University Press, 1983.

Sturgis, Howard. *Tim.* London: Macmillan, 1891.

Belchamber. 1904. Ed. Noel Annan. Oxford: Oxford University Press, 1986.

Taylor, Bayard. *Joseph and His Friend: A Story of Pennsylvania.* 1870. New York: Putnam's, 1881.

Warner, Sylvia Townsend. *Mr. Fortune's Maggot.* London: Chatto & Windus, 1927.

Waugh, Evelyn. *Brideshead Revisited: The Sacred and Profane Memories of Captain Charles Ryder.* 1945. Harmondsowrth: Penguin, 1962.

Whitman, Walt. *The Complete Poems.* Ed. Francis Murphy. Harmondsworth: Penguin, 1975.

Wilde, Oscar. *The Picture of Dorian Gray.* 1891. Ed. Isobel Murray. London: Oxford University Press, 1974.

Complete Works of Oscar Wilde. London and Glasgow: Collins, 1969.

The Artist as Critic: Critical Writings of Oscar Wilde. Ed. Richard Ellmann. London: W. H. Allen, 1970.

Wilde, Oscar, and Others. *Teleny.* Ed. John McRae. London: GMP Publishers, 1986.

Woolf, Virginia. *Flush: A Biography.* 1933. London: Hogarth, 1958.

Yeats, W. B. *Collected Poems.* London: Macmillan, 1950.

3 SECONDARY SOURCES

Anesko, Michael. *"Friction with the Market": Henry James and the Profession of Authorship.* New York and Oxford: Oxford University Press, 1986.

Appignanesi, Lisa. *Femininity and the Creative Imagination: A Study of Henry James, Robert Musil and Marcel Proust.* New York: Harper and Row, 1973.

Ariès, Philippe. *The Hour of Our Death.* Trans. Helen Weaver. Harmondsworth: Penguin, 1981.

Armstrong, Nancy. *Desire and Domestic Fiction: A Political History of the Novel.* New York and Oxford: Oxford University Press, 1987.

Armstrong, Nancy, and Leonard Tennenhouse, eds. *The Violence of Representation: Literature and the History of Violence.* London: Routledge, 1989.

Austen, Roger. *Playing the Game: The Homosexual Novel in America.* Indianapolis: Bobbs-Merrill, 1977.

Barthes, Roland. *The Pleasure of the Text.* 1973. Trans. Richard Miller. New York: Hill and Wang, 1975.

S/Z. 1973. Trans. Richard Miller. Oxford: Basil Blackwell, 1990.

Roland Barthes by Roland Barthes. Trans. Richard Howard. Basingstoke: Macmillan, 1975.

Incidents. Trans. Richard Howard. Berkeley, Los Angeles and Oxford: University of California Press, 1992.

Bartlett, Neil. *Who Was That Man?: A Present For Mr Oscar Wilde.* London: Serpent's Tail, 1988.

Bataille, Georges. *Erotism: Death and Sensuality.* Trans. Mary Dalwood. San Francisco: City Lights, 1986.

Bayley, John. 'The Master at War'. Rev. of *Henry James: The Imagination of Genius*, by Fred Kaplan. *New York Review of Books* 28 January 1993: 9–10.

Beaver, Harold. 'Homosexual Signs (In Memory of Roland Barthes)'. *Critical Inquiry* 8 (1981): 99–191.

Beckson, Karl, ed. *Oscar Wilde: The Critical Heritage.* London: Routledge & Kegan Paul, 1970.

Beer, Gillian. *Darwin's Plots: Evolutionary Narrative in Darwin, George Eliot and Nineteenth-Century Fiction.* London: Routledge & Kegan Paul, 1983.

Bell, Ian F. A., ed. *Henry James: Fiction as History.* London: Vision, 1984.

Henry James and the Past. Basingstoke and London: Macmillan, 1991.

Bender, John. *Imagining the Penetentiary: Fiction and the Architecture of Mind in Eighteenth-Century England.* Chicago: University of Chicago Press, 1987.

Benjamin, Jessica. *The Bonds of Love: Psychoanalysis, Feminism and the Problem of Domination.* London: Virago, 1988.

Bercovitch, Sacvan, ed. *Reconstructing American Literary History.* Cambridge, MA: Harvard University Press, 1986.

Bergman, David. *Gaiety Transfigured: Gay Self-Representation in American Literature.* Madison, WI: University of Wisconsin Press, 1991.

Berland, Alwyn. *Culture and Conduct in the Novels of Henry James.* Cambridge: Cambridge University Press, 1981.

Bernauer, James, and David Rasmussen, eds. *The Final Foucault.* Cambridge, MA and London: MIT Press, 1988.

Bernheimer, Charles, and Claire Kahane, eds. *In Dora's Case: Freud, Hysteria, Feminism.* London: Virago Press, 1985.

Bersani, Leo. *A Future for Astyanax: Character and Desire in Literature.* 1976. London: Boyars, 1978.

'The Subject of Power'. *Diacritics* 7.3 (1977): 2–21.

The Freudian Body: Psychoanalysis and Art. New York: Columbia University Press, 1986.

'Is the Rectum a Grave?' *Aids: Cultural Analysis, Cultural Activism.* Ed. Douglas Crimp. Cambridge, MA and London: MIT Press, 1988, pp. 197–222.

The Culture of Redemption. Cambridge, MA: Harvard University Press, 1990.

Boone, Joseph A. and Michael Cadden, eds. *Engendering Men: The Question of Male Feminist Criticism.* London: Routledge, 1990.

Borch-Jacobsen, Mikkel. *The Freudian Subject.* Trans. Catherine Porter. Stanford, CA: Stanford University Press, 1988.

Boren, Lynda S. *Eurydice Reclaimed: Language, Gender and Voice in Henry James.* Ann Arbor, MI: UMI Research Press, 1989.

Bowie, Malcolm. *Lacan.* London: Fontana, 1991.

Bradbury, Nicola. *Henry James: The Later Novels.* Oxford: Clarendon Press, 1979.

An Annotated Critical Bibliography of Henry James. Brighton: Harvester, 1987.

Brake, Laurel. *Subjugated Knowledges: Journalism, Gender and Literature in the Nineteenth Century.* Basingstoke and London: Macmillan, 1994.

Brennan, Teresa, ed. *Between Feminism and Psychoanalysis.* London: Routledge, 1989.

Brennan, Teresa. *The Interpretation of the Flesh: Freud and Femininity.* London and New York: Routledge, 1992.

Bristow, Joseph. '"Churlsgrace": Gerald Manley Hopkins and the Working-Class Male Body'. *ELH* 59 (1992): 693–711.

Effeminate England: Homoerotic Writing After 1885. Buckingham: Open University Press, 1995.

Brooks, Cleanth. *The Well Wrought Urn: Studies in the Structure of Poetry.* London: Denis Dobson, 1949.

Brooks, Peter. *The Melodramatic Imagination: Balzac, Henry James, Melodrama and the Mode of Excess.* New Haven, CT: Yale University Press, 1976.

'The Idea of a Psychoanalytic Literary Criticism'. In Meltzer, pp. 145–60.

Budd, John. *Henry James: A Bibliography of Criticism, 1975–1981.* Westport, CT: Greenwood Press, 1983.

Butler, Judith. *Gender Trouble: Feminism and the Subversion of Identity.* New York and London: Routledge, 1990.

Bodies That Matter: On the Discursive Limits of Sex. New York and London: Routledge, 1993.

'Imitation and Gender Insubordination'. In Fuss, *Inside/Out*, pp. 13–31.

Butler, Judith and Joan W. Scott, eds. *Feminists Theorize the Political.* New York and London: Routledge, 1992.

Carter, Angela. *The Sadeian Woman: An Exercise in Cultural History.* London: Virago, 1979.

Castle, Terry. *The Apparitional Lesbian: Female Homosexuality and Modern Culture.* New York: Columbia University Press, 1993.

Chase, Cynthia. *Decomposing Figures: Rhetorical Readings in the Romantic Tradition.* Baltimore: Johns Hopkins University Press, 1986.

Chauncey, George S. *Gay New York: Gender, Urban Culture, and the Making of the Gay Male World, 1890–1940.* New York: BasicBooks, 1994.

Cixous, Hélène. 'The Laugh of the Medusa'. Trans. Keith Cohen and Paula Cohen. *Signs* 1 (1976): 875–93.

Portrait de Dora, in *Théâtre: Portrait de Dora et La Prise de l'école de Madhubaï.* Paris: Editions des Femmes, 1986.

Cohen, Ed. *Talk on the Wilde Side: Towards a Genealogy of Male Sexualities.* New York and London: Routledge, 1993.

Conrad, Joseph. *Notes on Life and Letters.* London and Toronto: J. M. Dent and Sons, 1921.

Craft, Christopher. *Another Kind of Love: Male Homosexual Desire in English Discourse, 1850–1920.* Berkeley, CA: University of California Press, 1994.

Crimp, Douglas, ed. *Aids: Cultural Analysis, Cultural Activism.* Cambridge, MA and London: MIT Press, 1988.

'Mourning and Militancy'. *October* 51 (1989): 3–18.

Cunningham, A. R. 'The "New Woman Fiction" of the 1890's'. *Victorian Studies* 17 (1973): 177–86.

Davidson, Arnold I. 'How to Do the History of Psychoanalysis: A Reading of Freud's *Three Essays on the Theory of Sexuality*'. In Meltzer, pp. 39–64.

Davis, Lloyd. *Sexuality and Textuality in Henry James: Reading Through the Virginal.* New York: Peter Lang, 1988.

Dean, Tim. 'The Psychoanalysis of AIDS'. *October* 63 (1993): 83–116.

De Lauretis, Teresa. *Alice Doesn't: Feminism, Semiotics, Cinema.* London: Macmillan, 1984.

'Freud, Sexuality, and Perversion'. In Stanton, pp. 216–34.

De Man, Paul. *Blindness and Insight: Essays in the Rhetoric of Contemporary Criticism.* 1971. Revised second edition. London: Routledge, 1983.

Allegories of Reading: Figural Language in Rousseau, Nietzsche, Rilke, and Proust. New Haven, CT and London: Yale University Press, 1979.

The Rhetoric of Romanticism. New York: Columbia University Press, 1984.

The Resistance to Theory. Ed. Wlad Godzich. *Theory and History of Literature,* 33. Manchester: Manchester University Press, 1986.

Deleuze, Gilles. *Coldness and Cruelty.* Introduction to Leopold von Sacher-Masoch, *Venus in Furs.* Trans. Jean McNeil. 1971. New York: Zone Books, 1991.

Foucault. Trans. Seán Hand. London: Athlone, 1988. Trans. of *Foucault.* 1986.

Deleuze, Gilles and Félix Guattari. *Anti-Oedipus: Capitalism and Schizophrenia.* Preface by Michel Foucault. Trans. Robert Hurley, Mark Seem, and Helen R. Lane. London: Athlone, 1984.

Dellamora, Richard. *Masculine Desire: The Sexual Politics of Victorian Aestheticism.* Chapel Hill: University of North Carolina Press, 1990.

D'Emilio, John and Estelle B. Freedman. *Intimate Matters: A History of Sexuality in America.* New York: Harper & Row, 1988.

Derrida, Jacques. *Of Grammatology.* Trans. Gayatri Chakravorty Spivak. Baltimore: Johns Hopkins University Press, 1976.

Diamond, Irene and Lee Quinby, eds. *Feminism and Foucault: Reflections on Resistance.* Boston, MA: Northeastern University Press, 1988.

Dijkstra, Bram. *Idols of Perversity: Fantasies of Feminine Evil in Fin-de-Siècle Culture.* New York and Oxford: Oxford University Press, 1986.

Dollimore, Jonathan. *Sexual Dissidence: Augustine to Wilde, Freud to Foucault.* Oxford: Clarendon Press, 1991.

Donadio, Stephen. *Nietzsche, Henry James and the Artistic Will.* New York: Oxford University Press, 1978.

Donald, Adrienne. 'Coming out of the Canon: Sadomasochism, Male Homo-eroticism, Romanticism'. *The Yale Journal of Criticism* 3.1 (1989): 239–52.

Donoghue, Emma. *Passions Between Women: British Lesbian Culture 1668–1801*. London: Scarlet Press, 1993.

Donzelot, Jacques. *The Policing of Families: Welfare versus the State*. Trans. Robert Hurley. London: Hutchinson, 1979.

Dowling, Linda. 'The Decadent and the New Woman in the 1890's'. *Nineteenth Century Fiction*, 33 (1979): 434–53.

Language and Decadence in the Victorian Fin de Siècle. Princeton, NJ: Princeton University Press, 1986.

Hellenism and Homosexuality in Victorian Oxford. Ithaca and London: Cornell University Press, 1994.

Dreyfus, Hubert L. and Paul Rabinow. *Michel Foucault: Beyond Structuralism and Hermeneutics*. Brighton: Harvester, 1982.

Duberman, Martin. *About Time: Exploring the Gay Past*. Revised and Expanded Edition. New York: Meridian, 1991.

During, Simon. *Foucault and Literature: Towards a Genealogy of Writing*. London and New York: Routledge, 1992.

Eagleton, Terry. *The Ideology of the Aesthetic*. Oxford: Blackwell, 1990.

Edel, Leon. *Henry James: The Untried Years, 1843–1870*. London: Rupert Hart-Davis, 1953.

Henry James: The Conquest of London, 1870–1883. London: Rupert Hart-Davis, 1962.

Henry James: The Middle Years, 1884–1894. London: Rupert Hart-Davis, 1963.

Henry James: The Treacherous Years, 1895–1901. London: Rupert Hart-Davis, 1969.

Henry James: The Master, 1901–1916. London: Rupert Hart-Davis, 1972.

Edel, Leon. *The Life of Henry James*. Two volumes. Harmondsworth: Penguin, 1977.

Edel, Leon and Dan H. Laurence. *A Bibliography of Henry James*. Second edition. London: Rupert Hart-Davis, 1961.

Ellis, Havelock. *Sexual Inversion*. London and Watford: The University Press, 1897.

Analysis of the Sexual Impulse; Love and Pain; The Sexual Impulse in Women. 1903. Second edition. Philadelphia: F. A. Davis Co., 1924. Vol. 3 of *Studies in the Psychology of Sex*. 6 vols. 1924.

'A Note on Paul Bourget'. *Views and Review: A Selection of Uncollected Articles 1884–1932. First Series: 1884–1919*. London: Desmond Harmsworth, 1932, pp. 48–60.

Ellmann, Richard. *Oscar Wilde*. 1987. Harmondsworth: Penguin, 1988.

a long the riverrun: Selected Essays. London: Hamish Hamilton, 1988.

Esch, Deborah. 'A Jamesian About-Face: Notes on "The Jolly Corner"'. *ELH* 50 (1983): 587–605.

Faderman, Lilian. *Surpassing the Love of Men: Romantic Friendship and Love Between Women from the Renaissance to the Present*. London: The Women's Press, 1985.

Feher, Michael, Ramona Naddaff and Nadia Tazi, eds. *Fragments for the History of the Human Body*. 3 vols. New York: Urzone, 1989.

Felman, Shoshana. 'To Open the Question'. *Yale French Studies* 55/56 (1977): 5–10.

'Rereading Femininity'. *Yale French Studies* 62 (1981): 19–44.

Writing and Madness. Ithaca: Cornell University Press, 1985.

Fetterley, Judith. *The Resisting Reader: A Feminist Approach to American Fiction*. Bloomington and London: Indiana University Press, 1978.

Fletcher, John. 'The Haunted Closet: Henry James's Queer Spectrality'. Unpublished paper.

Forrester, John. *The Seductions of Psychoanalysis: Freud, Lacan and Derrida*. Cambridge: Cambridge University Press, 1990.

Forster, E. M. *Aspects of the Novel*. 1927. Harmondsworth: Penguin, 1990.

Foucault, Michel. *The History of Sexuality: An Introduction*. Trans. Robert Hurley. London: Allen Lane, 1979. Trans. of *La Volonté de Savoir*. Paris: Gallimard, 1976.

Power/Knowledge: Selected Interviews and Other Writings, 1972–1977. Ed. Colin Gordon. Brighton: Harvester, 1980.

The Foucault Reader. Ed. Paul Rabinow. Harmondsworth: Penguin, 1984.

The Use of Pleasure: The History of Sexuality, Volume 2. Trans. Robert Hurley. Harmondsworth: Penguin, 1987. Trans. of *L'Usage des Plaisirs*. Paris: Gallimard, 1984.

The Care of the Self: The History of Sexuality, Volume 3. Trans. Robert Hurley. Harmondsworth: Penguin, 1988. Trans. of *Le Souci de Soi*. Paris: Gallimard, 1984.

'The Social Triumph of the Sexual Will'. A conversation with Michel Foucault conducted by Gilles Barbadette. Trans. Brendan Lemon. *Christopher Street* 64 (May 1982): 36–41.

'Michel Foucault, An Interview: Sex, Power and the Politics of Identity'. Conducted by Bob Gallagher and Alexander Wilson. *The Advocate* 400 (7 August 1984): 26–30, 58.

Politics, Philosophy, Culture: Interviews and Other Writings, 1977–1984. Ed. Lawrence D. Kritzman. New York and London: Routledge, 1988.

Fowler, Virginia C. 'Milly Theale's Malady of Self', *Novel* 14 (1980): 57–74.

Henry James's American Girl: The Embroidery on the Canvas. Madison, WI: University of Wisconsin Press, 1984.

Freedman, Jonathan. *Professions of Taste: Henry James, British Aestheticism, and Commodity Culture*. Stanford, CA: Stanford University Press, 1990.

'Henry James and the Discourses of Antisemitism'. In *Between "Race" and Culture: Representations of "the Jew" in English and American Literature*. Ed. Bryan Cheyette. Stanford, CA: Stanford University Press, 1996, pp. 62–83.

Freud, Sigmund. *The Standard Edition of the Complete Psychological Works of Sigmund Freud*. Ed. J. Strachey. Trans. J. Strachey et al. 23 vols. London: The Hogarth Press and the Institute of Psycho-Analysis, 1953–66.

The Pelican Freud Library. 15 vols. Ed. Angela Richards (vols. 1–11) and Albert Dixon (vols. 12–15). Harmondsworth: Penguin, 1973–86.

Fuss, Diana. *Essentially Speaking: Feminism, Nature and Difference*. New York and London: Routledge, 1989.

ed. *Inside/Out: Lesbian Theories, Gay Theories*. New York and London: Routledge, 1991.

Fussell, Edwin Sill. *The Catholic Side of Henry James*. Cambridge: Cambridge University Press, 1993.

Gagnier, Regenia. *Idylls of the Marketplace: Oscar Wilde and the Victorian Public*. Stanford, CA: Stanford University Press, 1986.

Gallagher, Catherine and Thomas Laqueur, eds. *The Making of the Modern Body: Sexuality and Society in the Nineteenth Century*. Berkeley: University of California Press, 1987.

Gallop, Jane. *Feminism and Psychoanalysis: The Daughter's Seduction*. London: Macmillan, 1982.

Reading Lacan. Ithaca: Cornell University Press, 1985.

Thinking Through the Body. New York: Columbia University Press, 1988.

Gard, Roger, ed. *Henry James: The Critical Heritage*. London: Routledge and Kegan Paul, 1968.

Garson, Marjorie. *Hardy's Fables of Integrity: Woman, Body, Text*. Oxford: Clarendon, 1991.

Geismar, Maxwell. *Henry James and his Cult*. London: Chatto & Windus, 1964.

Gifford, James. *Dayneford's Library: American Homosexual Writing, 1900–1913*. Amherst, MA: University of Massachusetts Press, 1995.

Gilbert, Sandra M. and Susan Gubar. *The Madwoman in the Attic: The Woman Writer and the Nineteenth-Century Literary Imagination*. New Haven, CT: Yale University Press, 1979.

Sexchanges. New Haven, CT and London: Yale University Press, 1989. Vol. 2 of *No Man's Land: The Place of the Woman Writer in the Twentieth Century*.

Gilman, Sander. *Jewish Self-Hatred: Anti-Semitism and the Hidden Language of the Jews*. Baltimore and London: Johns Hopkins University Press, 1986.

Girard, René. *Deceit, Desire, and the Novel: Self and Other in Literary Structure*. Trans. Yvonne Freccero. Baltimore: Johns Hopkins University Press, 1965.

Glendinning, Victoria. *Vita: The Life of V. Sackville-West*. London: Weidenfeld and Nicholson, 1983.

Godden, Richard. *Fictions of Capital: The American Novel from James to Mailer*. Cambridge: Cambridge University Press, 1990.

Gooder, Richard. Introduction. Henry James. *The Bostonians*. Oxford: Oxford University Press, 1984, pp. viii–xxxiii.

Groos, Arthur. 'Amore e Morte: Dying of Consumption'. In programme for production of *La Traviata*. London: Royal Opera House, 1996, pp. 33–42.

Graham, Wendy. 'Henry James's Subterranean Blues: A Rereading of *The Princess Casamassima*'. *Modern Fiction Studies* 40.1 (1994): 51–84.

Grosskurth, Phyllis. *John Addington Symonds: A Biography*. London: Longmans, 1964.

Havelock Ellis: A Biography. London: Allen Lane, 1980.

Habegger, Alfred. 'Henry James's Rewriting of Minny Temple's Letters'. *American Literature* 58 (1986): 159–80.

Gender, Fantasy, and Realism in American Literature. New York: Columbia University Press, 1982.

Henry James and the 'Woman Business'. Cambridge: Cambridge University Press, 1989.

Hall, G. Stanley. *Adolescence: Its Psychology and its Relations to Physiology, Anthropology, Sociology, Sex, Crime, Religion and Education*. 2 vols. New York: D. Appleton and Company, 1904.

Hall, Richard. 'Henry James: Interpreting an Obsessive Memory'. *Journal of Homosexuality* 8.3 (1993): 83–47.

Haller, John. S. and Robin. M. Haller. *The Physician and Sexuality in Victorian America*. Urbana: University of Illinois Press, 1974.

Halperin, David M. *One Hundred Years of Homosexuality and Other Essays on Greek Love*. New York and London: Routledge, 1990.

Hartman, Mary S. and Lois W. Banner. *Clio's Consciousness Raised: New Perspectives on the History of Women*. New York: Harper & Row, 1974.

Hawkins, Peter S. 'Naming Names: The Art of Memory and the NAMES Project AIDS Quilt'. *Critical Inquiry* 19 (1993): 752–79.

Hayes, Kevin J., ed. *Henry James: The Contemporary Reviews*. Cambridge: Cambridge University Press, 1996.

Heath, Stephen. 'Difference'. *Screen* 19.3 (1978): 50–112.

The Sexual Fix. London: Macmillan, 1982.

'Psychopathia Sexualis: Stevenson's *Strange Case*'. *Critical Quarterly* 28.1–2 (1986): 93–108.

Henke, Richard. 'The Embarrassment of Melodrama: Masculinity in the Early James'. *Novel* 28.3 (1995): 257–83.

Hertz, Neil. *The End of the Line: Essays on Psychoanalysis and the Sublime*. New York: Columbia University Press, 1985.

Hoggart, Simon. 'All Present and Incorrect'. *The Observer* (15 December 1991): 37–8.

Holland, Laurence Bedwell. *The Expense of Vision: Essays on the Craft of Henry James*. Princeton, NJ: Princeton University Press, 1964.

Hyde, H. Montgomery, ed. *The Trials of Oscar Wilde: Regina (Wilde) v. Queensberry; Regina v. Wilde and Taylor*. Notable British Trials Series. London: William Hodge, 1948.

The Cleveland Street Scandal. London: W. H. Allen, 1976.

Hynes, Samuel. *The Edwardian Turn of Mind*. Princeton, NJ: Princeton University Press, 1968.

Irigaray, Luce. *Speculum: Of the Other Woman*. Trans. Gillian C. Gill. Ithaca and London: Cornell University Press, 1985.

James, William. *The Varieties of Religious Experience: A Study in Human Nature*. 1902. Ed. Martin E. Marty. Harmondsworth: Penguin, 1985.

Jardine, Alice and Paul Smith, eds. *Men in Feminism*. New York and London: Methuen, 1987.

Jeffreys, Sheila. *The Spinster and Her Enemies: Feminism and Sexuality 1880–1930*. London: Pandora, 1985.

Jordanova, Ludmilla. *Sexual Visions: Images of Gender in Science and Medicine Between the Eighteenth and Twentieth Centuries*. Madison, WI: University of Wisconsin Press, 1989.

Kaplan, Fred. *Henry James: The Imagination of Genius. A Biography*. London: Hodder & Stoughton, 1992.

Kappeler, Susanne. *Writing and Reading in Henry James*. London: Macmillan, 1980.

Katz, Jonathan Ned. *Gay American History: Lesbians and Gay Men in the U.S.A.* 1976. Revised Edition. New York: Meridian, 1992.

Gay/Lesbian Almanac: A New Documentary. New York: Harper and Row, 1983.

Keating, Peter. *The Haunted Study: A Social History of the English Novel 1875–1914*. London: Secker & Warburg, 1989.

Keynes, Geoffrey. *Henry James in Cambridge*. Cambridge: W. Heffer & Sons, 1967.

Kincaid, James R. *Child-Loving: The Erotic Child and Victorian Culture*. New York and London: Routledge, 1992.

Klein, Melanie. *The Psycho-Analysis of Children*. 1932. Trans. Alix Strachey. Revised edition. 1975. London: Virago, 1989.

Contributions to Psycho-Analysis 1921–1945. Intr. Ernest Jones. 1948. New York, Toronto and London: McGraw-Hill, 1964

The Selected Melanie Klein. Ed. Juliet Mitchell. Harmondsworth: Penguin, 1986.

The Psycho-Analysis of Children. 1932. Trans. Alix Strachey. Revised edition. 1975. London: Virago, 1989.

Love, Guilt and Reparation and Other Works 1921–1945. 1975. Intr. Hanna Segal. London: Virago, 1988.

Envy and Gratitude and Other Works 1946–63. 1975. Intr. Hanna Segal. London: Virago, 1988.

Koss, Stephen. *The Rise and Fall of the Political Press in Britain*. Two volumes. London: Hamish Hamilton, 1981–84.

Krafft-Ebing, Richard von. *Psychopathia Sexualis: With Especial Reference to the Antipathetic Sexual Instinct*. Translated from the twelfth German edition by Franklin S. Klaf, with a forward by Daniel Blain. London: Staples Press, 1965.

Kristeva, Julia. *Desire in Language: A Semiotic Approach to Literature and Art*. Ed. Leon. S. Roudiez. Trans. Thomas Gora, Alice Jardine and Leon S. Roudiez. New York: Columbia University Press, 1980.

Powers of Horror: An Essay on Abjection. Trans. Leon S. Roudiez. New York: Columbia University Press, 1982.

Revolution in Poetic Language. Trans. Margaret Waller. New York: Columbia University Press, 1984.

The Kristeva Reader. Ed. Toril Moi. Oxford and Cambridge, MA: Blackwell, 1986.

Kucich, John. *Repression in Victorian Fiction: Charlotte Brontë, George Eliot, and Charles Dickens*. Berkeley, CA: University of California Press, 1987.

Lacan, Jacques. 'Seminar on "The Purloined Letter"'. Trans. Jeffrey Mehlman. *Yale French Studies* 48 (1972): 73–117.

Ecrits: A Selection. Trans. Alan Sheridan. London: Tavistock, 1977.

The Four Fundamental Concepts of Psycho-Analysis. Trans. Alan Sheridan. London: The Hogarth Press, 1977.

Lanzer, Gertrud. 'On Masochism: A Contribution to the History of a Phantasy and Its Theory'. *Signs* 1 (1975): 277–324.

Laplanche, Jean. *Life and Death in Psychoanalysis*. 1970. Trans. Jeffrey Mehlman. Baltimore and London: Johns Hopkins University Press, 1976.

Laplanche, J. and J.-B. Pontalis. *The Language of Psycho-Analysis*. Trans. Donald Nicholson-Smith. London: Hogarth, 1973.

Laqueur, Thomas. *Making Sex: Body and Gender from the Greeks to Freud*. Cambridge, MA, and London: Harvard University Press, 1990.

Leavis, F. R. *The Great Tradition: George Eliot, Henry James, Joseph Conrad*. London: Chatto & Windus, 1948.

Lévi-Strauss, Claude. *The Elementary Structures of Kinship*. Revised edition. Trans. James Harle Bell, John Richard von Sturmer, and Rodney Needham (editor). Boston: Beacon Press, 1969.

Leys, Ruth. 'The Real Miss Beauchamp: Gender and the Subject of Imitation'. In Butler and Scott, pp. 167–214.

Litvak, Joseph. *Caught in the Act: Theatricality in the Nineteenth-Century English Novel*. Berkeley, CA: University of California Press, 1992.

Lukacher, Ned. *Primal Scenes: Literature, Philosophy, Psychoanalysis*. Ithaca: Cornell University Press, 1986.

Lunch, Out to. *So Much Plotted Freedom: The Cost of Employing the Language of Fetishized Domination: Poodle Play Explores the Sex Economy of Henry James' Lingo Jingo*. Reality Studios occasional papers 6. London: Reality Studios, 1987.

Lyotard, Jean-François. *The Postmodern Condition: A Report on Knowledge*. Trans. Geoff Bennington and Brian Massumi. Manchester: Manchester University Press, 1984.

Marcus, Stephen. *The Other Victorians: A Study of Sexuality and Pornography in Mid-Nineteenth-Century England*. London: Weidenfeld and Nicholson, 1966.

Marcuse, Herbert. *Eros and Civilization*. London: Sphere Books, 1969.

Martin, Luther H., Huck Gutman and Patrick H. Hutton, eds. *Technologies of the Self: A Seminar with Michel Foucault*. London: Tavistock, 1988.

Martin, Robert K. 'The "High Felicity" of Comradeship: A New Reading of *Roderick Hudson*'. *American Literary Realism* 11 (1978): 100–8.

Masters, Brian. *The Life of E. F. Benson*. London: Chatto and Windus, 1991.

Matthiessen, F. O. *Henry James: The Major Phase*. London and New York: Oxford University Press, 1946.

Mayne, Xavier [Edward Irenaeus Prime Stevenson]. *The Intersexes: A History of Similisexualism as a Problem in Social Life*. 1908. New York: Arno, 1975.

McNay, Lois. *Foucault and Feminism: Power, Gender and the Self*. Cambridge: Polity, 1992.

Meltzer, Françoise, ed. *The Trial(s) of Psychoanalysis*. Chicago and London: University of Chicago Press, 1988.

Meyer, Moe, ed. *The Politics and Poetics of Camp*. London and New York: Routledge, 1994.

Miller, D. A. *The Novel and the Police*. Berkeley: University of California Press, 1988.
Bringing Out Roland Barthes. Berkeley, Los Angeles and Oxford: University of California Press, 1992.

Miller, J. Hillis. 'The Figure in the Carpet', *Poetics Today* 1.3 (1980): 107–18.
The Ethics of Reading. New York: Columbia University Press, 1987.

Miller, James. *The Passion of Michel Foucault*. New York: Simon and Schuster, 1993.

Miller, Karl. *Doubles: Studies in Literary History*. London: Oxford University Press, 1987.

Mitchell, Juliet. *Psychoanalysis and Feminism*. London: Allen Lane, 1974.

Mitchell, Juliet and Jacqueline Rose, eds. *Feminine Sexuality. Jacques Lacan and the École Freudienne*. Trans. Jacqueline Rose. London: Macmillan, 1982.

Mizruchi, Susan L. *The Power of Historical Knowledge: Narrating the Past in Hawthorne, James, and Dreiser*. Princeton, NJ: Princeton University Press, 1988.

'Reproducing Women in *The Awkward Age*'. *Representations* 38 (1992): 103–30.

Modleski, Tania. *The Women Who Knew Too Much: Hitchcock and Feminist Theory*. New York and London: Methuen, 1988.

Moon, Michael. 'Sexuality and Visual Terrorism in *The Wings of the Dove*'. *Criticism* 28 (1986): 427–43.

'A Small Boy and Others: Sexual Disorientation in Henry James, Kenneth Anger, and David Lynch'. *Comparative American Identities: Race, Sex, and Nationality in the Modern Text*. Ed. Hortense J. Spillers. New York and London: Routledge, 1991, pp. 141–56.

Disseminating Whitman: Revision and Corporeality in Leaves of Grass. Cambridge, MA and London: Harvard University Press, 1991.

Moore, Lisa. 'Sexual Agency in Manet's *Olympia*'. *Textual Practice* 3.2 (1982): 222–33.

Morgan, Rosemarie. *Women and Sexuality in the Novels of Thomas Hardy*. London: Routledge, 1988.

Mort, Frank. *Dangerous Sexualities: Medico-moral Politics in England Since 1830*. London and New York: Routledge and Kegan Paul, 1987.

Mulvey, Laura. *Visual and Other Pleasures*. Basingstoke: Macmillan, 1989.

Myers, Frederick. 'Multiplex Personality'. *The Nineteenth Century* 20 (July-December 1886): 648–66.

Nietzsche, Friedrich. *The Will to Power*. Ed. Walter Kaufmann. Trans. Walter Kaufmann and R. J. Hollingdale. New York: Random, 1967.

Beyond Good and Evil: Prelude to a Philosophy of the Future. Ed. and trans. R. J. Hollingdale. Harmondsworth: Penguin, 1973.

Nordau, Max. *Degeneration*. London: William Heinemann, 1895.

Novick, Sheldon M. *Henry James: The Young Master*. New York: Random House, 1996.

Nunokawa, Jeff. '*In Memoriam* and the Extinction of the Homosexual'. *ELH* 58 (1991): 130–55.

Painter, George. *Marcel Proust: A Biography*. Revised and enlarged edition. London: Chatto and Windus, 1989.

Palmer, C. and Stuart Mason [C. S. Millard]. *Oscar Wilde: Three Times Tried*. London: The Ferrestone Press, 1912.

Pater, Walter. *The Renaissance: Studies in Art and Poetry*. Ed. Adam Phillips. Oxford and New York: Oxford University Press, 1986.

Person, Leland S., Jr. 'Henry James, George Sand, and the Suspense of Masculinity'. *PMLA* 106 (1991): 515–28.

Pick, Daniel. *Faces of Degeneration: A European Disorder. c. 1848 – c. 1918*. Cambridge: Cambridge University Press, 1989.

Plummer, Kenneth, ed. *The Making of the Modern Homosexual*. London: Hutchinson, 1981.

Poirier, Richard. *The Comic Sense of Henry James: A Study of the Early Novels*. New York: Oxford University Press, 1960.

Poole, Adrian. 'Henry James, War and Witchcraft'. *Essays in Criticism* 41 (1991): 291–307.

Poovey, Mary. *Uneven Developments: The Ideological Work of Gender in Mid-Victorian England*. Chicago: University of Chicago Press, 1988.

Posnock, Ross. *The Trial of Curiosity: Henry James, William James, and the Challenge of Modernity*. New York and Oxford: Oxford University Press, 1991.

Prince, Morton. *The Dissociation of a Personality: A Biographical Study in Abnormal Psychology*. New York, London and Bombay: Longmans, Green and Co., 1906.

Psychotherapy and Multiple Personality: Selected Essays. Ed. Nathan G. Hale, Jr. Cambridge, MA: Harvard University Press, 1975.

Przybylowicz, Donna. *Desire and Repression: The Dialectic of Self and Other in the Late Works of Henry James*. University, AL: University of Alabama Press, 1986.

Raitt, Suzanne. *Vita and Virginia: The Work and Friendship of V. Sackville-West and Virginia Woolf*. Oxford: Clarendon Press, 1993.

Rank, Otto. *The Incest Theme in Literature and Legend: Fundamentals of a Psychology of Literary Creation*. 1912. Trans. Gregory C. Richter. Baltimore and London: Johns Hopkins University Press, 1992.

Reade, Brian, ed. *Sexual Heretics: Male Homosexuality in English Literature from 1850 to 1900*. London: Routledge & Kegan Paul, 1970.

Reik, Theodor. *Masochism in Modern Man*. Trans. Margaret H. Beigel and Gertrud M. Kurth. New York: Grove Press, 1962.

Ricks, Beatrice. *Henry James: A Bibliography of Secondary Works*. Methven, NJ: The Scarecrow Press, 1975.

Robertson, W. Graham. *Time Was: The Reminiscences of W. Graham Robertson*. London: Hamish Hamilton, 1931.

Rose, Jacqueline. *Sexuality in the Field of Vision*. London: Verso, 1986.

The Haunting of Sylvia Plath. London: Virago, 1991.

Rosenzweig, Saul. 'The Ghost of Henry James'. *Partisan Review* 11 (1944): 436–55.

Rowbotham, Sheila and Jeffrey Weeks. *Socialism and the New Life: The Personal and Sexual Politics of Edward Carpenter and Havelock Ellis*. London: Pluto Press, 1977.

Rowe, John Carlos. *The Theoretical Dimensions of Henry James*. Madison, WI: University of Wisconsin Press, 1984.

Rubin, Gayle. 'The Traffic in Women: Notes on the "Political Economy" of Sex'. *Toward an Anthropology of Women*. Ed. Rayna Reiter. New York: Monthly Review Press, 1975, pp. 157–210.

Russo, Vito. *The Celluloid Closet: Homosexuality in the Movies*. Revised edition. New York: Harper & Row, 1987.

Sadoff, Dianne F. *Monsters of Affection: Dickens, Eliot and Bronte on Fatherhood*. Baltimore: Johns Hopkins University Press, 1982.

Said, Edward W. *Orientalism*. London: Routledge and Kegan Paul, 1978.

Literature and Society: Selected Papers from the English Institute, 1978. Baltimore and London: Johns Hopkins University Press, 1980.

Sarotte, Georges Michel. *Like a Brother, Like a Lover: Male Homosexuality in the American Novel and Theater from Herman Melville to James Baldwin.* Trans. Richard Miller. Garden City, NY: Anchor Press, Doubleday, 1978.

Savoy, Eric. '"In the Cage" and the Queer Effects of Gay History'. *Novel* 29.3 (1995): 284–307.

Sawicki, Jana. *Disciplining Foucault: Feminism, Power, and the Body.* New York and London: Routledge, 1991.

Schneiderman, Stuart, trans. and ed. *Returning to Freud: Clinical Psychoanalysis in the School of Lacan.* New Haven, CT and London: Yale University Press, 1980.

Scott, John. *The Upper Classes: Property and Privilege in Britain.* London: Macmillan, 1982.

Scura, Dorothy McInnis. *Henry James: 1960–1974: A Reference Guide.* Boston: G. K. Hall, 1979.

Sedgwick, Eve Kosofsky. *Between Men: English Literature and Male Homosocial Desire.* New York: Columbia University Press, 1985.

Epistemology of the Closet. New York: Harvester Wheatsheaf, 1991.

'Queer Performativity: Henry James's *The Art of the Novel*'. *GLQ* 1 (1993): 1–16.

Tendencies. London: Routledge, 1994.

'Shame and Performativity: Henry James's New York Edition Prefaces'. In *Henry James's New York Edition: The Construction of Authorship.* Ed. David McWhirter. Stanford, CA: Stanford University Press, 1995, pp. 206–39.

Seidman, Steven. *Romantic Longings: Love in America, 1830–1980.* New York and London: Routledge, 1991.

Seltzer, Mark. *Henry James and the Art of Power.* Ithaca: Cornell University Press, 1984.

Senf, Carol A. '*Dracula*: Stoker's Response to the New Woman'. *Victorian Studies* 26 (1982): 33–49.

Seymour, Miranda. *A Ring of Conspirators: Henry James and His Literary Circle 1895–1915.* London: Hodder and Stoughton, 1988.

Shand-Tucci, Douglass. *Boston Bohemia 1881–1900.* Volume One of *Ralph Adams Cram: Life and Architecture.* Amherst: University of Massachusetts Press, 1995.

Shephard, Simon and Mick Wallis, eds. *Coming on Strong: Gay Politics and Culture.* London: Unwin Hyman, 1989.

Showalter, Elaine. *The Female Malady: Women, Madness and English Culture, 1830–1980.* 1985. London: Virago, 1987.

Sexual Anarchy: Gender and Culture at the Fin de Siècle. London: Bloomsbury, 1991.

Showalter, Elaine, ed. *Speaking of Gender.* New York and London: Routledge, 1989.

Simpson, Colin, Lewish Chester and David Leitch. *The Cleveland Street Affair.* Boston: Little, Brown, 1976.

Silverman, Kaja. '*Histoire d'O*: The Construction of a Female Subject'. In Vance, pp. 320–49.

Male Subjectivity at the Margins. New York and London: Routledge, 1992.

Sinfield, Alan. *The Wilde Century: Effeminacy, Oscar Wilde and the Queer Movement.* London: Cassell, 1994.

Smith, Anna Marie. *New Right Discourse on Race and Sexuality: Britain, 1968–1990*. Cambridge: Cambridge University Press, 1994.

Smith-Rosenberg, Carroll. *Disorderly Conduct: Visions of Gender in Victorian America*. New York: Alfred A. Knopf, 1985.

Sontag, Susan. *Against Interpretation*. 1966. London: André Deutsch, 1987.

Illness as Metaphor. London: Allen Lane, 1979.

AIDS and its Metaphors. New York: Farrar, Straus & Giroux, 1989.

Stallybrass, Peter and Allon White. *The Politics and Poetics of Transgression*. London: Methuen, 1986.

Stanton, Domna C., ed. *Discourses of Sexuality: From Aristotle to AIDS*. Ann Arbor, MI: University of Michigan Press, 1992.

Stevens, Hugh. 'Queer Henry *In the Cage*'. In Jonathan Freedman, ed., *The Cambridge Companion to Henry James*. Cambridge: Cambridge University Press. Forthcoming.

Stewart, Susan. *On Longing: Narratives of the Miniature, the Gigantic, the Souvenir, the Collection*. Baltimore: Johns Hopkins University Press, 1984.

Strouse, Jean. *Alice James: A Biography*. London: Jonathan Cape, 1981.

Studlar, Gaylyn. *In the Realm of Pleasure: Von Sternberg, Dietrich, and the Masochistic Aesthetic*. New York: Columbia University Press, 1988.

Sulloway, Frank J. *Freud, Biologist of the Mind: Behind the Psychoanalytic Legend*. London: Burnett Books, 1979.

Symonds, John Addington. *Studies of the Greek Poets*. London: Smith, 1873.

Studies of the Greek Poets. Second series. London: Smith, 1876.

'A Problem in Greek Ethics'. 1883. Rpt. in *Sexual Inversion*. New York: Bell, 1984.

'A Problem in Modern Ethics'. 1891. Rpt. in *Sexual Inversion*. New York: Bell, 1984.

Memoirs. Ed. Phyllis Grosskurth. Random House: New York, 1984.

Tanner, Tony. *The Reign of Wonder: Naivety and Reality in American Literature*. Cambridge: Cambridge University Press, 1965.

Adultery in the Novel: Contract and Transgression. Baltimore and London: Johns Hopkins University Press, 1979.

Henry James: The Writer and His Work. Amherst: University of Massachusetts Press, 1985.

Scenes of Nature, Signs of Men. Cambridge: Cambridge University Press, 1987.

Tintner, Adeline R. '*Roderick Hudson*: A Centennial Reading'. *Henry James Review* 2 (1981): 172–98.

The Museum World of Henry James. Ann Arbor, MI: UMI Research Press, 1986.

Trachtenberg, Alan. *The Incorporation of America: Culture and Society in the Gilded Age*. New York: Hill and Wang, 1982.

Tyrwitt, Richard St. John. 'The Greek Spirit in Modern Literature'. *Contemporary Review* 29 (March 1877): 552–66.

Vaid, Krishna Baldev. *Technique in the Tales of Henry James*. Cambridge, MA: Harvard University Press, 1964.

Vance, Carole S., ed. *Pleasure and Danger: Exploring Female Sexuality*. Boston and London: Routledge & Kegan Paul, 1984.

Veeder, William. *Henry James – The Lesson of the Master: Popular Fiction and Personal Style in the Nineteenth Century*. Chicago: University of Chicago Press, 1975.

Veeder, William and Gordon Hirsch, eds. *Dr Jekyll and Mr Hyde After One Hundred Years*. Chicago and London: University of Chicago Press, 1988.

von Sacher-Masoch, Leopold. *Venus in Furs*. Intr. Gilles Deleuze. Trans. Jean McNeil. 1971. New York: Zone Books, 1991.

Vicinus, Martha, ed. *Suffer and Be Still: Women in the Victorian Age*. Bloomington: Indiana University Press, 1972.

A Widening Sphere: Changing Roles of Victorian Women. Bloomington: Indiana University Press, 1977.

Wardley, Lynn. 'Woman's Voice, Democracy's Body, and *The Bostonians*'. *ELH* 56 (1989): 639–65.

Warner, Eric and Graham Hough, eds. *Strangeness and Beauty: An Anthology of Aesthetic Criticism 1840–1910*. 2 vols. Cambridge: Cambridge University Press, 1983.

Warner, Marina. *Joan of Arc: The Image of Female Heroism*. London: Weidenfeld and Nicolson, 1981.

Weed, Elizabeth, ed. *Coming to Terms: Feminism, Theory, Politics*. London and New York: Routledge, 1989.

Weeks, Jeffrey. *Coming Out: Homosexual Politics in Britain from the Nineteenth Century to the Present*. 1977. Revised edition. London and New York: Quartet Books, 1990.

Sex, Politics and Society: The Regulation of Sexuality Since 1800. London and New York: Longman, 1981.

Sexuality and its Discontents: Meanings, Myths and Modern Sexualities. London and New York: Routledge, 1985.

White, Allon. *The Uses of Obscurity: The Fiction of Early Modernism*. London, Boston and Henley: Routledge and Kegan Paul, 1981.

Yeazell, Ruth B. *Language and Knowledge in the Late Novels of Henry James*. Chicago and London: Chicago University Press, 1976.

Yeazell, Ruth B. ed. *Sex, Politics and Science in the Nineteenth-Century Novel: Selected Papers for the English Institute, 1983–84*. Baltimore and London: Johns Hopkins University Press, 1986.

Index

215